CW00505721

HEALING THROUGH REMEMBERING

MAKING PEACE WITH THE PAST

OPTIONS FOR TRUTH RECOVERY REGARDING THE CONFLICT IN AND ABOUT NORTHERN IRELAND

PRODUCED AND PUBLISHED BY HEALING THROUGH REMEMBERING

WRITTEN BY

PROF. KIERAN McEVOY

OCTOBER 2006

ISBN 1 905882 07 6 (10 DIGIT)
ISBN 978 1 905882 07 6 (13 DIGIT)

To be ordered directly from
Healing Through Remembering
Alexander House, 17a Ormeau Avenue, Belfast
Tel: +44 28 9023 8844 Email: info@healingthroughremembering.org
Reports can also be downloaded from www.healingthroughremembering.org

This report was developed by the following members of the
Healing Through Remembering Truth Recovery and Acknowledgement Sub Group

Sarah Alldred
Marie Breen Smyth
Emily Brough
Pat Conway
Séamas Heaney
Gareth Higgins
Avila Kilmurray
Patricia Lundy
Stephen Martin
Roy McClelland
Kieran McEvoy
Jackie McMullan
Raymond Murray
Paul O'Connor
David W. Porter
Dawn Purvis
Andrew Rawding
Joe Rice
Mike Ritchie
Tom Roberts
Mark Thompson
Irwin Turbitt
Alan Wardle

Written by
Kieran McEvoy

Core Consultant and Facilitator
Brandon Hamber

Project Co-ordinator
Kate Turner

Support Staff
Lainey Dunne
Elaine Armstrong
Sara Templer

Overseen and supported by the Board of Healing Through Remembering

Marie Breen Smyth
Sean Coll
Claire Hackett
Maureen Hetherington
Alan McBride
Roy McClelland
Jackie McMullan
Dawn Purvis
Geraldine Smyth
Oliver Wilkinson

Acknowledgements

Healing Through Remembering would like to thank a number of people who have been extremely helpful in the writing and production of this document.

First the members of the Healing Through Remembering Sub Group on Truth Recovery and Acknowledgement have been deeply involved from the genesis and in developing the options. Many of them have also made available their own writings and other resources on the subject. They have provided detailed and constructive commentary on the numerous drafts, as well as various forms of moral and physical sustenance when they were most needed. They have been immensely supportive and good humoured. This process is proof-positive that people of good will from very different political perspectives do not necessarily have to agree with one another in order to work coherently on a difficult and sensitive topic related to the conflict in and about Northern Ireland.

We are also deeply appreciative of the work and contribution of Kieran McEvoy. He took on the task of researching the international and local aspects, and of writing up this report. This proved to be a much more substantial piece of work than any of us had envisaged. Our thanks go to Kieran for the thorough and professional way in which he tackled this work - his meticulous research, coherent writing skill, clear grasp of concepts and good grace in accepting redrafting from the Sub Group members. His assiduous approach has produced what we believe is a significant document.

HTR would also like to thank the staff and consultants - Brandon Hamber, Kate Turner, Lainey Dunne, Sara Templer and Elaine Armstrong - who helped bring this document to fruition. They have worked tremendously hard in commenting themselves, editing the document, as well as shepherding the comments of others and facilitating the Sub Group meetings. The Healing Through Remembering Board, too, have provided useful insights and feedback at key moments. Kirsten McConnachie provided excellent research assistance in the early stages and valuable comments and feedback as various drafts emerged. Sue Williams facilitated a residential Sub Group meeting at which the document was initiated and she also worked on the Executive Summary. Barbara English proofread and edited the document transcripts. Healing Through Remembering also received excellent feedback from Maggie Beirne, Brice Dickson, Priscilla Hayner, Lorna McGregor and Marny Requa. We appreciate their input.

Prof. Roy McClelland, Chair, Healing Through Remembering

Preface

The Truth Recovery and Acknowledgement Sub Group is part of the Healing Through Remembering Project. It comprises individuals from a wide range of backgrounds and experiences of the conflict in and about Northern Ireland.

This document was produced after almost two years of research, reflection and debate about truth recovery. While there is a range of opinions within the Sub Group on how best to deal with the issue of truth recovery, we are all agreed on the need for a debate as to how to deal with the issue.

We share the view that a lack of information, understanding or acknowledgement has left many people with burning questions concerning truth and justice in relation to past events. The risk of not addressing these questions is that they will continue to cause pain and to destabilise the present. While there is no easy way to deal with these issues, we believe that a mature and honest discussion could contribute to the development of a sustainable peace. This document is meant to be an aid to such conversation, and is intended as a tool for deepening and furthering the discussion.

Any consideration on how to deal with the past must recognise the particular circumstances of the conflict in and about Northern Ireland. We believe there has been a disproportional media focus on the option of a truth commission, and in particular on the South African Truth and Reconciliation Commission. Truth recovery is a wide process and can involve many different mechanisms. We therefore offer in this document a number of options for truth recovery, of which a truth commission is one.

Although we recognise the limits of international comparison, we are also of the opinion that lessons can be drawn from other societies. Hence this document explores examples from all over the world. That said, no model can simply be imported and there is a need for options appropriate to our own particular circumstances. We hope this document will move us some way towards a solution appropriate to the local context.

The options outlined are examples of approaches that might be taken and are not meant to be a definitive list. Any consideration of options should be inclusive and open. Any process of truth recovery has to consider the needs of those who suffered most, but must also be a society-wide consideration. Some feel that the best way to address the past is to "do nothing" and "move on". Their voices must be heard alongside those who propose specific models.

The process around the issue of truth recovery is not an easy one. This document is the outcome of a process which often proved difficult even within the Sub Group, since we come from a wide range of backgrounds, experience and opinions. We are convinced of the value of the research, reflection and debate. We hope this document will facilitate reflection, discussion and debate across society. We encourage all to read the document and to reflect on truth recovery. We believe that respecting diversity of opinion is an essential part of addressing the legacy of the conflict in and about Northern Ireland.

We offer this document as a practical and symbolic expression of our willingness to acknowledge the deep hurt that many people have suffered and our desire to achieve a more secure and tenable future. We hope it can be a contribution to "making peace with the past".

Sarah Alldred, Marie Breen Smyth, Emily Brough, Pat Conway, Séamas Heaney,
Gareth Higgins, Avila Kilmurray, Patricia Lundy, Stephen Martin, Roy McClelland,
Kieran McEvoy, Jackie McMullan, Raymond Murray, Paul O'Connor, David Porter,
Dawn Purvis, Andrew Rawding, Joe Rice, Mike Ritchie, Tom Roberts, Mark Thompson,
Irwin Turbitt, Alan Wardle

Belfast
September 2006

Table of Contents

Executive Summary

Healing Through Remembering

Healing Through Remembering is a project which emerged from discussions held in 1999 with a range of individuals concerning the issue of dealing with the past. The project was formally launched in 2001, and the first focus was a consultation based on the question:

> How should people remember the events connected with the conflict in and about Northern Ireland and in so doing, individually and collectively contribute to the healing of the wounds of society?

The Report on this consultation was published in 2002. This led to the establishment of sub groups to work on each of five recommendations identified in the Report: Storytelling, Day of Reflection, Living Memorial Museum, Network of Commemoration and Remembering Projects, and Truth Recovery and Acknowledgement.

This latest report, *Making Peace with the Past*, has been produced by the Sub Group on Truth Recovery and Acknowledgement.

Truth Recovery and Acknowledgement Sub Group

The Truth Recovery and Acknowledgement Sub Group was established in August 2004. Its membership comprises a diverse range of individuals acting in a personal capacity, including people from loyalist, republican, British Army, and police backgrounds, as well as individuals from different faith backgrounds, victims groups, academics, and community activists.

Healing Through Remembering and the Truth Recovery and Acknowledgement Sub Group present this report in the hope of fostering further discussion among all interested parties on options for making peace with the past.

Making peace with the past

The question of how to deal with the past in relation to the conflict in and about Northern Ireland evokes strong and conflicting emotions. The question is often associated with South Africa's Truth and Reconciliation Commission, and many advocate or reject the idea of truth recovery according to what they believe about the South African model. This report challenges this approach and expands the discussion beyond the South African case to other international experiences. Specifically, the *Making Peace with the Past* document suggests five different options with regard to truth recovery (including one which explores drawing a line under the past), and describes how each of these options might help to meet different needs.

The options proposed are the product of a group of people whose experience as victims, combatants, and members of civil society and local communities encompass many of the conflicting points of view brought together by the Healing Through Remembering Initiative. This group of individuals known as the Truth Recovery and Acknowledgment Sub Group met over the last two years, commissioned studies, considered local and international viewpoints, and discussed options for truth recovery in depth. The members considered the many recent and ongoing inquiries and initiatives which are part of the process of truth recovery, such as the Bloody Sunday Inquiry, the post-Cory inquiries, the work of the Police Ombudsman, the Patten Commission, the Historical Enquiries Team, the Stalker Inquiry, and so forth. The Sub Group also considered other truth-related issues such as the wrangling over the so-called "On The Runs" Legislation and ongoing revelations and allegations about collusion. Consideration of all these developments reinforced the Sub Group's view that, however one views the issue of truth recovery, the past continues to destabilise the present.

In addition to considering local developments, the Sub Group studied the international legal context including international courts and tribunals, as well as models of truth recovery used over recent years in many countries, including Chile, East Timor, Argentina, Guatemala, Rwanda, South Africa, and Uganda. As a result of these deliberations, the Sub Group agreed on a range of options which could be used singly or in combination to begin to meet the diverse needs and realities of truth recovery related to the conflict in and about Northern Ireland. The options are grounded in a comprehensive review of available evidence and are presented for public discussion to facilitate the debate on dealing with the past.

Over the past 30 years the conflict in and about Northern Ireland has resulted in enormous levels of trauma, distress, and suffering. In recent years, the political situation has changed significantly, and many people are anxious to find a way to make sense of the past and look towards the future.

Some people are fearful of any process to determine the truth about the past. Some are apprehensive because of what they and others have done or experienced. Others are worried that the process might only open old wounds without resolving anything; and some people are concerned that the fragile peace process and any chance of political progress may be jeopardised. Others are anxious that there will be no attempt to deal with the past, and that instead, the violence and injustices will be allowed to fester, or take on the appearance of having been normal, justifiable, and acceptable.

In such a conflicted situation, with high emotional, social, and political stakes, it can seem threatening even to discuss these questions. The legacy of the conflict includes lack of trust in the "other side", ingrained pessimism about whether change is possible, and cynicism about the motivation of other actors. These concerns and the associated issues are explored in depth in this report. Without movement towards an agreed process, the suffering and conflict will not be acknowledged, still less resolved.

This report is the product of just such an agreed process, in which people with very different experiences and political and cultural viewpoints found the space and the will to discuss many options for truth recovery. Agreement was reached on five options of potential utility. The Sub Group also identified ways in which the various players involved had to change and to build trust and confidence with opponents. That such a diverse group was able to discuss and agree on alternative ways forward suggests that society as a whole may be able to engage in a purposeful consideration of these issues provided the necessary structures and processes are put in place.

The aims of this report are to:

- Broaden and deepen the public debate on the important issue of truth recovery;
- Increase awareness of the different ways people have tried to deal with the past, in a variety of conflict situations, and how their approaches have worked;
- Critique the assumption that a single truth-recovery model must be selected, by describing different approaches which could be used singly or in combination;
- Identify broad principles and values which are likely to frame any process of truth recovery;
- Offer options for truth recovery with regards to the conflict in and about Northern Ireland in a complex, nuanced way, including alternative ways of dealing with a variety of needs;
- Describe practical issues and likely reactions to different options; and
- Offer for public debate and scrutiny five options for truth recovery that hopefully can provide a basis for moving the "dealing with the past" debate forward.

The options
Based on extensive research into a broad range of international contexts, Healing Through Remembering has identified five options which might be applicable to dealing with the consequences of the conflict in and about Northern Ireland:

- "Drawing a Line Under the Past"
- Internal Organisational Investigations
- Community-Based "Bottom-Up" Truth Recovery
- A Truth-Recovery Commission
- A Commission of Historical Clarification

Healing Through Remembering has described and assessed each option in the light of the following:

- Different interpretations of "truth";
- Broad principles for processes of truth recovery;
- Purposes of truth recovery; and
- Likely advantages, disadvantages, and reactions to each model.

The purposes of truth-recovery mechanisms
While some may feel that no truth-recovery process is needed in the context of the conflict in and about Northern Ireland (see Option 1 below), on the basis of international experiences, a number of useful reasons have emerged for an engagement in some form of truth recovery in the wake of violent conflict. These include:

- To make known the truth, in all its forms, about the conflict;
- To take seriously the needs of victims from all sections of the community;
- To increase understanding of the conflict and the systems which underlay it, and the consequent need for political processes which accommodate different and competing political and national traditions;
- To build in society the capacity to distinguish the truth of the past from lies about it, which will serve in building a stable political future;

- To learn lessons about the past in order to guard against future conflict;
- To broaden ownership of and responsibility for the process of conflict transformation;
- To hold accountable those inside and outside the jurisdiction who played a part in the conflict; and
- To explore conditions under which political actors can nurture greater trust, confidence, and generosity towards each other.

In addition, where a truth-recovery process is established, lessons from international evidence suggest it should also be based on the following principles:

a. **Prioritising the needs of victims** is broadly accepted as a key principle in dealing with the past. This serves as a reminder that "moving on" is not the main priority, at least not until victims' needs have been addressed.

b. The aim is **recovery** of truth, not the imposition of false reconciliation. Victims should not be under pressure to forgive, nor should ex-combatants be required to be contrite.

c. The broad legal principle is that individuals have the **right to a remedy**; that is, the right to have wrongs reversed or replaced if possible,[1] and to have grievances addressed and injustices ended. In any case, transitional or peace processes must not allow injustices or violations of rights to continue.

d. International courts consistently order or recommend **reparations**, usually in the form of financial compensation. Increasingly, international bodies are recommending other forms of reparation, including public apologies or appropriate commemoration of the dead and injured. Broadly, there is acceptance of a variety of forms of restitution, compensation, rehabilitation, and "satisfaction" to recompense victims, knowing that such measures can never make up for what happened to victims. Reparations and compensation is seen both as a moral imperative and as a sound basis for reconciliation.

e. International legal standards reflect the notion that there is an arguable **right to truth**. That right is often expressed in order to ensure both that perpetrators do not enjoy impunity from being held to account and that the rights of victims are protected. This right is seen to be both an individual and a societal right; that is, individuals have the right to know the truth about their individual cases, and society has the right to know about the patterns and systems which permitted or fostered victimisation and violations of human rights. As will be seen in the analysis of individual models of truth recovery, there may sometimes be conflict between discovering truth about events for the individual, and acknowledging the role in the conflict of political, social and economic institutions. While conflicted societies often continue to argue about the causes of conflict, what actually happened, and its significance to the society, a process of truth recovery should dramatically increase society's understanding and acceptance of the facts, and severely limit the possibilities of lying about or wilfully misinterpreting history.

f. While some form of amnesty has often featured as an element of the broader post-conflict reconciliation packages, in recent years such amnesties are increasingly circumscribed by international legal standards. This means, for example, that blanket amnesties of specified groups of actors over a particular timeframe of conflict are not lawful under international law. Similarly, crimes which are deemed so serious as to be "international" in nature (e.g. genocide, crimes against humanity) cannot be lawfully amnestied. That said, where states are involved in "genuine" efforts at national reconciliation or reconstruction which may involve forsaking prosecutions in lieu of truth recovery, they are given considerable latitude, providing such efforts are not a mask for an unwillingness to prosecute.

g. Any truth-recovery mechanism or process must be, and be accepted as, **independent** of the state, combatant groups, political parties, civil society, and economic interests.

Options for truth recovery regarding the conflict in and about Northern Ireland[2]
Below are the five options developed by the Truth Recovery and Acknowledgement Sub Group for discussion. They are presented here and in the *Making the Peace with the Past* document as discrete options. However, the debate that follows this report may consider how they might be developed or changed, and what might be transferable between options, thus developing, if necessary, new options.

Option 1: "Drawing a Line Under the Past"
The "drawing a line under the past" or the "do nothing else" option would mean that the ongoing patchwork of processes would continue. However, no additional formal steps would be taken towards a process of truth recovery.

---

1 There may be legal remedies in the case of seizure of property, for example, or revocation of citizenship, while this is unlikely in cases of death, torture, or illegal imprisonment.
2 See Chapter Four for a detailed description and analysis of each of these options.

Those who favour this option believe that any process of truth recovery is not necessary, is not possible at this time, or is likely to:

- Open old wounds without resolving anything;
- Destabilise the already fragile political system; and
- Criminalise those who were actively involved in violence, without changing the systems and structures which gave rise to and encouraged the conflict.

Discussion: The absence of an official process to establish a broader "social truth" would mean that the ongoing patchwork of truth recovery (e.g. the various post-Cory inquiries, the work of the Historical Enquiries Team, the work of the Office of the Police Ombudsman, individual cases before the courts, and disclosures from former informers and agents) would continue.

Option 2: Internal Organisational Investigations

In this option, organisations which have been involved in acts of violence take primary responsibility for assisting as much as possible in providing victims with the truth about what happened to their loved ones. The organisations would become involved voluntarily, in order to meet victims' requests for information, and would build on their experience in conducting internal investigations. A variety of possible formats, including tribunals or investigations by group members at an internal level, could be available.

Discussion: This option could provide ex-combatants and the security forces with the opportunity to make a commitment to healing and reconciliation. At the same time, there might be considerable public mistrust of organisations investigating incidents in which they themselves had been involved. This option might deliver information about what happened to individuals, if victims and families were prepared to ask for investigations. It would not lead to prosecution or the naming of names, nor would it directly help in transforming institutions or political leadership. However, a willingness to participate in such a process might show some commitment to trying to resolve past grievances.

Option 3: Community-Based "Bottom-Up" Truth Recovery

There are existing models of communities devising and carrying out their own forms of truth recovery. The involvement of local people in collecting and documenting local truth would take advantage of this skills base, and would itself be a mechanism for communal healing and reconciliation. This model could take into account structural issues, combine with storytelling and local history as well as "top-down" truth recovery, and could vary from one community to another. It could give voice to victims and marginalised communities, record previously untold stories, underline the validity of different experiences between and within communities, and emphasise the importance of individual and grassroots experiences, thus providing an alternative to dominant "macro" narratives.

Discussion: "Bottom-up" truth recovery may promote community development, open up space for reflection, and resonate with other ongoing activities such as storytelling and community testimony. It offers particular possibilities of healing when there are internal communal divisions. Such deliberations could in turn feed into a broader societal process of truth recovery, whether or not there was a formal, state-sponsored mechanism. As a localised mechanism, it risks varying greatly from one community to another, or focusing within single identities, and therefore not holding to account all institutions and protagonists. This option would not lead to prosecution or the naming of names, but a broad collection of stories and narratives about the past.

Option 4: Truth-recovery Commission

Such a commission would focus on events of the past over a specified period of time. It would explore the causes, context, and consequences of violence as well as examine specific events and patterns. Set up by legislation by the Irish and British governments, with independence from both, it would have the power to compel witnesses, grant amnesty, recommend prosecution, order reparations, and present a report with recommendations. A Truth-recovery Commission could build on the truth-recovery work that has already taken place, but do so in a much more inclusive fashion, which would not only cover a broader range of incidents, but also find, investigate, and document events in a broader framework of the causes, nature, context, and consequences of violence. Such a Commission would collect testimony from victims. It could also try and persuade those that committed acts of violence to reveal information by, for example, offering to expunge criminal records or a guarantee against future prosecutions in exchange for truth telling.

Discussion: This would be a practical and symbolic expression of the willingness of society to deal with its violent past as part of the transition to becoming a more inclusive society. It offers the possibility to document individual events, as well as organisational and institutional aspects of the conflict. It could have both "carrots" and "sticks" to reach the truth. Such a commission need not be exactly like the South African Truth and Reconciliation Commission, nor exactly like any of the previous inquiries here in Northern Ireland. It would work best if it were independent, included eminent international figures, avoided an overly adversarial and legalistic way of working, and saw itself as part of the wider process of making peace with the past rather than the only vehicle. Whether it could be established, and succeed, would depend greatly on the trust, participation and confidence of victims, ex-combatants, and institutions within society to participate in it.

Option 5: A Commission of Historical Clarification

The primary focus of this option is historical, the causes of conflict, with less emphasis on either victims or those who had been involved in past acts of violence. The focus would be on devising an independent, authoritative, historical narrative about what occurred during the conflict and why, in order to encourage a broader sense of collective (rather than individual) responsibility for what happened. An agreed narrative would limit misperceptions and disagreements about what actually happened, and thus help to prevent future cycles of violence based on grudges and manipulation. This narrative would be developed by an independent body over a period of time.

Discussion: This option would probably generate less political opposition, be less expensive, and could be the start of a broader public debate on what happened. It would produce a report, and could make recommendations. However, this type of Commission would have no evidentiary powers, no power to compel witnesses, grant amnesty, or prosecute, so it would not enable individuals to discover what happened in particular incidents, nor would it be able to name names or push for prosecution. Also, it would be unlikely to meet the needs of victims, and would risk seeming distant and scholarly, both of which would limit public ownership of its results.

Conclusion

The *Making Peace with the Past* document from Healing Through Remembering is not designed to offer a definitive view on how or whether Northern Ireland should have some form of truth-recovery process. Indeed, considerable attention has been given to considering the option of not introducing any new form of institutional truth-recovery process beyond the ongoing initiatives. Rather, this report is intended to provide sufficient detail and context to help focus the debate concerning truth recovery regarding the conflict in and about Northern Ireland on realistic options for the future.

The report presents five options for truth recovery and it is hoped that, through public debate and consultation, this will lead to the development of a method for dealing with the past by either drawing on the options presented here to create a new option, or to a specific approach being adopted. Combinations of options should be considered, as well as changes to the options presented. Considering such developments should not, however, preclude the option of agreeing to "draw a line in the sand". It is hoped this report will lead to informed and dynamic debate. The process of producing this report is also a sign of hope and, in our view, proof positive that people from very diverse backgrounds, and holding very different points of view, can have a reasoned debate on this difficult and emotive topic.

Of course, any process of truth recovery could become a place in which competing versions of history would be strongly advocated by the various protagonists. Truth recovery is not, however, a political "free-for-all". Instead, formalised truth recovery usually entails a systemic attempt to uncover, research, record, and validate as much as possible what actually happened. An objective and respected source of truth narrows the capacity of politicians, ex-combatants, victims or other actors to simply assert partial or untrue versions of history.

The absence of trust has been widely viewed as core to the stop start nature of the peace process in and about Northern Ireland. For advocates of truth recovery, it is precisely the capacity to distinguish between the truth and the lies of the past that is required to build the trust required for a stable political future. One of the features of engagement in truth recovery in other contexts has been the notion that individual and national engagement in such a process contributed to a greater spirit of political generosity amongst the political protagonists. At its best, this is evidenced by diminution in absolute moral certainties concerning the past actions of "their side", and a concurrent greater willingness to see beyond the victimhood of one's own community to countenance the suffering of the "other". Despite appearances to the contrary, all of the main political actors in Northern Ireland have shown themselves capable of generosity to political opponents, both within and without their own communities. Again, for those who support truth recovery this is its key virtue; it exposes the myth of blamelessness. In doing so, it would also provide both a context and a framework to build upon and embed the notion that political generosity is required for the good of our society as a whole.

Finally, across all sectors in society there is a widespread consensus on the desirability of processes and structures which prioritise the needs of victims. If we accept that many victims want to know the truth about what happened to them or their loved ones and why, then there is a moral imperative for all of us affected by the conflict to engage seriously in a debate on truth recovery.

CHAPTER ONE

Background

Healing Through Remembering

In February 1999 Victim Support Northern Ireland (VSNI) and the Northern Ireland Association for the Care and Resettlement of Offenders (NIACRO) jointly invited Dr Alex Boraine to visit Northern Ireland.

Dr Boraine, then Deputy Chair of the Truth and Reconciliation Commission (TRC) in South Africa, met many groups and individuals to discuss the experience of truth and reconciliation in South Africa and to consider what relevance such experiences might have to the process of conflict transformation in Northern Ireland. Following that visit, a small working group was formed, comprising those who had coordinated the visit, together with representatives from the Community Relations Council (CRC). Funded by the CRC the group produced a report of the discussions which had taken place during Dr Boraine's visit (NIACRO & Victim Support 2000), which was launched in 2000. Following the launch of that report, a broad-based board was created to oversee a project, the principal objective of which was to submit a written report to the British and Irish governments and the Offices of the First and Deputy First Ministers which would identify a programme of action designed to assist with dealing with the past in the jurisdiction affected by the conflict. The project was named the Healing Through Remembering Project (HTR) and formally launched in 2001.

Since its inception, HTR has sought to ensure through its language, working practices, and group membership "that anyone from any background would feel comfortable with approaching at least one member of the Board and that voices could be heard from all sections of society" (Healing Through Remembering 2006a). The project launched a public consultation considering "How should people remember the events connected with the conflict in and about Northern Ireland and, in so doing, individually and collectively contribute to the healing of the wounds of society?" This question, together with a number of related issues, formed the basis of a public consultation which included placing advertisements in 56 local newspapers, distributing over 5,000 leaflets, and receiving a total of 108 submissions from individuals, groups, and organisations - all of which were anonymised before consideration by the Board. In 2002 the report of that consultation was launched (Healing Through Remembering 2002). Following further consultation, in June 2004 five sub groups were formed and began working on the recommendations identified in the report. These were Storytelling, Day of Reflection, Living Memorial Museum, Network of Commemoration and Remembering Projects, and Truth Recovery and Acknowledgement.

The current document has been produced by the HTR Truth Recovery and Acknowledgement Sub Group (see Appendix 1 for biographies of the group members) with the support of the HTR Board.

The Truth Recovery and Acknowledgement Sub Group

The Truth Recovery and Acknowledgement Sub Group was established in August 2004. Its membership involves a diverse group of individuals acting in a personal capacity. The Sub Group includes a number of people from loyalist, republican, British Army, and police backgrounds, as well as individuals from different faith backgrounds, victims' groups, academics, and community activists. Following lengthy internal discussions on the issues with regard to truth recovery, as well as a number of bilateral meetings with key actors, the Sub Group agreed that it could make a useful contribution to the broader debate concerning the conflict in and about Northern Ireland by producing an options document on the subject. Although there is some obvious overlap between the concepts, the Sub Group also commissioned a separate scoping study on the notion of acknowledgement (Healing Through Remembering 2006b) which will be referred to at various junctures throughout this document. This notion of acknowledgement had been envisaged in the 2002 report as a necessary precursor to a broader analysis of truth recovery.[3]

Rationale, methodology and structure

It is important to stress that this document is not intended to offer a prescriptive view on how or whether Northern Ireland should have some form of truth commission. Indeed, one of the options discussed in detail below is referred to as the "drawing a line under the past" option. Rather, the purpose is to provide as much relevant detail and context as possible to inform the broader debate. People in Northern Ireland, the Irish Republic, Britain, and elsewhere affected by the conflict will of course come to their own conclusions on the

---

[3] The Report concluded that "...all organisations and institutions that have been engaged in the conflict, including the British and Irish States, political parties and loyalist and republican paramilitaries, honestly and publicly acknowledge responsibility for past political violence due to their acts of omission and commission. This could be the first and necessary step towards the potentiality of a larger process of truth recovery." (Healing Through Remembering 2002: v-vi).

complex and sensitive issues concerning truth recovery. Indeed, there are a variety of views within both the Truth Recovery and Acknowledgement Sub Group and the broader HTR membership.

However, many who have been involved with HTR share a common frustration that, all too often in the period since the IRA and loyalist cessations, public discussion on this issue has narrowed to (a) whether or not people are in favour of a "truth process"; and (b) the impact that a South African-style "Truth and Reconciliation Commission" would have on the affected jurisdictions, and whether such a process is needed. While we are not averse to learning relevant lessons from South Africa, we believe that the debate requires an understanding of the broader range of international experiences, as well as a more subtle and nuanced appreciation of the particularities of the Northern Ireland context.

The methodology for producing this document has therefore entailed:

(a) Intensive discussions with the HTR Truth Recovery and Acknowledgement Sub Group. Often these discussions were informed by dialogue facilitated by individual members of the group within their own constituencies and areas of work. These discussions involved regular monthly meetings, a number of residentials at which the document structure, options to be discussed, and broad themes were agreed, as well as reviews of the various drafts of the document;
(b) A number of bilateral meetings with key individuals and organisations to better understand their views on truth recovery and acknowledgement;
(c) An extensive survey of the relevant academic and policy literature on the international experience of truth recovery and acknowledgement;
(d) A similar survey of the range of materials available on the various ongoing truth-recovery initiatives concerning the conflict in and about Northern Ireland;
(e) Comments and feedback from a number of prominent international experts in the field as well as Board members from the HTR Project; and
(f   Commissioning a legal opinion to consider the issues with regard to prosecutions emerging from the work of the Historical Enquiries Team.

The structure of this document is as follows:

The remainder of Chapter One offers a very brief background to the debate regarding truth recovery and the conflict in and about Northern Ireland.

Chapter Two reviews different styles of truth-recovery initiatives which have been developed internationally over the past number of years, as well as some thematic discussion concerning the international legal context within which such initiatives may occur. These international developments are explored in particular in terms of their relevance to the Northern Ireland context.

Chapter Three outlines the various types of truth-recovery initiatives which have either occurred in the past or are currently ongoing with regard to the conflict in and about Northern Ireland.

Chapter Four offers an outline of five options for truth recovery which the Truth Recovery and Acknowledgement Sub Group consider of particular possible relevance to the Northern Ireland context.

Chapter Five offers a brief summary of some of the key themes and issues addressed in the document.

Terminology
As in many other contexts, it is important to be politically sensitive in the language used to discuss the process of truth recovery. The use of language is something that was given considerable thought in the work of HTR in general and in the production of this document in particular. For current purposes the HTR Sub Group on Truth Recovery and Acknowledgement adopted the following terms.

Truth Recovery
This term refers to the broad range of processes designed to uncover the causes, context, and extent of acts of political violence in the conflict.

In and about Northern Ireland
This phrase was one previously agreed by HTR in recognition that the conflict affected a number of jurisdictions outside Northern Ireland, including the Irish Republic, Britain, other European jurisdictions, and elsewhere. The name "Northern Ireland" is not universally regarded as neutral, particularly by republicans and nationalists. However, its usage for the purposes of convenience was accepted by those who worked on

this initiative with the caveat that this should not be viewed as a reflection of the opinion of all of those involved in HTR as to the desired constitutional status of the jurisdiction.

Ex-combatants and security forces

"Ex-combatant" is an internationally recognised phrase which generally refers to both state and non-state actors who have been involved in violent conflict. Some individuals who have been involved in violent acts from republican and loyalist backgrounds have objections to the phrase, pointing out that it suggests that they are no longer involved in struggle (albeit political rather than armed struggle) or that it reduces their identity to a single dimension which does not capture the complexities of their post-conflict life in their communities, families, workplaces, and so forth. For those who were engaged in conflict on the side of the state, some from both military and policing backgrounds have held prominent public dialogues with former paramilitary activists framed as "ex-combatants talking to one another". However, others bridle at the bunching of state forces with those they regard as "terrorists", suggesting (for example, with regard to the failed "On The Runs" Legislation discussed below) that such a linkage creates an unacceptable "myth of equivalence" between the two sets of actors. Still others, particularly some of those who served in the RUC, have argued that the reality of their posting or particular area of work meant that they were only minimally involved in the conflict since much of their professional lives was actually directed towards the policing of "ordinary crime".

Mindful of these various positions, the reservations of the different actors, and the desire not to needlessly alienate readers through the use of language, the HTR Sub Group nonetheless had to adopt some terminology which would refer to those who had been involved in acts of armed conflict. Ultimately the group opted to use "ex-combatants" to refer broadly to former loyalist and republican activists who were involved in hostilities. British Army members, or members of the RUC who were also involved in hostilities are generally referred to as the "security forces", and the members of the various intelligence agencies are referred to as such, or as "security services". The terminology employed reflects no value judgements on the actions of any of the individuals or organisations involved.

Victims

In Northern Ireland, as elsewhere, there is a lively debate on the use of the word "victim". In particular, many of those who have been directly affected by violence question the use of the term and its suggestion of powerlessness, passivity, and unidimensionality. In some jurisdictions, a number of alternative terms have been suggested, with "survivor" probably being the most widely employed. As is discussed in some detail below, Northern Ireland has seen quite a heated debate as to the definition of victim and hierarchies of victims, a distinction suggested between "innocent" and "guilty" victims, and debate concerning whether people who have been involved in armed actions can also be regarded as victims when they or their families also suffered violence. The HTR Sub Group was well aware of all of these complexities. The use of the term "victim" in this document is a broad one. It refers to all of those killed or injured physically or psychologically during the conflict, their surviving relatives or those who care for them, and those who mourn their dead (OFMDFM 2004: 3).[4] The term makes no distinction whatsoever between victim types.

The truth-recovery debate regarding the conflict in and about Northern Ireland

Despite the lack of reference to the need to establish a formal truth-recovery institution in the 1998 Agreement (also known as the Good Friday Agreement or Belfast Agreement, hereafter the Agreement),[5] a range of "piecemeal" initiatives and campaigns concerning specific incidents or events has featured prominently on the political landscape in recent years. Many families of victims from a range of backgrounds have campaigned for what they call "truth" about their cases, in some cases for decades. The notion of considering an official and structured way of looking at truth recovery, however, is fairly new and has only been debated in this last decade.

Although many of the relevant developments are discussed in greater detail in Chapter Three, it might be useful at this juncture to offer a very brief overview of the historical developments and current "state of play" with regard to the truth-recovery debate concerning the conflict in and about Northern Ireland.

A number of published works were produced in the 1990s which explored the issue of truth recovery. One of the earliest of these was written by Bill Rolston (1996). Rolston compared the impact of truth commissions in South Africa, Chile, the Philippines, and Brazil. While he concluded that the timing was not right for a truth commission (particularly one which was not entirely free from government interference), and suggested that other methods of truth recovery might prove more effective, he did not rule out the possibility of a truth

---

[4] This definition is also utilised in the OFMDFM Victims Strategy Document (Victims Unit 2002).
[5] According to An Taoiseach Bertie Ahern, the issue of a truth commission was discussed in the negotiations before and after the signing of the Agreement but at that stage "all sides agreed that it was not the way to go." Dáil Debates 8th March 2005.

commission. In his 1998 investigation into victims' issues (discussed in detail in Chapter Three), Kenneth Bloomfield also does not close the door on the idea of a truth commission although he suggested that it could only occur in the context of a more far-reaching political accommodation (Bloomfield 1998: 38). In 1998, shortly after the Agreement, another study looked at the possibility of a truth commission for Northern Ireland. It concluded at that time that:

> Most political players demand truth from those they perceive as the other side or sides, but seem unwilling to offer the truth from their side, or acknowledge and take responsibility for their actions. This is mostly due to fear that such acknowledgement (public or otherwise) will weaken in the new dispensation and that the truth may be used against them within the context of the delicate peace that prevails. There are also those in Northern Ireland who refuse to accept that they did anything wrong or that their action (or inaction) was complicit in perpetuating the conflict (Hamber 1998: 80-81).

At the same time, this study also concluded that although there was little appetite at the time for such a process, the issues of truth and justice would have to be dealt with at some point.

But perhaps the largest investigation into the possibility of looking at options for truth recovery came from the HTR Project as part of their initial consultation (discussed above). That consultation found mixed views, with as many people being in favour of a truth commission as those being against the idea. In the final instance it recommended that:

> ...all organisations and institutions that have been engaged in the conflict, including the British and Irish States, the political parties and Loyalist and Republican paramilitaries, should honestly and publicly acknowledge responsibility for past political violence due to their acts of omission and commission. We see this as the first and necessary step having the potentiality of a larger process of truth recovery. When acknowledgement is forthcoming, we recommend that measured, inclusive and in-depth consideration be given to the establishment of an appropriate and unique truth recovery process (Healing Through Remembering 2002: 50).

Given the mixed results of the consultation, the project concluded that more needed to be done to lay the ground work for any truth-recovery process. One key issue highlighted by the report was the notion of acknowledgement, which was framed as a potential first step to exploring truth-recovery options further. In addition, the use of the phrase "truth recovery" was deliberate because it was viewed as conveying a broader approach than simply whether or not a truth commission should be established (Hamber 2003b). In the broadest sense, the report argued that truth recovery could imply mechanisms such as truth commissions run domestically or internationally, but also commissions of enquiry, tribunals or special prosecutions, or perhaps historically based truth-recovery processes driven by victim narratives (Hamber 2003b). Furthermore, the report was at pains to point out that any such process should relate to and not replace other formal truth-finding structures that exist, namely those within the existing criminal justice system and other associated mechanisms such as inquests, police investigations, prosecutions, and inquiries.

Since the publication of the HTR 2002 Report, there has also been a steady increase in the academic debate about the idea of truth recovery, much of which is featured throughout this report. Two journal collections have featured essays on the possibilities and pitfalls of truth recovery in Northern Ireland. One such collection, entitled Truth, was published by Race and Class in 2002 (Volume 44, Number 1), and another by the Fordham Law Journal in 2003 (Volume 26, Number 4) also contained a number of essays on truth-related issues. A survey of attitudes to a truth commission in 2003 in Northern Ireland found that some 65% of people were in favour of a truth commission (Cairns, Mallet, Lewis & Wilson 2003); subsequent surveys have found less favourable results (see Lundy & McGovern 2005a, discussed below).

The Northern Ireland Human Rights Commission also gave considerable focus to the issue in its 2003 report on Victims/Survivors (Northern Ireland Human Rights Commission 2003). This report is fairly bold, noting "In due course it will be appropriate to develop some kind of truth-recovery mechanism in Northern Ireland" (Northern Ireland Human Rights Commission 2003: 7). However, it goes on to say that there is little support amongst the victim community for such a process to be initiated, and the role of the Human Rights Commission is to facilitate discussion on the issue and not to run such a process.

Despite the considerable interest from NGOs, academics, and elements of civil society, the issue was given comparatively little attention by the British government until the last two years (discussed below). There has been no response or follow-up to the idea of acknowledgement as proposed by HTR. The Victims Strategy (Victims Unit 2002) mentioned that it would be reviewing the HTR Report to assist it with truth and justice issues in relation to victims, but subsequent developments have not addressed the issue, restricting the focus on victims largely to service delivery.

However, on 1 April 2004, at his monthly Downing Street press conference, British Prime Minister Tony Blair responded to the publication of the Cory Reports into collusion between the security forces and paramilitary groups with the following statement:

> We will abide by the commitments that we have given. I do think it is important that we do try in Northern Ireland to move beyond the past. These things have to be gone into but we should start to move beyond the past. I do not know whether necessarily a Truth and Reconciliation Commission is the right way to do it but I think there needs to be some way of trying to both allow people to express their grief, their pain and their anger in respect of what has happened in Northern Ireland without the past continually dominating the present and the future and that is what we will try to do.

In May 2004 the then Secretary of State Paul Murphy made an announcement in Parliament that he would be embarking on a series of discussions on dealing with the past.[6] Although there was considerable controversy amongst victims' organisations as to the nature and extent of the consultation by Paul Murphy, he followed up that announcement with a visit to South Africa to explore the workings of the South African Truth and Reconciliation Commission.[7] The British government has received support for such an initiative from the Irish government, who appeared to share concerns regarding the incremental approach to truth recovery which has been the dominant approach to date.[8] Ultimately, the British government announced in March 2005 that, in a context of a lack of political progress and insufficient consensus on the issue, the timing was not right for such an initiative. The Secretary of State's activities on the question of the past coincided with the decision of the Northern Ireland Affairs Committee to conduct a series of hearings and produce a document called *Dealing with the Past in Northern Ireland*.[9] The focus of that report was ultimately narrowed somewhat to the particular needs of victims by the time it was published in April 2005. This was due in part to the impending general election, but also to the government's announcement to suspend its consultation on truth recovery. The Committee did, however, indicate that it was broadly in support of some form of truth commission, although it concurred with the judgement of the government that the timing was not yet right.[10]

Support for the increased government interest in the question of a more holistic approach to dealing with the past has also emerged from a number of prominent members of the policing establishment. In June 2003, the year before the Prime Minister's statement, the Chief Constable of the Police Service of Northern Ireland Hugh Orde (now Sir Hugh Orde) announced that some form of truth process should be considered. The Chief Constable admitted that many of the unsolved murders of the conflict in and about Northern Ireland were

---

[6] "I want to proceed in a way which respects the feelings of all concerned and which takes nothing for granted. Over the weeks ahead I will be embarking on a programme of discussion with a wide range of people with relevant experiences and expertise. These discussions will initially take the form of private soundings which will in due course lead to wider consultation. I will also be commissioning work of relevant international experience which will cover the sort of processes which others have used in seeking to come to terms with the past." NIO Press Statement 17 May 2004.

[7] "A Telling Contribution: The British Government Wants South Africa to Convince Northern Ireland to Start Talking", *The Guardian*, 9 June 2004.

[8] "... an endless number of groups have been formed which are concerned with various atrocities. As time passes, instead of the healing process setting in, bitterness arises. I can understand that having met numerous groups of families. The more they see one case getting prominence, the more they feel they have not served their families' interest. I do not know what is the best way to do it. The South African way proved to be an effective short means, but I do not know if it solved the problems for people. It certainly seems to have done so, but perhaps somebody will correct me some years from now and say that has not been the experience. Something must happen. I have made the point to the Secretary of State, Paul Murphy, on a number of occasions and to the Northern Ireland Office that we must find some process." An Taoiseach Bertie Aherne, Dáil Debates 8 March 2005.

[9] The lessons learned from the soundings and reflections of the Secretary of State and his visit to South Africa were presented to the Northern Ireland Affairs Committee. They included: "(a) the difficulty in importing a ready-made approach to Northern Ireland; (b) the importance to many of resolving unanswered questions about the past; (c) the need to ensure proper respect and protection for victims and survivors; (d) the need for any solution to command widespread acceptance across all sections of the community in Northern Ireland, and the implications that this has for Government's role in the process." (NIO Evidence in NIAC, 2005: Ev235).

[10] "One initiative which was mentioned frequently is that of a formal and official 'truth recovery' process, an idea which the government has decided against pursuing for the time being. This is an idea that may have its place in the healing process in Northern Ireland, but which is complicated and contentious at present. We are supportive of the idea, particularly where an independent element is included, but are not convinced that this is the right time to begin to put it into practice. Community consensus about the nature of such a process, and a positive political context would be required to enable a wide variety of groups and individuals in Northern Ireland to participate in such a process with sufficient confidence for it to be worthwhile. Unfortunately, this essential context has not yet been created, and we are concerned that to embark on this process now would not achieve the aim of truth recovery and could exacerbate inter-community tensions. We expect the government to keep the appropriateness of initiating a truth recovery process under constant review." (NIAC 2005: Ev4).

unlikely to be satisfactorily resolved and that what was required was a much broader process.[11] These comments were endorsed the following February when they received support from both the Chair of the Policing Board, Professor Des Rea, and Vice Chair Denis Bradley, albeit speaking in their private capacity. Professor Rea suggested that the two governments should establish a commission "which would deliberate on the past, consult with the public, and make proposals on a constructive way forward". He also suggested that the process could involve an amnesty for the perpetrators of crimes related to the conflict in and about Northern Ireland, including the unsolved murders referred to by the Chief Constable.[12]

The views of the major political parties in the jurisdiction on the topic are diverse.

Amongst the nationalist political parties, there has been an incremental increase in support for some form of truth-recovery process. In 2004 the SDLP called for the establishment of a Truth and Survivors Forum, which would be tasked with designing a truth and remembrance process. The SDLP went on to recommend:

> establishing a 'truth, recognition and remembrance archive' which would be overseen by an independent international Truth Body. This would allow victims to record their experiences, allege who they felt was responsible and then the individual named would be permitted to come forward and deny or contradict the allegation and the Truth Body could make a ruling on whether there is sufficient evidence to support the allegation. The opening of police files to victims, survivors and their families either by the police or – when requested – by the Truth Body which would then also be responsible for any redaction that was strictly necessary. Where recommended by the Police Ombudsman, who would continue to operate as at present, or where there is sufficient evidence, victims and survivors could seek a criminal reinvestigation. However it would be for the Truth Body to carry out the reinvestigation of pre-Good Friday Agreement killings, not the PSNI. Victims, survivors and their families also to have the right to waive a criminal investigation and possible prosecution in return for truth. However, the Truth Body could refuse to accept the waiver on public interest grounds – not least to protect against intimidation.[13]

With regard to republicans, there has been a gradual clarification in their position towards the issue of truth recovery over the past few years. While, like the SDLP, Sinn Féin has usually been supportive of the Bloody Sunday families and other families who have been campaigning on issues of state collusion with loyalists,[14] some republican commentators have historically appeared suspicious of a broader truth process. For example, the former Sinn Féin Director of Publicity and now author and journalist Danny Morrison expressed serious concerns that the calls by Professor Rea were a deliberate attempt to undermine the Public Inquiries recommended by Judge Cory.[15] A debate has however clearly been ongoing within the broader republican community. In 2002, a community-based initiative from Eolas which included individuals from the republican ex-prisoners organisation Coiste na n-Iarchimí amongst its participants produced a document which included three options for truth recovery (discussed in more detail in Chapter Three). In 2003, Sinn Féin produced a discussion document which expressed their "willingness to discuss the issues involved with all interested parties" and outlined a number of principles which it argued should underpin the public debate on truth recovery.[16] Recently the issue of truth recovery has been linked with a range of issues more traditionally associated with the republican position.[17]

---

[11] "I have made it very clear when I have met families of victims that in an evidential sense we are going to be struggling to secure convictions...A conviction is an unlikely outcome even if you put a lot of resources for a long period of time into one or two cases...one way forward is a truth forum, where paramilitaries, victims and security forces could come forward and speak publicly about the past. There needs to be something that gives everyone an opportunity to say their piece, to get the best explanation they can on what happened to their families, their loved ones so they can then get on with their lives." *Irish News*, 11 June 2003. As is discussed below, the Chief Constable has gone on to reiterate this position a number of times.

[12] "Northern Ireland Commission 'Could Heal Wounds'", *BBC News*, 18 February 2004.
See http://news.bbc.co.uk/1/hi/northern_ireland/3499613.stm

[13] SDLP Press Release, Does Northern Ireland Need a Truth Commission, 12 September 2004.
See http://www.sdlp.ie/prdurkanlabourpartyfringesept04.shtm

[14] See further discussion in Chapter Three concerning the abandoned "On The Runs" Legislation.

[15] For example, "A Truth That Tells A Lie". Danny Morrison, *Andersonstown News*, 24 February 2004.

[16] These principles included that: "[A]ll processes should be victim-centred. Victims have a right both to acknowledgement of their pain and to contribute to a changing society; full co-operation and disclosure by all relevant parties is essential to the success of any truth process; there should be no hierarchy of victims; all processes should be politically neutral; it is crucially important that any panel/commission would be international and independent; an objective of any process should be healing - both for victims and for society in general; consideration should be given to the South African formulation that the purpose of a truth process is to examine 'the causes, nature and extent' of the conflict; all processes should be informed by a desire to learn the lessons of the past so that mistakes will not be repeated; the focus of any truth process should not be restricted to combatant groups. Other institutions require scrutiny so as to recover the truth. This includes the media, judiciary, state institutions, civic society etc; ... A common aim should be to enable society to build the peace" (Sinn Féin 2003: 4-5).

As is explored in more detail in Chapter Three, the views of the main unionist parties towards forms of truth recovery such as truth commissions have been more negative, with the DUP in particular expressing the strongest opposition.[18] For example, Ian Paisley Jr. reacted to the comments by Des Rea by saying "Professor Rea has now lost the confidence of ordinary unionists through his outrageous comments. What the chairman of the Policing Board is saying is that he has no confidence in the police to capture the perpetrators of 30 years of violence". His party colleague Arlene Foster, formerly of the Ulster Unionists, released a longer statement articulating her party's opposition to a truth commission.[19] The Ulster Unionist Party position has been more measured. One prominent party member has indicated that he is in favour of a truth commission as a mechanism both to bring an end to the number of single issue inquiries which have been established, and in order to hold republicans accountable for past misdeeds.[20] Interviewed on the BBC Radio programme Talkback before he became Party leader, Sir Reg Empey said:

...a debate is raging over the issue [the establishment of a Truth Commission]. I personally have mixed feelings about the idea but I would be interested in the views of those who have been directly affected. My concern is that such a commission would be turned into a political football and it may therefore only reopen the wounds of those who have suffered but I am willing to listen to the arguments.[21]

More recently Party Victims' spokesperson Derek Hussey referred to "...a debate taking place within the Ulster Unionist Party as to how [we] can satisfactorily draw a line under the past and move forward as society" and invited opinions from as broad a range of views as possible (but particularly victims and victims groups) to contribute to the debate.[22] The Alliance Party has for a number of years been in favour of some form of victims forum to take forward the debate on truth recovery.[23]

---

[17] "Over recent days both the Taoiseach and the British Secretary of State have said that urgent progress is necessary in restoring the political institutions. Sinn Féin has been pressing for early progress and we will pursue this with the two governments over coming weeks. In the interim the two governments should move quickly on issues under their direct control. These include the issue of political policing, the need for an effective truth recovery process, including the case of Pat Finucane and the issue of OTRs". Gerry Adams Responds to OTR Announcement, Sinn Féin Press Release, 11 January 2006.

[18] The distinct views of loyalism are explored in some detail in Chapter Three.

[19] "We could never be confident that a truth commission would get at the whole truth. The British Government and the security forces would inevitably be compelled to give evidence and would effectively be put on trial. Any commission would amount to nothing more than a 'Brit bashing session'. Would we ever learn the whole truth from the terrorists? Would they be as forthcoming with what they know about the horrors of the last thirty years? I doubt it. Martin McGuinness's behaviour at the Bloody Sunday Inquiry, when he failed to divulge all he knew about the IRA, showed us exactly how the IRA would engage with a commission. Are we expected to take the word of the IRA even in the format of a truth commission? They have made lying and deceit an art form." DUP Press Release, 'Truth Commission And Amnesty The Last Thing Northern Ireland Needs' Says Foster, 19 February 2004.

[20] "Let us draw a line in the sand and have a truth commission. However, the problem with a truth commission is that everyone has to tell the truth. I look forward to having Martin McGuinness tell the truth about his activities in the past 34 years. I would also like to hear Gerry Adams, Stakeknife and Johnny Adair. Let them all come to a truth commission to explain why they did what they did and say, 'We now believe it was wrong and unjustified. Let's bring it to an end.' That is what the law-abiding people of Northern Ireland want, not another biased, pro-republican, pro-nationalist inquiry, which is the only thing that the Hon. Gentleman has campaigned for in this House for the past 30 years." Former Ulster Unionist MP David Burnside, Hansard, 14 May 2003, Col 85WH. See also D. Burnside in Hansard, 1st April 2004, Col 1766. "With humility, on behalf of the families of 1,007 members of the Royal Ulster Constabulary, the Regular Army, the Ulster Defence Regiment and the Royal Irish Regiment, may I ask the Secretary of State why is there not a truth commission in Northern Ireland? Does he agree that the main problem with having a truth commission, which, I hope, will bring to an end the conflict, is the inability of the Provisional IRA, Gerry 'I've never been in the IRA' Adams and Martin McGuiness to tell the truth rather than deal in lies? Is that not the major difficulty in relation to setting up a truth commission to deal with the problems and bereavement of the families of those 1,007 members of our security forces?"

[21] See http://www.bbc.co.uk/northernireland/talkback/askempey.shtml

[22] "UUP wants to Move Forward", Letters to the Editor, *Belfast Community Telegraph*, 20 January 2006. In March 2006 the Unionist Group, an informal "coming together" of members of the Ulster Unionist Party, produced a document which, although it expressed some misgivings about a "semi-judicial commission" designed to achieve truth recovery, also suggests that initiatives such as Days of Reflection, Memorials and Oral Histories which it suggests might "...coincide with extensive and widespread opportunities for personal narrative telling" (Unionist Group 2006: 1-2).

[23] For example, "This will be a tortuous process for many people, but we cannot rush into something as important to bringing the conflict to a close without listening to victims. It may be that we need to set up a form of public consultation involving a commission to try and gauge consensus and make proposals to the Government. Alliance and others have already suggested a Victims Forum as part of a victim-centred truth telling process, but we are willing to listen." Alliance Press Release by Eileen Bell, then Party Victims Spokesperson, 2 April 2004.

The views of the general public in Northern Ireland would seem to broadly reflect the variances of the different political actors. In their analysis of the Life and Times Survey of Attitudes [24] towards truth recovery, Lundy & McGovern (2005a) discerned some interesting findings. Amongst the most noteworthy from quite a complex range of data were that :

- A slight majority (52%) of all respondents felt that a truth commission was either very or fairly important, with only 28% declaring that they believed it would be either fairly or very unimportant.
- There were some differences in community attitudes. Catholic respondents were far more likely (60%) to support calls for a truth commission and far less likely to express disapproval (21%). For Protestants, opinions were more evenly divided with 44% expressing broad approval and 34% against.
- Given the focus of a truth commission on re-constituting future relations, perhaps just as significant was the high level of support for a truth commission amongst the young. Over two-thirds (69%) of 18-24 year old respondents thought that a truth commission was either fairly or very important while a mere 16% thought that it was not.
- There is currently little public support for an amnesty in return for giving evidence to a truth commission. In the survey, only 19% agreed or strongly agreed with the suggestion that people should "be free from possible prosecution for past actions, including killings" if they gave evidence to a truth commission, 61% disagreed.
- Even with the majority support for a truth commission, there was also a large degree of scepticism as to whether or not a truth commission could achieve its ends. 85% of respondents agreed (either strongly or otherwise) with the statement that "you would not necessarily get the truth from a truth commission".
- 92% of all respondents did not trust the British government to run a truth commission (95% of Catholics and, 89% of Protestants).

It is important to remember that this survey occurred in a context where there has arguably been a dearth of informed public debate. For example, as Lundy & McGovern (2005a) point out, the levels of knowledge concerning the international experience of truth recovery appeared quite limited. When asked if they were aware of a truth commission having taken place in another country, only 25% of people answered positively to this question, and the vast majority indicated knowledge of the South African Truth and Reconciliation Commission.

To sum up with regard to the various political actors, the British government (supported by the Irish government) appeared for a period to be steering the political process towards a major initiative on truth recovery. The energy applied towards that end has been linked by some commentators to a view that the Blair government had apparently formed that truth recovery should form a part of a broader "mega-deal" designed to achieve devolved government which would include Sinn Féin and the DUP sharing power (Guelke 2005). However, the impetus for that initiative appeared to dissipate in early 2005 when the government concluded that there was insufficient consensus on the question of how to take truth recovery forward and that the political timing was not right. Both nationalist parties appear now to be broadly in favour of some formal truth-recovery initiative. Similar to both these parties, the Alliance Party is also in favour of some form of victim-centred approach to truth recovery. The unionist parties are much less enthusiastic, the DUP remains the most vociferously opposed, while the Ulster Unionist Party is currently engaged in a debate on the issue. Loyalist misgivings are the most advanced, and they are considered in detail in Chapter Three.

Outside these macro-political actors, again as is outlined in Chapter Three, a myriad of truth-recovery initiatives have either been completed or are ongoing with regard to the conflict in and about Northern Ireland. A number of church-based discussions have taken place to explore the views of the members of the different churches towards the establishment of truth-recovery mechanisms.[25] As is detailed elsewhere (Kelly 2005), there have been a wide variety of community, NGO, and civil society-based storytelling, commemoration, and other initiatives, many of which also entail elements of truth recovery. Beyond this plethora of projects and programmes, general survey data suggests a slight majority of the population at large are in favour of some form of truth-recovery initiative such as a truth commission, although the public debate does not seem particularly well informed on the intricacies of any likely process. This relative lack of public knowledge, both of the international context, and of the developments within Northern Ireland and the other jurisdictions affected by the conflict in and about Northern Ireland, is the reason for this contribution to the debate from HTR.

---

24   For methodological details on this comprehensive survey that has been running annually since 1998 see http://www.ark.ac.uk/nilt

CHAPTER TWO

Truth Recovery: The International Context

Introduction

Before examining a number of different international truth-recovery models, this chapter considers some of the relevant legal issues and international standards which will inevitably shape any such discussions in Northern Ireland. This is not to suggest that the truth-recovery debate or indeed any other aspects of the broader transition from conflict should be the exclusive preserve of lawyers. Indeed, the subject matter of transition from violent conflict has long been enriched academically and practically by sociologists, psychologists, political scientists, and by others in civil society who are engaged in a broad range of activities such as storytelling, memorialisation, mediation, reconciliation, and other types of grassroots work.[26] A perfunctory glance at the different styles of truth-recovery processes which emerged in Latin America in the 1970s, Eastern Europe and elsewhere in the 1980s, and from the South African Truth and Reconciliation Commission (SATRC) onwards in the 1990s reflect very different approaches to what Richard Wilson (2001: 17) has described as "legal fetishism", the reduction of the politics of transition to "lawyer talk".

That said, without a genuine adherence to some basic shared legal principles by the state or other key actors in the transition, it is often very difficult for those involved in such work to maximise their practical effectiveness. As is discussed below, states and other political actors do not have "carte blanche" when it comes to considering different ways of dealing with the past. Thus, each of the options discussed below with regard to dealing with the past in Northern Ireland will inevitably be shaped by a range of legal strictures. It is therefore useful to offer a brief overview of both the legal limitations and the legal possibilities before considering in greater detail how these options might work in practice.   As will be evidenced throughout the discussions, such legal analysis will then be framed by the realities of the social, economic, and political conditions within which any such model may operate.

Truth recovery and the rule of law

The notion of some form of truth recovery as part of a broader process of post-conflict recovery has become an increasingly familiar element of what is now often regarded as the "transitional justice template" for post-conflict reconstruction. As the name suggests, transitional justice refers to the styles of legal formations (e.g. international courts, localised prosecutions, truth commissions) which emerge in the transition from a violent political conflict (McAdams 1986; Campbell, Ní Aoláin & Harvey 2003). Since such political conflicts have often been marked by a disregard for the rule of law by both state and non-state actors, legal mechanisms are often viewed as a crucial element to re-establishing (or in some instances establishing for the first time) a respect for the rule of law (UN Security Council 2004).[27] Transitional justice mechanisms are required to be both backward-looking at past abuses, and also forward-looking as a building block for a new society.

---

[25] By way of illustration, in February 2004 the General Board of the Presbyterian Church rejected the idea of a South African-style Truth and Reconciliation Commission as "an inappropriate means of dealing with the past in Northern Ireland." A report commissioned by the General Board concluded that "...the search for truth and justice could all too easily become a weapon with which to inflict further damage on each other for the next 30+ years." However, the relevant committee was encouraged by the General Board to explore further the idea of creating official opportunities for victims to tell their stories. Press statement 27 February 2004, http://www.presbyterianireland.org. The Centre for Contemporary Christianity in Ireland (formerly ECONI) has produced a series of booklets which examine themes such as Forgiveness, Reconciliation, Justice, and Truth from an evangelical Christian tradition. In their submission to the Northern Ireland Affairs Select Committee, after discussing at length some of the difficulties and challenges presented by truth recovery, the CCCI suggested that "[C]hurches could consider modelling a truth-telling process so that if and when the time is right for a process to begin in the community there is a local model already operating on a micro scale which can be replicated in the macro setting. 'Truth' needs to be spoken publicly between the churches about the nature of their relationships and ongoing contribution to the divisions of Northern Ireland which in the telling would model the kind of truth-telling to be encouraged in the community." (NIAC 2005: Ev342). In his submission to the NI Affairs Committee, drawing upon the work of the Catholic Commission on Social Affairs, the Catholic Archbishop Sean Brady argued for "...the need to hand over the whole process of assessing the desire for dealing with the past in Northern Ireland and making recommendations for the structure and form of such a process, to an independent commission with expertise across a range of related disciplines and a mix of local and international membership, at the earliest possible stage. While current initiatives and consultation are important and welcome, a process which does not have this level of independence and broad political agreement between the two governments and the main political parties in Northern Ireland, is unlikely to receive widespread support and is therefore unlikely to be effective" (NIAC 2005: Ev 338).

[26] See e.g. Williamson, Scott & Halfpenny (2000) and Bell & Keenan (2004).

[27] The UN Security Council has defined transitional justice thus: "The notion of transitional justice... comprises the full range of processes and mechanisms associated with a society's attempts to come to terms with a legacy of large-scale past abuses, in order to ensure accountability, serve justice and achieve reconciliation. These may include both judicial and non-judicial mechanisms, with differing levels of international involvement (or none at all) and individual prosecutions, reparations, truth-seeking, institutional reform, vetting and dismissals, or a combination thereof" (UN Security Council 2004: 4).

Of course, given the contested political nature of transitions, tensions may arise in transitions concerning the role of law. Peace processes may emerge because of messy and unpalatable political compromises. In such contexts, the rule of law becomes a highly contested notion. For some, the introduction of legal structures such as a new constitution or a Bill of Rights may constitute a particular historical moment, as a new relationship between the state and individual is established that guarantees the rights of the latter and limits the power of the former (McEvoy & Morison 2003). In such instances, law may be viewed as a means of drawing a line under the past and establishing a new beginning. More often though, the legal formations which emerge in a transition will contain some efforts to come to terms with the past.[28] For example, law in transition is often required to wrestle with the difficulties of balancing a desire to hold accountable those who have been guilty of abuses during a conflict with the political, social or practical difficulties in achieving that aim. In some instances such as Rwanda (discussed below), where literally hundreds of thousands of people are suspected of having been engaged in genocide, it may be simply logistically impossible to give all the lengthy sentences that common sense would suggest befit the gravity of their crimes (Drumbl 2000a). In other instances, such as Chile, where delicate power relationships may be characterised by a military dictatorship reluctantly handing over power to a nascent democracy, widespread prosecutions may be deemed (at least in the short term) as politically unfeasible (Ensalaco 1999). Transitional justice mechanisms are also required to consider other key issues such as how best to deal with the pain and suffering of victims; how to transform organisational cultures in state agencies, such as the police or military; how to disarm, demobilise and resettle non-state combatants; how to find agreed mechanisms by which societies can remember and acknowledge their past, and so forth. In sum, the rule of law in the transitional context requires a much more ambitious gaze than simply punishing the perpetrators of violence.[29]

That said, the fact that transitional justice mechanisms are often required to focus beyond punishment does not mean that states have a free hand with regard to the breadth and scope of the particular mechanism they employ. As one would expect, there is a lively debate amongst international lawyers concerning the extent to which international legal standards may limit the flexibility of nation states in establishing such mechanisms. So, for example, some international lawyers would argue that the international imperative to punish those most responsible (i.e. leaders and planners rather than "foot soldiers") for the most serious human rights abuses transcends the particularities of national contexts (e.g. Orentlicher 1991a).[30] Others would argue that international law has traditionally allowed considerable latitude to local responses where genuine efforts are being made at truth recovery in often difficult circumstances. Thus, for example, William Schabas (2004) suggests that there was considerable sympathy when the statute of the International Criminal Court (ICC) (discussed below) was being drafted that the Court should not become involved in decisions to prosecute perpetrators in instances where local countries were involved in "genuine" or "sincere" truth commission projects (as compared to naked attempts by outgoing or incumbent regimes to obfuscate their past misdeeds). He argues that such circumstances might persuade the prosecutor to look elsewhere (Schabas 2004).[31] The broader point, however, is that decisions in any local jurisdiction must consider at least the likely legality or otherwise of provisions such as truth commissions or amnesties under international law as part of their planning process. Below are a number of issues which are likely to be of relevance.

A right to truth?

There is no specific right to truth referred to in any of the better-known human rights instruments such as the UN Charter or the European Convention on Human Rights. Despite this, however, Amnesty International and Human Rights Watch (two prominent international human rights non-governmental organisations) have for a considerable time asserted that their work in this area is premised on an international "right to truth" (Kritz 1995: 217-219).[32] For example, almost a decade ago Priscilla Hayner was asserting that she too agreed that

---

[28] As has been discussed elsewhere, the Good Friday Agreement is conspicuous amongst such international political accords in that it does not contain an explicit legal method for institutionalised truth recovery. However, provisions such as those relating to the early release of prisoners, victims, the establishment of the Patten Commission, Criminal Justice Review and so forth may certainly be viewed as efforts to "deal with the past" (Bell 2003; Bell & Keenan 2004).

[29] "...establishment of the rule of law within a liberalising state is often considered to depend on exercises of individual accountability. Thus punishment most clearly instantiates the concern with individual responsibility central to law within the liberal state...In its transitional variant, however, not only is punishment informed by a mix of retrospective and prospective purposes, but also the question of whether to punish or to amnesty, to exercise or restrain criminal justice is rationalised in overtly political terms. Values of mercy and reconciliation commonly considered to be external to criminal justice are an explicit part of transitional deliberation. The explicit politicisation of criminal law in these periods challenges ideal understandings of justice and turns out to be a persistent feature of jurisprudence in the transitional context" (Teitel 2000: 217).

[30] For a self-styled "pragmatic" critique of this approach, see the response by Carlos Santiago Nino in the 1991 issue of the Yale Law Review. Nino was legal adviser to President Alfonsín regarding trials of military officers in Argentina's "Dirty War". See also Orentlicher's (1991b) spirited response to that critique in the same issue.

[31] The background to the International Criminal Court is discussed below.

[32] See also Article 19 (2000), especially Chapter One.

there is such a "right to truth" (1997), a position she reiterated in her 2001 book, *Unspeakable Truths* (Hayner 2001). Those who assert that such a right exists tend to do so from two broadly overlapping areas of international law: the desire to assure that perpetrators do not enjoy impunity from being held to account and the desire to ensure that the rights of victims are protected.

Hayner has received strong support for her position in the highly influential *Principles on Impunity* published in 1997 by UN Special Rapporteur, Louis Joinet. These were updated in 2005 by Diane Orentlicher (Orentlicher 2005). In the original principles, Joinet suggests in Principle 3 that the right to truth is a right for victims and their families to know the fate of their relatives, irrespective of any legal proceedings (Joinet 1996). The updated principles go further in recognising an "inalienable right to the truth" as a component of a broader "right to know" (hereafter Orentlicher 2005).[33] In broad terms, as Ratner and Abrams (1997) have concluded, the legal rationale under international law for truth commissions and other truth-recovery mechanisms may rest upon an implied duty of states to investigate and disseminate the truth about human rights violations, stemming from the right of individuals to be apprised of the truth. More broadly, the first of the Joinet Principles suggests that the right is also the right of society "...to know the truth about past events and about circumstances and reasons which led, through the consistent pattern of gross violations of human rights, to the perpetration of aberrant crimes". The Joinet Principles further describe mechanisms for ensuring the right to truth, namely commissions of inquiry (e.g. truth commissions) and the preservation of archives to prevent abusive authorities from destroying the evidence of their wrongdoings.

Although the Joinet Principles were not formally adopted by the United Nations, their impact was considerable in various international and regional legal fora (Orentlicher 2004).[34] For example, the Inter-American Commission on Human Rights established under the American Convention for Human Rights (the broadly equivalent structure in the Americas to the European Court of Human Rights or ECHR in Europe) has held that the right to the truth arises as a basic and indispensable consequence for all state parties, given that not knowing the facts related to human rights violations means that, in practice, there is no system of protection capable of guaranteeing the identification and possible punishment of those responsible.[35] The Inter-American Commission has also recognised the right "to know the full, complete, and public truth" and has affirmed that this is a collective rather than simply an individual right.[36] In 2002 the Inter-American Court affirmed that "society has the right to know the truth" regarding "atrocities of the past...so as to be capable of preventing them in the future".[37] In Europe, in the *Srebrenica* case, the Human Rights Chamber of the Hybrid Court (made up of local and international judges) ordered authorities of Republika Srpska "to conduct a full, meaningful, thorough, and detailed investigation" into the events surrounding the Srebrenica massacre with a view to making its own role known to "the applicants, all other family members, and the public".[38]

The notion of a right to truth is also contained in the UN *Basic Principles* document for victims of human rights abuses.[39] By way of background, this important document was adopted by the UN High Commission on Human Rights in April 2005 after 15 years of painstaking drafting. Similar to the Joinet/Orentlicher Principles, it is not of itself legally binding. As stated in the preamble to the document, it is however intended to summarise existing legal obligations under international human rights and humanitarian law.[40] As such, it is reasonable to argue that it constitutes an articulation of existing customary international law. These *Basic Principles* offer a definition of who should qualify as a victim of a conflict.[41] Principle 24 states:

---

[33] See Principle 2, "The inalienable right to the truth", in Part II, "The Right to Know" in Orentlicher (2005).

[34] The Updated Principles (Orentlicher 2005) have been adopted by the Human Rights Commission, but while this increases the Principles' status, they remain non-binding.

[35] Lucio Parada Cea et al. v. El Salvador, Caso 10.480, Informe No. 1/99, Inter-Am. CHR, OEA/Ser.L/V/II.95 Doc. 7 rev. en 531 (1998).

[36] See Report No. 3700, para. 148.

[37] Bámaca Velásquez Inter-American Court of Human Rights, vol. 70, Series C, paras. 159-166 (25 November 2000).

[38] Cases Nos. CH/01/8365 et al.

[39] The full title is the *Basic Principles and Guidelines on the Right to a Remedy and Reparation for Victims of Violations of International Human Rights and Humanitarian Law*. C.H.R. res. 2005/35, U.N. Doc. E/CN.4/2005/ L.10/Add.11 (19 April 2005).

[40] International human rights law refers to the set of international legal standards which have historically concerned the relationship between the state and individual (e.g. the European Convention on Human Rights or the United Nations Charter of Individual Rights and Freedoms). These are traditionally concerned with holding states rather than individuals to account. International Humanitarian Law refers to the laws of war (e.g. the various Geneva Conventions) and has historically been applied to both state and non-state actors and individuals.

[41] Principle 8 states that "...victims are persons who individually or collectively suffered harm, including physical or mental injury, emotional suffering, economic loss or substantial impairment of their fundamental rights, through acts or omissions that constitute gross violations of international human rights law, or serious violations of international humanitarian law. Where appropriate, and in accordance with domestic law, the term 'victim' also includes the immediate family or dependants of the direct victim and persons who have suffered harm in intervening to assist victims in distress or to prevent victimization". Principle 9 also states that "A person shall be considered a victim regardless of whether the perpetrator of the violation is identified, apprehended, prosecuted, or convicted and regardless of the familial relationship between the perpetrator and the victim".

...victims and their representatives should be entitled to seek and obtain information on the causes leading to their victimization and on the causes and conditions pertaining to the gross violations of international human rights law and serious violations of international humanitarian law and to learn the truth in regard to these violations.

Principle 23 also suggests that victims are entitled to "satisfaction" which may include "Verification of the facts and full and public disclosure of the truth" and/or "Public apology, including acknowledgement of the facts and acceptance of responsibility."

In brief, in light of the jurisprudence of the Inter-American human rights system in particular, and both the UN *Basic Principles* document on victims and the Joinet\Orenticher Principles, the status of a "right to truth" under customary international law is at least arguable. Further evidence of an emerging right to truth is afforded by a recent resolution of the United Nations Commission on Human Rights.[42] This resolution, although diplomatically avoiding the use of imperatives, acknowledges prior recognition of a right to truth by organs and agencies of the United Nations and "recognises the importance of respecting and ensuring the right to truth so as to contribute to ending impunity and to promote and protect human rights." This consolidation of a "right to truth" appears likely to continue.

The right to a remedy
Unlike the "right to truth", there is definitive national and European jurisprudence on the meaning of the long established right to remedy. For example, the ECHR has found:

the notion of an effective remedy entails that in addition to the payment of compensation where appropriate, a thorough and effective investigation capable of leading to the identification and punishment of those responsible and including effective access for the complainant to the investigatory procedure.[43]

While the state is afforded some leeway regarding the process for uncovering the truth, the means by which justice is achieved and reparations are provided has also been discussed in some detail by the ECHR. Thus, for example, in four important decisions made in May 2001 regarding cases emanating from the conflict in and about Northern Ireland (discussed in greater detail below), the ECHR insisted that in order to comply with the procedural requirements of Article 2 of the European Convention on Human Rights (the right to life), investigations of killings need to be independent, thorough, prompt, and effective, and the prosecution system needed to be fully accountable (Bell & Keenan 2005).[44]

The UN *Basic Principles* are also a useful source on the notion of the right to a remedy. They point to the long-established victims' "right to a remedy" contained in a plethora of international instruments (at p.2). They go on to describe this right to a remedy as consisting of the victim's rights to "access to justice"; "reparation for harm suffered and other appropriate remedy"; and, as noted above, "access to factual information and other relevant information concerning the violations". Although the emphasis in the *Basic Principles* is upon victims having access to a judicial remedy, they continue that "other remedies available to the victim include access to administrative and other bodies, as well as mechanisms, modalities and proceedings conducted in accordance with domestic law". There appears here to be a recognition of the possibility of other forms of recourse, including non-prosecutorial truth-recovery mechanisms satisfying the redress requirements under international law (Mallender 2005).

The legality of amnesty laws?
A third obvious relevant consideration with regard to the relationship between international law and possible truth-recovery mechanisms is the question of the legality or otherwise of amnesty provisions. It is important to be clear that international law does not prohibit amnesty laws per se. In fact, Additional Protocol II to the Geneva Conventions actually encourages states to grant the "broadest possible amnesty" at the end of hostilities in non-international armed conflicts. Although the International Committee of the Red Cross has subsequently tried to narrow the reading of this clause,[45] it is difficult to ignore the fact that this important instrument of international humanitarian law actually foresees and encourages the use of amnesties in certain contexts. However, it is true that certain amnesties in certain circumstances for certain crimes may be deemed unlawful.

---

[42] Resolution of the Commission on Human Rights on the Right to the Truth, Human Rights Resolution 2005/66 (20 April 2005).
[43] Askoy v Turkey, 1996, No. 100/1995/606/694, para. 98.
[44] Jordan v UK, (2003) 37 EHRR 2, Kelly v UK, Application No.30054/96, Judgement of 4 May 2001; and McKerr v UK (2002) 34 EHRR 553 and Shanaghan v UK, Application No. 37715/97, Judgement of 4 May 2001.
[45] See e.g. Ŝimonović (2004).

In broad terms, what has been happening at both the national and the international level is that courts have been narrowing the terms upon which amnesties may be deemed unlawful. For example, blanket amnesties "for all crimes committed between x date and y date" or "for all offences committed by x group or y group" have been found to be unlawful (Roht-Arriaza 1996; Cassese 2003; Mallender 2005). Blanket amnesties in places such as Chile and Argentina have been consistently eroded both by the national courts and international fora such as the Inter-American Court of Human Rights (Chigara 2002). Often it is because the amnesty provisions (e.g. in Peru, Haiti, and Uruguay) effectively remove the right to a remedy from those who have been victims of human rights violations, that they are found to be unlawful under international law.[46] Similarly, courts have found unlawful amnesties which included some of the most heinous offences such as genocide, crimes against humanity, and other crimes deemed so serious that they are viewed as "international" in nature, that it is not open to local states to permit the perpetrators of such acts to be amnestied (Bassiouni 1996). Thus, for example, with regard to Article 9 of the controversial Agreement between the government and rebel forces in Sierra Leone which provided for de facto blanket amnesty for both sets of protagonists, the UN Secretary General entered a proviso that "...the UN interprets that the amnesty and pardon in Article 9 of the Agreement shall not apply to international crimes of genocide, crimes against humanity, war crimes, and other serious violations of international humanitarian law" (United Nations 1999: 777 cited in Human Rights Watch 1999). This means that theoretically, while someone charged with such offences might benefit from an amnesty in their own country, under the rules of universal jurisdiction for such offences, they might be subject to prosecution if they travelled to a country which was so minded.[47]

Perhaps the most significant recent authoritative discussions concerning the legal status of amnesties can be seen in the discussion surrounding the Rome Statute, which governs the operation of the ICC. As was noted above, Schabas (2004) and other influential commentators have detected a sensitivity to local truth recovery and amnesty initiatives in the drafting of the relevant section concerning the decision to prosecute at the Court. Prosecutions under the Rome Statute may be restricted in a number of circumstances that could conceivably protect an amnesty. The UN Security Council has the power to defer an investigation or prosecution if it "promotes international peace or stability". The Prosecutor may choose not to initiate an investigation where a:

> prosecution is not in the interests of justice, taking into account all the circumstances, including the gravity of the crime, the interests of victims and the age or infirmity of the alleged perpetrator, and his or her role in the alleged crime.[48]

Finally, the ICC shall find cases inadmissible if a state with appropriate criminal jurisdiction prosecutes that case or investigates it and decides not to prosecute. A local decision not to prosecute stands, so long as it does not flow from "unwillingness or inability or prosecute". The statute does not explicitly say that a local amnesty process will automatically trump the "unwillingness to prosecute" hurdle, rather it leaves what Philippe Kirsch, chair of the drafting committee, referred to as "creatively ambiguous" provisions (Newman 2005). It would certainly be arguable that a lawfully established truth commission or amnesty process was not in fact evidence of an unwillingness to prosecute, but rather spoke to a conscious decision not to prosecute in the broader interests of national reconciliation.[49]

To summarise, apart from those crimes noted above which are deemed "international" in nature, the current state of international law with regard to amnesty processes would appear to suggest a leaning towards giving states a considerable degree of latitude, based largely on judgements of whether or not such amnesty initiatives are part of "genuine" processes of reconciliation or nation building.

---

[46] For example in Rodríguez v Uruguay [Communication No. 322/1988, U.N. Doc. CCPR/C/51/D/322/1988 (1994) at p. 12] the UN Human Rights Committee argued that a Uruguayan law called the Limitations Act 1986 was unlawful because it "...effectively excludes in a number of cases the possibility of investigation into past human rights abuses and thereby prevents the State Party from discharging its responsibilities to provide effective remedies to the victim of those abuses. Moreover the Committee is concerned that, in adopting this law, the State party is contributing to an atmosphere of impunity which may undermine the democratic order and give rise to further grave human rights violations."

[47] Cassese (2003: 316) suggests that even where individuals were suspected of such crimes and travelled to a different jurisdiction, if the amnesty had been granted by a specific judicial decision or a Truth and Reconciliation Commission rather than where the individual had benefited from a blanket amnesty, then "The exigencies of justice could be held to be fulfilled and foreign courts should refrain from adjudicating those crimes."

[48] Rome Statute of the International Criminal Court (1998) Article 52, 3(c) available at http://www.un.org/icc/part5.htm

[49] However UN Secretary General Kofi Annan has stated, "The purpose of the clause in the statute is to ensure that mass-murderers and other arch-criminals cannot shelter behind a State run by themselves or their cronies, or take advantage of a general breakdown of law and order. No one should imagine that it would apply to a case like South Africa's, where the regime and the conflict which caused the crimes have come to an end, and the victims have inherited power. It is inconceivable that, in such a case, the Court would seek to substitute its judgment for that of a whole nation which is seeking the best way to put a traumatic past behind it and build a better future". See Asmal (2000).

The right to reparations

A final issue of relevance to discussions on truth recovery which has received increased prominence in international legal circles in recent years is the notion of reparations (De Greiff 2006). Reparations are normally associated with those who have suffered as victims of violence during a conflict, although as the conflict in and about Northern Ireland highlights, sometimes the distinctions between victims and perpetrators are less clear cut than might appear at first (e.g. Morrissey & Smyth 2002). There are different forms of rights to reparations that can be ordered or recommended by an international court, including the rights to restitution, compensation, rehabilitation, and satisfaction, and guarantees of non-repetition (Mallender 2005). International courts consistently order or recommend reparations, usually in the form of financial compensation, although increasingly, organs such as the Inter-American Commission are recommending other forms of reparations, including the erection of memorials, public apologies or appropriate commemoration of the dead and injured (McEvoy & Conway 2004).

Again, the UN *Basic Principles* document is highly instructive. It argues that the extent of reparations should be proportionate – that is, proportionate to the gravity of the violations and the harm suffered. The right to reparations entails both individual as well as collective measures. The international guidelines on victims' rights all have sections – in most cases quite substantial sections – dedicated to the right of reparation. In general terms, however, there are four broad courses of action required to give effect to the right to reparation.

These are:

- Restitution: seeking to restore victims to their previous state by measures such as the restoration of liberty, citizenship, and employment.
- Compensation: providing damages for physical or mental injury, including compensation for lost opportunities, physical damage or harm to reputation.
- Rehabilitation: providing medical care, including psychological and psychiatric treatment.
- Satisfaction and guarantees of non-repetition: taking measures to ensure that there is a cessation of hostilities and closure provided for victims, including a search for those who have disappeared and an official acknowledgement of responsibility and apology, in addition to preventative measures instituted to prevent recurrence of violations.

Any programme of reparations as a result of a truth-recovery process would be expected to contain all of these elements. Indeed, there is a growing preference for comprehensive reparations packages which include measures of symbolic reparation (such as a national day of commemoration) or collective reparation to communities (such as targeted funding packages for community development or memorialisation) (De Greiff 2006).[50]

Conclusion

The preceding discussion is not a comprehensive review of the relevant international legal jurisprudence, standards and scholarly interpretation. Such a review could easily form the substance of a stand-alone legal academic text. Rather, it is intended to make the broad point that any truth-recovery option must be consistent with established international legal principles and to indicate some of the likely themes to emerge in such a process. Truth-recovery models are to some extent "creatures of law" in the sense that they often require legislation to become established and they must operate lawfully. As was noted above, law in the transitional context does have a particular political role to play, and international legal bodies are not unsympathetic to genuine efforts at using law to effect the process of conflict transformation. Questions such as the notion of a right to truth, the availability of a remedy for victims, the legality of any amnesty provisions, and the requirement for victim reparations are all complex legal issues which will inform the benchmarks by which the various truth-recovery options discussed below should be judged. Before looking in more detail at the Northern Ireland context, it may be useful at this juncture to offer an outline of the styles of truth-recovery models which have been employed in other transitional settings.

---

50 For example, the programme of reparations proposed by the Peruvian Truth and Reconciliation Commission has won particular plaudits as an example of best practice in concretising the notion of reparations in the truth recovery context (Orentlicher 2004). The Comprehensive Reparations Plan (PIR) involved extensive consultations with victims' organisations and other elements of civil society. It contains an explicit acknowledgment by the TRC that reparations are a moral, political and legal obligation of the State and that recognition of victims as human beings whose fundamental rights were violated is "the central goal" of reparations. It is also comprehensive, making reparations available to all victims of serious violations. At the same time, the proposed PIR allows individuals to pursue individual remedies instead of participating in the comprehensive programme if that is their preference. It also contains a range of complimentary programmes, measures of symbolic reparation, health and education-oriented programmes, and economic compensation.

International models of truth recovery & responses to widespread abuses

In the work which led to the production of this document, the HTR Truth Recovery and Acknowledgement Sub Group discussed a broad range of truth-recovery mechanisms in order to inform our debate on the Northern Ireland context. Some are of more direct relevance to Northern Ireland than others. Nonetheless, the group felt that it was important to provide some of those details in this document, both to underline again the breadth and complexity of the subject matter and to provide information about the models we considered were most relevant to engendering a productive discussion on the Northern Ireland context.

1. International retributive tribunals

Although there were failed attempts at trials after the First World War (Bass 2000), those which took place of Nazi and Japanese leaders by International Military Tribunals (IMT) after the Second World War in Nuremberg and Tokyo respectively may be seen as the first sustained effort at international truth recovery. Although these tribunals were primarily retributive in nature, focused upon the punishment of those guilty of the most heinous of offences, the need to establish a public "truth" about what had happened at the behest of these political and military leaders was also at the forefront of the minds of those who set them up. As Cassese (2003: 330) argues with regard to Nuremberg, "…the trial was designed to render great historical phenomena plainly visible, and was conceived of as a means of demythologising the Nazi State by exposing their hideous crimes for all to see". The public nature of these trials was explicitly designed to undermine the capacity for denial in the states and political cultures which had led to such atrocities being committed in the first place (Cohen 2001).

The terms of reference for the IMT were that they had jurisdiction to try Crimes against Peace (i.e. an "aggressive" war), Crimes of War,[51] and Crimes against Humanity[52] (namely murder, extermination, enslavement, or other inhuman acts perpetrated against civilians). The Nuremberg Tribunal tried 24 major Nazi war criminals, leaving the prosecution of minor ones to the states in which they had occurred. One defendant killed himself, another was declared unfit to stand trial, three were acquitted, 12 sentenced to death, three to life imprisonment, and four to determinate prison terms. The Tokyo tribunal tried 24 suspects including the former Japanese Prime Minister (Pritchard 1996; Maga 2001). While there were initial hopes that Nuremberg and Tokyo would begin the institutionalisation of a judicial response to atrocities, such aspirations foundered on the rocks of Cold War realpolitik. The international prohibitions against mass atrocities, codified in the aftermath of Nuremberg, withered as states systematically failed to enforce these norms. The West criticised the human rights record of Soviet states and their allies (and vice versa), but ignored the human rights records of right-wing governments in Latin America, Africa, and elsewhere who were anti-Soviet. The post-World War Two refrain of "never again" appeared hollow in the light of repeated acts of genocide in which the international community appeared incapable or unwilling to act, and arguably encouraged further acts of barbarism by despotic regimes.[53] Richard Goldstone, the first Prosecutor of the International Criminal Tribunal for the Former Yugoslavia, has concluded that the failure to prosecute Pol Pot (Cambodia), Idi Amin (Uganda), and Saddam Hussein (Iraq), among others, encouraged the Serbs to launch their policy of ethnic cleansing in the former Yugoslavia (1991-1995) and the Hutus to commit their genocide in Rwanda (Goldstone 2000).

Despite such failures, following the end of the Cold War, there has been something of a renaissance in the field of international criminal law. In the 1990s, following considerable pressure from the Germans, the French, and the US under Clinton, the UN agreed to the establishment of an ad hoc tribunal to deal with crimes in the former Yugoslavia, the International Criminal Tribunal for the Former Yugoslavia (ICTY). A similar ad hoc

---

[51] Crimes of War drew upon the long established traditions of humanitarian law. Humanitarian law or "the laws of war" can be traced to at least the 17th Century. It is premised on the notion that since war was a "normal aspect of foreign policy" it should be conducted in as civilised a fashion as possible. Thus rules emerged that armies should not deliberately kill civilians, loot cities, rape, attack someone carrying a white flag, attack people engaged in treating the wounded, kill or torture prisoners and so forth. The first Geneva Convention was signed in 1864 and has been further codified on several occasions since, mostly notably in 1929, 1949 and 1977 (Roberts & Guelff 2000).

[52] Crimes against Humanity were drawn up as a specific set of rules to deal with both the scale of the Nazi atrocities but also the fact that many such atrocities were carried out against their own citizens e.g. German Jews. While mass murder of civilians from another states was covered by war crimes, this new "crimes against humanity category" was required to cover heinous crimes carried out against one's own citizens. These kinds of crimes trumped any traditional consideration of the sovereignty of the state. Article 6(c) of the International Military Tribunal charter distinguished two types of crimes against humanity – firstly, murder, extermination, enslavement, deportation, and other inhuman acts against civilians, and secondly, persecution on political, racial or religious grounds.

[53] For example, four million people were murdered in Stalin's purges (1937-1953), five million were killed in China's Cultural Revolution (1966-1976), two million died in Cambodia's killing fields (1975-1979), 30,000 disappeared in Argentina's Dirty War (1976-1983), 200,000 were massacred in East Timor (1975-1985), 750,000 were murdered in Uganda (1971-1987), 100,000 Kurds were gassed in Iraq (1987-1988), and 75,000 peasants were slaughtered by death squads in El Salvador (1980-1992).

tribunal, the International Criminal Tribunal for Rwanda (ICTR), was also established to try individuals charged with offences related to the genocide there. In both instances, establishing the truth about what happened to provide redress to victims as well as to establish secure platforms for reconciliation were prominent rationales for their establishment (Barria & Roper 2005). Both are staffed by international judges, based outside the jurisdictions where the events occurred (the ICTY is based in the Hague in Holland and the ICTR is located in Arusha, Tanzania), and have their own prosecution, investigation and research units, appeal system, places of detention, and associated administrative and logistical support. In effect, they operate as mini criminal justice systems.[54] Both have jurisdiction to try (a) grave breaches of the 1949 Geneva Conventions "war crimes"; (b) violations of the laws or customs of war; (c) genocide; and (d) crimes against humanity. The ICTY has indicted 161 individuals, 131 of whom have so far appeared for trial, including most famously former Serbian President Slobodan Milosovic who died before his trial could be completed.[55] Since it was set up in 1997, the ICTR has delivered 19 judgments involving 25 accused, 23 of whom were convicted. In addition, 25 persons are currently on trial, which brings the number of persons whose trials have either been completed or are in progress to 50. They include one Prime Minister, 11 Government Ministers, four Prefects, and many other high-ranking personalities (UN 2005).

Following on from the establishment of these ad hoc tribunals, there have been a number of other developments in the field of international criminal law of broader relevance to the notion of truth recovery. In Sierra Leone, East Timor, Kosovo, and more recently Cambodia, "hybrid models" have been established which are, in effect, combinations of international and local lawyers and judges operating in conjunction to bring prosecutions for war crimes, crimes against humanity, genocide, and other serious crimes (Roper & Barria 2005). In some instances, such as East Timor and Sierra Leone, these retributive hybrid models operate alongside local truth commissions which are more reconciliation-focused, a relationship which has created some practical, political, and jurisdictional difficulties (Schabas 2003). In addition, as noted above, and despite persistent hostility from the US administration, the Rome Statute which established the Permanent ICC entered into force in July 2002. It too now has jurisdiction to take referrals of cases from either the UN or nation states concerning genocide, crimes against humanity, and war crimes where national courts are unwilling or unable to conduct genuine prosecutions (Schabas 2004; McGoldrich, Rowe & Donnelly 2004). In 2004, it took referrals with regard to three cases from Congo, Sudan, and Uganda. In the case of Uganda, the ICC is examining in particular the actions of the rebel group, the Lord's Resistance Army.

A key aim for all of these internationally-led initiatives has been to challenge the effective impunity of those responsible for planning or implementing the most serious of international crimes. While debates remain as to whether or not they have been fully effective, lessons have been learnt since Nuremberg and Tokyo and there is now considerably greater attention paid to meeting the needs of those victims most affected by such abuses in the ways in which such trials are conducted (Findlay & Henham 2005). The other great advantage of such trials is that they have the effect of having unpalatable truths "written into the record". As Michael Ignatieff has argued:

> the great virtue of legal proceedings is that their evidentiary rules confer legitimacy on otherwise contestable facts. In this sense, war crimes trials make it more difficult for societies to take refuge in denial - the trials do assist the process of uncovering the truth (2000: 113).

As to their specific relevance to the process of truth recovery with regard to the conflict in and about Northern Ireland, at first blush these models may seem of only limited interest. There are a number of political, temporal, as well as legal factors which would make it highly unlikely that such proceedings would commence with regard to the conflict in and about Northern Ireland.

Throughout the conflict in and about Northern Ireland the British government was highly resistant to attempts to "internationalise" the conflict. Thus, for example, when the Irish government attempted to use the offices of the United Nations to examine British policy in Northern Ireland, they met with the sternest opposition from Britain as one of the permanent members of the Security Council (O'Brien 1996). The idea that a British government would cede prosecutorial authority to any international tribunal for events which occurred within the United Kingdom would have appeared highly unlikely at any stage of the conflict in and about Northern Ireland. It would seem even more remote in a context where Northern Ireland is almost a decade on from the end of much of the organised political violence and is already engaged in the myriad of truth-recovery processes discussed below. With little likely pressure coming from an international community arguably concerned with abuses of a more contemporary and egregious scale, international retributive tribunals as a mode of truth recovery would appear politically unlikely in the extreme.

---

[54] One of the by-products of the scale of the infrastructure surrounding the international tribunals has been a spiralling of related costs. For example, by 2003 the ICTY had a staff of over 1,000 and an annual running budget of $223,000,000 (Kerr 2004).
[55] http://www.un.org/icty/glance/index.htm

As for the legal obstacles, they, too, are formidable. They are, however, worth developing in a little detail, not least because phrases discussed below which have a specific legal meaning have appeared in some of the public discourse in the wake of the conflict in and about Northern Ireland.[56] All of the legal tribunals above have been focused on the prosecution of those responsible for planning and implementing genocide, crimes against humanity, "war crimes", and other serious breaches of humanitarian law.

With regard to the ICC, under the Rome Statute, it cannot prosecute cases which occurred before 1 July 2002. With regard to genocide, it would appear highly unlikely that the events of the conflict in and about Northern Ireland would meet the extremely high threshold of this "crime of crimes".[57] As for "crimes against humanity", these require actions to be committed against civilians and committed in pursuance of a broader policy (Hirsh 2003). They must be "widespread" or "systematic" (Kittichaisaree 2001; Cassese 2003). While historically it was assumed that these were limited to states and carried out in pursuance of a state policy, this has been broadened in recent years to include non-state actors. However, it is only applicable when such groups can exercise de facto control over a particular territory.[58] While republicans might have met this threshold during the brief period of the "no-go areas" in the 1970s, it is a threshold that probably rules out much of both republican and loyalist activity for the vast majority of the conflict in and about Northern Ireland.

The categories of war crimes and other serious violations of the laws and customs of international humanitarian law are more interesting in relation to Northern Ireland. War crimes have traditionally been understood as "grave" breaches of the Geneva Conventions and until recently had explicitly not applied to conflicts such as the conflict in and about Northern Ireland, which were deemed in international law as "internal armed conflicts" (Schabas 2004: 57). However, following developments at the Yugoslav and Rwanda tribunals, the Rome Statute of the ICC now includes a lengthy section concerning war crimes committed in internal armed conflicts (Rowe 2004).[59] Although, as discussed above, the chance of the criteria being met for actual prosecutions by international tribunals are slight in Northern Ireland, these legal constructs may still be of relevance.

One of the difficulties arising in this context is that, in reality, there was little systemic application of the laws of war standards to the conflict in and about Northern Ireland while it was ongoing (McEvoy 2001, 2003). As noted above, the British government was at considerable pains to stress that the laws of war did not apply to "the Troubles", and neither loyalist nor republican paramilitaries made any serious effort to identify publicly their respective targeting strategies with the strictures of the laws of war. However, as Colm Campbell (2005) has argued recently, the need to find appropriate legal standards within which to frame the actions of these non-state actors in particular[60] may mean that previous armed actions will be benchmarked retrospectively against humanitarian law requirements, as occurred in the South African TRC process. Thus, for example, if a truth-recovery mechanism in Northern Ireland was to reach a finding that x or y protagonists had been guilty of war crimes, this might have a considerable social and political effect, perhaps exacerbating divisions and polarisation.

Thus, while the legal mechanism of an international retributive tribunal may be politically unlikely to occur, the legal classifications provided by the developments in this field may ultimately prove to be of quite considerable importance indeed.

---

[56] See e.g. website of Families Acting for Innocent Relatives (FAIR) which makes a number of allegations of genocide carried out against the Protestant community in South Armagh. http://www.victims.org.uk/future.html

[57] What distinguishes genocide from other crimes which involves murder is what is often referred to as the "specific intent" rule wherein the actions must be committed with the specific intent to destroy in whole or in part a national, ethnic, religious or racial group. There would also seem to be an implicit requirement that the acts be committed as part of a widespread or systemic attack, or as part of a general plan to destroy the group (Schabas 2004: 38-39).

[58] Prosecutor v Tadic (Case No IT-94-1-T) before the ICTY, Opinion and Judgement 7 May 1997, para 654.

[59] For example, part of Article 8 of the Rome Statute applies to civilians or combatants who are taking no part in active hostilities and includes a range of offences defined as grave breaches of humanitarian law including "violence to life and person, in particular murder of all kinds, mutilation, cruel treatment and torture; ...the passing of sentences and the carrying out of executions without previous judgement pronounced by a regularly constituted court; ...intentionally directing attacks against the civilian population as such or against individual civilians not taking part in hostilities...".

[60] State actors can be adjudged guilty of breaches of human rights standards such as the European Convention on Human Rights as well as Humanitarian Law standards. As states are the only signatories to international treaties, it is only they who can be adjudged guilty of breaches of human rights standards.

2. Truth commissions

Over the past two decades there has been a phenomenal growth in the utilisation of different models of "truth commissions" as mechanisms for dealing with the transition from violent conflict. In her 2001 book, Priscilla Hayner details a total of 21 truth commissions. In addition to those considered in her book, commissions have been established in recent years in a number of other jurisdictions, including East Timor, Ghana, Peru and Morocco. Past commissions have been known by a variety of names. Previous versions of truth commissions have included Commissions on the Disappeared in Argentina, Uganda, and Sri Lanka, and Truth and Justice Commissions in Haiti and Ecuador. More recently, the trend has been to include the term reconciliation; thus South Africa, Sierra Leone and Peru all set up Truth and Reconciliation Commissions, East Timor established a Commission for Reception, Truth and Reconciliation, a National Reconciliation Commission in Ghana, and in Morocco a Commission on Equity and Reconciliation was set up. Despite this trend, however, some critics have argued that the use of the term "reconciliation" implies a transformative effect that a commission will be hard-pressed to achieve, thus unnecessarily and unfairly raising public expectations of the process (Wilson 2001). Indeed, recently it has been suggested that what is required is the establishment of a permanent international global truth commission to assist countries emerging from their violent past (Forsberg & Teivainen 2004).

Despite the variety of nomenclature, truth commissions share certain key features. Hayner (2001: 14) suggests that the common characteristics shared by truth commissions are:

- Truth commissions focus on the past;
- They investigate a pattern of abuses over a period of time rather than focus on a specific event;
- A truth commission is a temporary body, typically in operation for six months to two years and typically completes its work with the submission of a report; and
- Commissions are officially sanctioned, authorised or empowered by the state (and sometimes also by armed opposition groups wherein, for example, a truth commission has been agreed as part of a broader peace agreement).

There are a number of websites that provide comprehensive overviews of the work of these commissions, as well as offering a basic "how-to" set of guidelines concerning the establishment and management of commissions.[61] Rather than reproducing such work, this document considers a range of thematic issues of broader relevance to the debate on truth recovery in Northern Ireland. The thematic issues addressed are a combination of those identified in the literature and those raised during the process which has led to this document.

Challenges of Truth Commission Design

Challenges concerning the design of truth commissions arise in a number of overlapping areas:

(i)   Determining the goals of a commission, e.g. determining what is truth? What is reconciliation?
(ii) Deciding upon the mechanism for commission independence, selection, and recruitment
(iii) Determining the mandate of the commission
(iv) Determining the role of reconciliation in the work of a commission
(v)   Determining whether a commission should name names
(vi) Determining the commission functions and whether hearings should be held in public
(vii) Determining commission powers, methods of achieving institutional accountability
(viii) Determining commission powers in relation to any amnesty provisions
(ix) Determining what happens after a commission

Within these broad sectors are discrete design challenges such as criteria for commission selection and recruitment; the question of naming/not naming individual perpetrators in a final report; whether proceedings should be conducted in public or private; and ways of exploring institutional accountability and linkages with other mechanisms of transitional justice, including prosecutions and amnesty. Each of these thematic issues is discussed further below. It is also important to note that these thematic issues are also of relevance to other models of truth recovery, such as those outlined in Chapter Four, and are therefore worth exploring in some detail.

(i)   What is truth?

At first glance, the notion of truth in this context might seem relatively straightforward – it would appear to equate with uncovering the "facts" as to what occurred during a violent political conflict. However, the experience of truth-recovery mechanisms elsewhere has underlined just how complex the idea may become in a transitional process. The South African experience on this issue is particularly instructive.

The SATRC began its work with quite a simplistic concept of truth as establishing the facts of the apartheid era (Posel 1999). However, the final SATRC report actually defines four notions of truth which guided the Commission during its work. These were:

(1) *Factual or forensic truth*: the familiar legal or scientific notion of bringing to light factual, corroborative "evidence".
(2) *Personal or narrative truth*: the individual truths of victims and perpetrators, attaching value to oral tradition and story-telling and linking the role of such narrative truth to healing.
(3) *Social truth*: established through interaction, discussion, and debate, social truth acknowledges the importance of transparency and participation and affirms the dignity of human beings.
(4) *Healing and restorative truth*: framing or understanding the narratives of the past in such a way that they are directed towards goals of self-healing, reconciliation, and reparation – a process which requires acknowledgement that everyone's suffering was real and worthy of attention.[62]

Although, as Cohen (2001) points out, the Commission report in practice narrowed to focus predominantly on notions of forensic and narrative truth, such sub-categorisations reflect the complexity of reality. Forensic truth focused upon two levels, the individual and the social. At the individual level, it meant finding out what exactly happened to whom, where, when, how, and who either carried out such actions or ordered them. At the social level, it meant recording the context, causes, and patterns of violations. Often during the process of the SATRC, this broadly legalistic approach was juxtaposed with the narrative and subjective aspects of truth recovery. At various times, one was preferred over the other, with the narrative approach being particularly dominant during the televised hearings, but the legalistic forensic version becoming more significant in the latter stages, as the actual report was prepared and written up (Wilson 2001: 38).

Similar to most truth commissions, the SATRC was operating in a highly politicised environment (Tutu 1999; Boraine 2000; Orr 2000). In order to deal with these pressures and to demonstrate their bona fides and impartiality, the Commission increasingly relied upon the scientific nature of their truth-recovery methods. Thus, they made use of "Infocomm", a large-scale human rights database which had been used elsewhere (e.g. in El Salvador and Haiti) to manage their data. Statements were catalogued, placed in a database, categorised into different types of abuses, the names of victims and perpetrators, and short narratives were recorded. The information was then corroborated and assessed by a team of over 60 investigators, either accepted or rejected, and then passed from regional-level findings to the national task group (South African Truth and Reconciliation Commission 1998). As the data processors were forced to reduce the statements to 30 words or fewer to fit on the database, many were uncomfortable that, in effect, the data-recording process was driving the tone and content of the ultimate findings.[63]

The subsequent critiques of the South African process (e.g. Posel 1999; Wilson 2001) are a useful corrective to bear in mind in the debate on truth recovery in Northern Ireland. Obviously, the desire for a definitive account concerning questions such as "what happened", "who planned and ordered it", and "who was responsible" are likely to be the dominant focus in truth recovery in this context as elsewhere. This is both understandable and politically necessary, since arguably the conflict in and about Northern Ireland was sustained at different junctures by what historians might term "workable" but largely mutually exclusive versions of history between the various protagonists (e.g. O'Leary & McGarry 1995). However, this comparatively narrow version of truth will be somewhat anaemic unless it is informed by a process that includes space for more subjective, narrative-based accounts. Put simply, one cannot hope to explore or understand the actions and reactions of those who have either been involved in violence and/or been on the receiving end of such violence, unless one has the opportunity to understand better their subjective experiences and world views as actors in such events. This is not to argue that such experiential or subjective accounts should "trump" forensic truth. Rather, it is to suggest that the subjective or narrative truths of the actors involved should inform the political, social, and ideological context by which their actions are understood.

---

[62] For a critical discussion on these formulations see Posel (2002).
[63] "The emotional part of the story wouldn't go on the computer, remember it was just a machine. You'd lose a lot – we couldn't put style or emotion into the summary. We were inputting for counting purposes. We lost the whole of the narrative...we lost the meaning of the story. It was tragic, pathetic. It became dry facts" (Interview with Chief SATRC data processor in Johannesburg Office, cited in Wilson, 2001: 46).

(ii) Commission independence, selection and recruitment

The establishment of a truth commission requires a degree of political will on the part of the government concerned. Although, as is discussed below, there is often a lively debate as to whether governments are genuinely interested in full truth recovery, the fact that any truth commission should be seen to be independent from the government of the day is now a generally accepted axiom of the truth literature. As Jeremy Sarkin (1999: 803) has argued, "If the commission is not seen as independent of the government, this will affect the public's perception of the commission's objectivity...the state and not the government must establish the commission by law". Other than the need for independence from government and other parties to the conflict, the question of who manages and staffs any truth-recovery institution is also of crucial importance to its credibility and effectiveness, and may ultimately determine whether a truth commission succeeds or fails (Freeman & Hayner 2003). As the figureheads and guides to the investigative process, commissioners, in particular, are likely to play a crucial role. For example, in the South African context, Krog (1998) has described Archbishop Tutu as the "compass" of the SATRC. Much of the reconciliatory and nation-building tone traditionally associated with the South African Commission has been attributed directly to his personality and Christian approach to conflict transformation (Wilson 2001).

Commissioners should be appointed following a selection process that is transparent, inclusive, democratic, representative, non-discriminatory, and appropriate to the commission's goals and broader societal needs. Although commissioners are often presidentially appointed (such as those in Chile, Sri Lanka, Ghana, and Peru), a participative selection process can encourage media engagement and public ownership of the process from the outset. For example, the commissioners in South Africa were appointed after a transparent and inclusive process of public nominations, short-listing by a dedicated committee, and public interviews. A similar public selection process for commissioners of the Commission for Reception, Truth and Reconciliation (CAVR) in East Timor received 300 nominations. The CAVR mandate also stipulated that 30% of the commissioner panel be female.

Commissioners are usually selected in consideration of attributes such as nationality, experience, reputation, and human rights track record. An obvious issue for consideration is whether appointees should be local or international. Local or national appointees have the advantage of in-depth knowledge of the conflict and the local "politics of truth". However, it may be difficult to find suitably qualified local candidates who are perceived as neutral. Thus for example, Nepal's Commission of Inquiry dissolved after two of its three members resigned in protest over the appointment of a chair they viewed as having collaborated with the prior regime (Hayner 2001: 57).

The degree of international involvement has varied widely. At one end of the spectrum is the CAVR in East Timor, which (though established by the UN Transitional Administration for East Timor) is staffed almost wholly by East Timorese, with limited international technical support. At the other extreme, the El Salvador Commission on the Truth was staffed wholly by non-nationals. Mixed boards of international/national commissioners chaired the Sierra Leone Truth and Reconciliation Commission. In Guatemala, two Guatemalans and one foreigner chaired the Commission for Historical Clarification (CEH). This latter body had over 200 staff members at the height of operations, though none of the administrative managers was Guatemalan, for fear of reprisals against nationals in those positions.

Selection criteria focused on status and reputation may stipulate that appointees be of "national and international prestige" (Argentina) or possess "high moral character, impartiality and integrity" (East Timor).[64] Demonstrated commitment to human rights principles is also often specified. Other staffing requirements will depend on the context. For example, in Sierra Leone, special training of commission staff to deal with women and child victims was seen as a necessity. In other contexts, the skills of forensic anthropologists, psychologists and archaeologists may be valuable. The total number of staff members within a commission has varied from fewer than 30 (El Salvador, Sri Lanka), 40-60 (Argentina, Chile, Sierra Leone) to several hundred (East Timor, South Africa).

It would be difficult to envisage a successful truth-recovery process in Northern Ireland that did not have significant international input. Indeed, one of the marked tendencies of the process of conflict transformation in the jurisdiction has been to involve international actors of high reputation in the most difficult and demanding aspects of the peace process (McEvoy & Morison 2003). Thus, for example, the chairing of the political negotiations, the Patten Commission, the Sentence Review Commission, the Independent International Commission on Decommissioning have all drawn heavily from international expertise in order to

---

[64] Regulation No. 2001/10 on the Establishment of a Commission for Reception, Truth and Reconciliation in East Timor, UNTAET/REG/2001/10 13 July 2001, s.4(1). "Nunca Mas: Report of the Argentine Commission on the Disappeared" Transitional Justice: How Emerging Democracies Reckon With Former Regimes. Volume III: Laws, Ruling and Reports (Washington DC: United States Institute of Peace Press) excerpted in Kritz (1995).

underline their impartiality and enable these various entities to carry out their task more effectively. Whether any truth-recovery institution would also include local commissioners would be a matter for political negotiation. Certainly, there is considerable experience of finding an appropriate balance with regard to community background on public bodies in the jurisdiction. However, as evidenced by recent controversies regarding similar public appointments, the need for an open and transparent appointment process with, for example, a suitable emphasis on a proven commitment to human rights principles or other selection criteria drawn from the international experience would be of central importance to maximising the credibility of any such truth-recovery initiative.

In addition, it would be important to ensure that any truth-recovery initiative was properly staffed and resourced to carry out its functions. As is discussed in further detail below, with regard to the specific options proposed, there are a number of complex tasks which will be required from any such institution. Statement-taking, investigation, psychological support, research, data management and authentication, public consultation and public relations – these and other functions will all require significant administrative and financial support. As Murray and Livingstone (2004) argue persuasively, one of the key aspects that undermined the effectiveness of the Northern Ireland Human Rights Commission in its first years was a lack of financial and political support from the government. Without doubt, the extent of resourcing in terms of staff and budget of any truth-recovery institution would be a crucial benchmark by which to judge the commitment of the British and Irish governments to the process.

(iii) Terms of reference: defining the mandate

The mandate of a truth commission, by its delineation of the types of violation which a commission will investigate, the period of time which will be under investigation, and the period of time which is available for investigation, is a critical determinant of the type and extent of truth elicited. An obvious potential pitfall is a commission which is given an overly narrow substantive scope of investigation. For example, the Chilean National Commission on Truth and Reconciliation (1990) was mandated to investigate state abuse of human rights resulting in death or disappearance but not violations such as torture or illegal detainment; thus excluding tens, perhaps hundreds, of thousands of victims from the investigation. The failures of that commission led to the issue being revisited more than a decade later, by a National Commission on Political Imprisonment and Torture (2003-2004) which documented around 28,000 testimonies of victims of torture and political imprisonment who had been excluded by the narrow terms of reference of the 1990 Commission.

The mandate of any truth commission must be sufficiently broad to explore the historical causes or other events surrounding a period of conflict, but sufficiently focused in order to render the project "doable". This is what Hayner (1997: 179) has referred to as a "flexible but strong" mandate which allows a commission some leeway in shaping the parameters of the investigation.

It would be possible to have the primary focus of a truth commission or other truth-recovery mechanism related to the conflict in and about Northern Ireland focused upon, for example, the period between 1966 and the signing of the 1998 Agreement (also known as the Good Friday Agreement or Belfast Agreement, hereafter the Agreement), but with context-setting sections in the truth commission's final report to reflect on the periods before and after those dates. As is discussed in greater detail below, the remit of any such institution should be broad enough to encompass a focus upon events which have led to deaths and injuries during the conflict in and about Northern Ireland, but also the role played by various institutions in contributing or otherwise to the context within which events occurred. As for the period in which a commission should be operable, although these have varied internationally, a broad rule of thumb might be that a period of around two years should be sufficient to conduct most commission investigations (Orentlicher 2004: 19(h)). Finally, any commission must inevitably focus upon the role that reconciliation should play in its ethos and working practices.

(iv) The meaning of reconciliation

One of the most oft-stated rationales for a truth commission is that there is an intrinsic relationship between the search for truth and the potential for reconciliation in transitional societies (Kriesberg 2004). "Knowing" the truth about what happened and an acknowledgement of what happened and its impact upon victims is often portrayed as a necessary precursor to individual, communal or societal reconciliation (Tutu 1999). The trend in recent years has been to include the term reconciliation in the name of truth commissions (e.g. in South Africa, Sierra Leone, Peru, East Timor, Ghana, Morocco) to underscore its centrality in the objectives, ethos, and working practices of the different commissions.

However, the complexities of the notion of reconciliation are borne out by the failure of a number of truth commissions to define properly its meaning. For example, as Richard Wilson (2001) points out, whilst it was included in the nomenclature of the SATRC, the Commission never actually defined what was meant by reconciliation in that context.[65]   Similarly, the relevant statute for the East Timorese Commission on Reception, Truth and Reconciliation contains no such definition, although a criterion is laid down as to how individuals may qualify for community-based reconciliation as opposed to prosecution.[66] In both instances the lack of a clear definition of what is meant by reconciliation has led to political and practical confusion as to its meaning and also how its effectiveness may be measured or evaluated. As Sarkin and Daly rhetorically ask about reconciliation in transitional societies more generally:

> But what does 'reconciliation' mean in these different countries? Is it national unity? Is it peace? Is it healing? Is it relationship building? Is it stability? Is it harmony? Is it developing a democracy that ensures the fullest sense of inclusivity and opportunity, as well as access to resources for those who reside in the country? Is it all of these? Or none? Is it just moving on? (Sarkin & Daly 2004: 662).

Hamber and Kelly (2005: 13) point out that the notion has been subject to a number of quite distinct interpretations internationally, including as a "soft" concept or euphemism for political compromise, a profound process involving forgiveness and repentance (which often carries theological overtones), or as a practical programme of work designed to re-establish workable relationships in deeply divided societies. Some commentators have described reconciliation as akin to varying degrees of co-existence, from "integrated" societies in which members of different ethnic, racial, or religious groups live in harmony with one another, to a more minimalist approach which requires "only that members of such groups live together without killing each other" (Afzali & Colleton 2003: 3). It has been variously described as the "rebuilding of a moral order" (Stevens 2004: 42-43), creating a "sense of belonging" amongst all citizens (Porter 2003: 94) or, more cynically, the "second best alternative when justice is impossible" (Sarkin & Daly 2004: 668).

For many academics, reconciliation is viewed as an ongoing process rather than a seminal "moment" such as the completion of a truth commission. For example, Huyse (2003) argues that there are three stages to reconciliation: replacing fear by non-violent coexistence, building confidence and trust, and moving towards empathy. For him, empathy also does not imply forgiveness or absolute harmony, and does not exclude feelings of anger. In order to achieve these objectives, Huyse argues that a variety of mechanisms are required, including truth-telling, reparations, restorative justice, and processes to promote healing (cited in Hamber & Kelly 2005: 21). Similarly, after their comprehensive review of the literature, Hamber and Kelly (2005: 7) conclude that reconciliation should best be viewed as a voluntary process which involves addressing conflictual and fractured relations through a number of practical interwoven strands.   These include developing a shared vision of an interdependent and fair society; acknowledging and dealing with the past; building positive relationships; significant cultural and attitudinal change; and substantial social, economic, and political change.

To summarise, any truth commission that seeks to contribute to reconciliation must recognise the complexity of the term "reconciliation", the fact that dealing with the past may be but one part of a broader societal process, and that the relationship between truth recovery and reconciliation is often a complex one. While the most common articulation of that relationship is that truth is necessary as a precursor to reconciliation, it might equally be argued that in some instances truth may actually impede reconciliation, where the horrors of past acts are so painful as to harden attitudes, and make forgiveness and empathy all but impossible (e.g. Sarkin & Daly 2004). There are real difficulties in assessing or measuring the extent to which reconciliation has actually been achieved (Gibson 2004b). There are also issues concerning the danger of reconciliation in a process of truth recovery creating an ethos which pressurises victims towards forgiveness of those who have killed or injured their loved ones or which masks a failure to hold accountable individual perpetrators or institutions which have been guilty of previous gross violations of human rights (Wilson 2001). The particular challenges of reconciliation as a part of truth recovery in the Northern Ireland context are discussed in Chapter Four, option four.

---

[65] "...reconciliation was to be a secondary outcome which flowed from the other, more important, activities of investigation and indemnification for offenders...Defining exactly what was meant by reconciliation remained one of the incomplete tasks of the TRC. This stemmed from a number of factors including the pragmatic realisation on the part of the Commissioners that if they defined a key objective, then they could be held accountable for not achieving it, and it was obvious to Commissioners that attempts at reconciling individuals would achieve only mixed results. In the context of a largely critical media, unleashing such a messy and unmanageable process would be leaving a hostage to fortune. In addition, reconciliation like all central unifying metaphors, would function best as a kind of social glue when it was left indeterminate. Different groups with dissimilar agendas could then appeal to reconciliation to advance their objectives" (Wilson 2001: 100-101).

[66] Individuals must submit a statement to the Commission with a full description of the acts, an admission of responsibility, an explanation of their linkage to the conflict, and a renunciation of violence to achieve political ends. Regulation No. 2001/10 On The Establishment Of A Commission For Reception, Truth And Reconciliation in East Timor, Section 22.

(v) Naming names

The question of whether a commission can identify individual perpetrators may be addressed in its mandate (e.g. the SATRC was mandated to name individual perpetrators while the Guatemalan CEH and the recent Moroccan Equity and Reconciliation Commission (Instance Équité et Réconciliation (IER)) were both mandated not to), although it has also often been left to the individual commission's discretion.[67] Commissions in Chad, El Salvador, and Rwanda opted to identify individual perpetrators, but the overwhelming majority of past commissions have chosen not to.

Deciding whether or not to name individual perpetrators is a contentious issue that will require a complex balancing of the competing demands of victims and the wider process of conflict transformation. Naming perpetrators may address a public desire for retribution, the naming and shaming of "the guilty men and women" (Osiel 1997). For victims, some would argue that public identification of the person(s) responsible may provide some sense of closure (Findlay & Henham 2005). On a collective level, naming perpetrators of atrocities may be seen as contributing to the formation of a more comprehensive record of past events, and may assist to unravel the role of state institutions, collusion, and patterns of political violence amongst paramilitary protagonists (Crocker 2000). A further compelling justification for identification of individuals is where the alternative is impunity. If there is no effective judicial process which can attribute individual responsibility, and a truth commission possesses overwhelming evidence of such responsibility, it may consider failure to identify the individual concerned to be both unjust and offensive to the victims (Hayner 2001).

The arguments against naming names are also strong in some contexts. One concern is the rights of those accused. As José Zalaquett has argued with regard to the Rettig Commission in Chile (of which he was a commissioner), "naming culprits through an official commission appointed by the executive, which did not have subpoena powers and could not conduct trials, would have been analogous to publicly indicting individuals without due process" (1992: 1435). Such due process concerns can be at least partially alleviated by adoption of clear policies regarding corroboration and standards of proof. For example, the UN Truth Commission for El Salvador named perpetrators where their guilt was established by two credible and independent sources, while the SATRC named individual perpetrators if their identities were clear and the Commission could give them notice of its intention to name them. One reliable information source was considered sufficient to corroborate victim testimony regarding a perpetrator's identity. As a basic standard, the Joinet *Principles on Impunity* (1996) recommend that a commission must try to corroborate any information gathered, and that any person implicated by a commission's findings is entitled to be notified and given an opportunity to refute the charges against them (Principle 8: Guarantees for Persons Implicated). This was affirmed as best practice in the follow-up *Independent Study on Impunity* by Professor Diane Orentlicher (2004: 19 (d)) and the Updated Principles (2005: Principle 9).[68] Drawing upon submissions by Human Rights Watch to the SATRC, Hayner has similarly argued that, while attention must be paid to due process considerations in the operation of a truth commission, it is important to distinguish these from the standards required for a criminal trial.[69]

Apart from due process concerns, the compelling reasons offered for not "naming names" are usually associated with the political context in which the truth-recovery institution is established. Thus, for example, in circumstances where the move to democracy is seen as fragile or reversible, commissions have historically tended not to name individuals, lest it herald a reversion to authoritarian rule in order to protect those with much to lose from the previous regime. Also, where the legal powers of compulsion of a commission are limited, or indeed the political circumstances are such that, in effect, a truth-recovery mechanism is relying upon the co-operation of former combatants, then the prospect of perpetrators being publicly named would appear to be a powerful disincentive to cooperation (Ensalaco 1994). There appears to be a sliding scale apparent in the operation of commissions, between balancing the level of involvement of those named and the

---

[67] Although some past commissions have been given discretion on whether or not to identify perpetrators, it is generally better to have such an important matter clarified at the earliest stage possible.

[68] "If a truth commission has authority to identify suspected perpetrators of violations or if individuals may be implicated in the commission's proceedings, those individuals should be provided appropriate opportunities to provide to the commission their version of the events in question." This right does not necessarily extend to permitting the accused to confront their accusers if the Commission believes that this might put the witnesses at risk.

[69] "While due process is important, it is widely agreed that the guarantees required for a commission are less than those of a criminal trial. In a trial, certain minimal requirements are almost universally accepted: the accused must be informed in advance of the charges, and must be given adequate time and opportunity to defend him or herself, including the right to counsel and right to call and confront witnesses. But due process requirements are in part determined by the severity of punishment that may result. The consequences of being named by a commission are far less severe than the consequences of being found guilty in court. While perhaps damaging a person's reputation, a commission generally has no powers to punish the named. It may recommend prosecutions or other civil penalties, but these will usually require yet another layer of review before being implemented" (Hayner 2001: 129).

resultant social or personal consequences where such individuals remain in the community where the offences took place. As Hayner (2001: 132) argues, such a logic would suggest omitting the names of low-level perpetrators in light of the risks to them or their victims, but a stronger inclination towards naming those involved at senior military/paramilitary or political levels who authorised or organised massive abuses or who knowingly allowed such abuses to take place "under their watch".

Finally there is an argument that in focusing upon the attribution of individual culpability associated with the public naming of the guilty, there is a risk of obscuring broader institutional or societal responsibility for past atrocities. Put simply, an exclusive focus upon the naming of the 18-year-old paramilitary who carries out a sectarian or racist murder obfuscates the role of the sectarian or racist demagogue who inspired him to take up an AK 47 or a machete in the first place. As Hans Steinert (1997) has pointed out, such an approach not only produces a handful of the guilty but many more "false innocents". To counter this danger, individual accountability for particular acts must be framed within the broader context within which violence occurred.[70]

The question of whether the "naming of names" will form part of any truth-recovery initiative in Northern Ireland will be one of the most difficult choices of those involved. The delicate balance to be struck will be between (a) the understandable desire of some victims to know the identity of those involved in killing or injuring their loved ones; (b) the due process considerations of those named in any such proceedings; and (c) the likely impact on the effectiveness of the process when the application of such sanctions includes either all perpetrators, or even only those in more senior political or military positions, and the arguably stronger public interest in the naming of those in higher positions. (See the discussion below on lustration.)

(vi) Commission functions and the public/private debate

The traditional functions associated with truth commissions include activities such as public dialogue and education, victim and witness statement-taking, research and investigation, conduct of hearings and the ability to draft recommendations, and (the process which is generally seen as the primary task of a truth commission) the construction of a report which establishes the occurrence of and culpability for incidents, patterns, and policies of human rights abuses.[71] All of these various functions require consideration and perhaps dedicated training processes (in, for example, statement-taking, or dealing with children or victims of sexual violations). Apart from the logistical tasks of a commission in carrying out its work, the broad political and sociological functions are usually associated with the notion of educating and informing the affected society or societies about what has actually occurred in their past (Landsman 1996; Shea 2000). In assuming responsibility for this educative function, truth commissions have increasingly had to decide whether or not their hearings, or at least part of them, should be heard in public.

Older commissions such as those held in Argentina, Chile, and El Salvador tended to hold their deliberations in private closed-door sessions. As the Truth Commissions Project argues,

> the less stable the political environment, the higher the power of former perpetrators, and the more pervasive fear and distrust in a society, the less feasible public hearings are. They can only be held in the context of irreversible transition and in the presence of safety and protection for victims and witnesses.[72]

However, since the SATRC, the tendency has been a presumption at least in favour of holding hearings in public, with the capacity (where necessary) to hold in-camera hearings. The SATRC held 76 public hearings, at which approximately 2000 individuals gave testimony. More recently (2002), the Peruvian TRC – the first commission in Latin America to conduct public hearings – involved close to 10,000 people in a public hearings process conducted in 15 separate communities. Similarly, the recent commissions in Ghana, East Timor, and Morocco have held at least part of their proceedings in public.

The public aspects of the hearings are primarily educative and commemorative, or what Mark Osiel has referred to as "making public memory publicly" (2000: 192). Although South Africa is renowned for its public hearings, as Hayner (2001: 227) points out, in fact less than 10% of the total number of victims who gave

---

[70] As Major Craig Williamson, a former security police spy in South Africa told the South African Truth and Reconciliation Commission: "Our weapons, ammunition, uniforms, vehicles, radios and other equipment were all developed and provided by industry. Our finances and banking were done by bankers who even gave us covert credit cards for covert operations. Our chaplains prayed for our victory and our universities educated us in war. Our propaganda was carried by the media and our political masters were voted back into power time after time with ever increasing majorities" (cited in Martin 2004: 16).

[71] See http://www.truthcommission.org/ for further details. The Truth Commissions Project is a collaboration between the Program for Negotiation at Harvard Law School, Search for Common Ground (an international NGO based in Washington, D.C.), and the European Centre for Common Ground (based in Brussels). The project was established to assist political leaders who are considering the establishment of a truth commission as part of the process of conflict transformation.

[72] http://www.truthcommission.org

statements also gave these statements at the public hearings. Given the logistics of holding public hearings, only a small representative sample of victims was called to give such evidence (Wilson 2001). At such hearings, little "new" evidence was presented that had not already been placed before the commissioners.

Issues which might militate against holding proceedings in public might include the security of victims, witnesses, accused perpetrators, and commission staff; the impact on the wider process of conflict transformation; and the psychological impact on victims. Victims may experience real problems associated with public testimony. For example, the South African Trauma Centre for Victims of Violence and Torture in Cape Town found 50-60% of those who testified before the SATRC suffered difficulties after the hearing or regretted taking part (cited in Stanley 2005).

Apart from the safety issues for both victims and perpetrators, one would expect objections to be raised by state agencies in particular to public hearings on the grounds of national security. The complex arrangements designed to ensure the anonymity of military personnel during the Bloody Sunday tribunal (Hegarty 2003) and the ongoing dispute concerning the likely impact of the Inquiries Act (2005) with regard to any inquiry into the murder of Pat Finucane are surely indicative of likely objections to be raised by such agencies in any truth-recovery process related to the conflict in and about Northern Ireland. Similarly, one would expect little enthusiasm for public hearings from either loyalist or republican paramilitaries.

That said, the potential power of witnessing (either at first hand or more likely through the media) the suffering of human beings perhaps traditionally viewed as "other" is such that it arguably creates a moral impetus for creativity in considering the practical and political implications of public hearings. Despite the considerable difficulties outlined above, it is certainly arguable that, in line with recent commissions, there should be a presumption in favour of holding at least some such hearings in public with, for example (as occurred in Ghana), a discretion given to the truth-recovery institution to hold certain proceedings in private "for good cause".

(vii) Commission powers and institutional accountability

In common with many of the details concerning the operation of truth commissions, the powers of such bodies tend to reflect the political power balances that led to their creation. Generic issues that inevitably arise regarding such entities include whether the commission has powers to compel access to evidence (e.g. in state security or policing files); whether the commission has the power to subpoena witnesses, perpetrators or victims; the precise legal status of any recommendations and whether these must be acted upon; and the relationship between a truth commission and the formal justice system (e.g. whether or not the commission can refer cases for prosecution).

International experiences concerning these different themes vary. In Argentina and Chile the commissions had no subpoena powers and no judicial powers, although their findings could be utilised as supportive evidence before the courts. In El Salvador, the commission had no subpoena powers and no judicial powers; however, its recommendations were binding on the government.[73] The SATRC enjoyed a more robust set of legal powers which included subpoena powers as well as judicial powers such as the power to grant amnesty (South African Truth and Reconciliation Commission 1998). More recently, the Moroccan Commission has been established without powers of investigation such as subpoena, search and seizure powers, although public officials in the country are under a legal obligation to cooperate with all requests for information and evidence (Goldstein 2004).

In the literature on commission powers there appears a largely shared assumption that the greater the legal powers given to a commission, the more effective it is likely to be at uncovering the truth. There are, of course, good reasons for such an assumption, many of them well rehearsed in the various debates on the different styles of inquiry concerning the conflict in and about Northern Ireland which have been conducted to date and the recent passage of the Inquiries Act (e.g. Rolston & Scraton 2005 – discussed in greater detail below). However, a broad rule of thumb to be borne in mind is that, the more powerful the legal powers of any commission, the more likely the political and legal pressures will be to safeguard the due process rights of those accused of being perpetrators, which will inevitably make any process more legalistic.

Perhaps the issue which has received most attention in the debate concerning the powers of commissions is their capacity to deliver institutional accountability for human rights abuses in determining the extent to which violations were sanctioned, authorised or conducted by the state or other powerful institutions. For example, in 1992 the German Parliament established two Enquetekomission/Commissions of Inquiry to examine the operation and activities of Communism in East Germany, which held public hearings across East Germany on issues such as power, the justice system, the intelligence services, and the church (Borneman 1997, 2005).

---

[73] http://www.truthcommission.org

On the recommendation of the second commission, a foundation was established to address issues connected with the Communist years and provide services including legal and psychological support to victims.[74]

An approach taken by several past commissions has been to supplement investigation of violations against individuals with institutional and/or thematic hearings which examine the role of specific institutions in human rights abuse and explore patterns of abuse in the context of broader social conditions. Such a process also allows a commission to make appropriate recommendations for institutional reforms.

Again, the South African experience is particularly instructive. In addition to its hearings with victims of human rights violations and perpetrator amnesty hearings, the SATRC held a series of institutional/thematic hearings into the political, economic, and social environment that gave rise to abuses of human rights. The findings of these hearings are detailed in Volume IV of the 1998 Report (South African Truth and Reconciliation Commission 1998), which in its foreword poses the question, "How did so many people, working within so many influential sectors and institutions, react to what was happening around them?".

The institutional hearings addressed:

- Business and labour: the role of white business, black business, and labour, including issues of culpability, collaboration, and involvement in human rights violations.
- The faith community: considered as both agents and victims of oppression.
- The legal community: the fact that the judiciary did not appear before the Commission was noted with disappointment by the TRC in its Final Report (see also Dyzenhaus 1998).
- The health sector: the activities of members of the medical profession who failed to fulfil their moral and ethical responsibilities (see Orr 2000).
- The media: the role of different media organisations and attempts by the state to control the media.
- Prisons: through the testimony of political prisoners, an exploration of the link between the prison system and apartheid, and the particularly cruel treatment of political prisoners.

Three additional special hearings were held on Compulsory Military Service, Children and Youth, and Women. Sometimes the SATRC was successful in obtaining the participation of all role-players (e.g. the health hearing), and sometimes it was not (e.g. the legal hearing). The health sector hearing was reported as one of the success stories of the TRC for its degree of participation from stakeholders in the health sector who saw it as an opportunity for self-reflection and for furthering transformation (van der Merwe 2000). The Minister for Justice participated in the hearing on the legal profession, but judges did not. Some of the individual judges and attorneys-general apologised and asked for forgiveness. On the other hand, there were judges and attorneys-general who argued bluntly that there was nothing to apologise for. In the joint submission of the judges, there was also no apology for the role of the judiciary during the apartheid era (Rombouts 2002).

Thematic and/or institutional hearings have also been conducted in East Timor's CAVR. Five thematic hearings were held on: political prisoners; women; international actors; displacements and famine; and civil war and political parties.   Sierra Leone's Truth and Reconciliation Commission schedule for thematic/institutional hearings[75] lists participants as including several Government Ministers, including the Minister of Economic Planning, the Minister for Social Welfare, and the Minister for Education.

Thematic and/or institutional hearings allow a commission to explore patterns of abuse in the context of broader social conditions and to consider whether or not specific institutions were particularly egregious in their complicity with or involvement in human rights abuses. They also allow exploration as to who benefited from the violence. Ultimately, institutional explorations can allow a commission to address recommendations to areas where institutional reforms are required. The difficulty, however, is that acceptance of institutional responsibility requires both evidence of the previous wrongdoing and the cooperation of the institution/government and its officials. The level of destruction of official documentation in South Africa was commented on in the SATRC Final Report, and undoubtedly impacted on its ability to ascertain institutional guilt (see Hayner 2001).

Measures in other nations regarding institutional accountability have included a signed letter of apology from the Chilean president on behalf of the state to the family of each victim identified in the Rettig Report, and the partial funding of the Peruvian Truth Commission with recovered funds that had been misappropriated by the prior government (Orentlicher 2004).

While creative attempts to render institutions accountable are to be applauded, the obvious (and sometimes insurmountable) problem remains that it is difficult to analyse institutional responsibility if the institution does not want to be investigated. For example, the UN Truth Commission for El Salvador theoretically had full access to state and military files, but lacked subpoena powers with which to enforce this, and thus investigations were severely hindered by uncooperative government and military officials (Hayner 2001). Taking on board the fact that increased powers may lead to an increased sense of legalism in the proceedings, in reviewing the operation of a number of past commissions, it is abundantly clear that if commissions have judicial powers to subpoena evidence and compel cooperation with their work, the potential scope of investigation is greatly enhanced. Of course, as was evidenced in South Africa, increased legal powers do not necessarily preclude the shredding of incriminating documentation (South African Truth and Reconciliation Commission 1998). They do, however, increase the chances of greater public awareness that such shredding has in fact taken place.

In the Northern Ireland context, therefore, the range of institutions which could be required to account for their conduct during the conflict in any truth-recovery process would include the various elements of the security forces and intelligence services; the criminal justice system including the judiciary, legal profession, prosecution, and prison services; the broad range of government departments whose functions were affected by and impacted upon the conflict in and about Northern Ireland; business and labour organisations; media (both broadcast and print) in the way that they reported the conflict; the churches; and a number of other institutions.[76] The difficulties in engaging such institutions in truth recovery should not be underestimated. For many such institutions, the notion of their own individual independence (e.g. with regard to the judiciary) are long standing and genuinely held aspects of organisational culture. For others, organisational notions of independence intersect with discourses of professional self-image (e.g. "we were neutral or above the conflict", "we were only doing our job", "we were holding the line in the face of a terrorist onslaught"), all of which also militate against the notion of accounting for past actions during the conflict in and about Northern Ireland. Engaging with such institutions, therefore, will require not only the necessary legal powers, but a broader process of education and explanation as to the role and function of such institutional accountability in the broader process of transition from conflict.

(viii) Commissions and the granting of amnesty

A further key issue with many truth commissions is whether or not the process for truth recovery is linked to one of amnesty. Although there is no inherent relationship between truth commissions and amnesty, previous truth commissions have been established in the context of an existing amnesty for political offences (Chile), as a brokered compromise for granting amnesty in order to gain peace (Sierra Leone) or, in the unique case of South Africa, a truth commission had the power to grant amnesty. The significance of amnesty may change during a commission's work. In Peru, for example, annulment of amnesties that had been granted by the previous Fujimori regime opened up the possibility of domestic prosecutions at the same time that the truth commission was operating (Cueva 2004). In sharp contrast is the case of El Salvador, where amnesty only became relevant after the commission had completed its work, and a controversial blanket amnesty was enacted to protect all those identified in its report.

An inter-relationship between amnesty and truth was most fully developed in South Africa, where the truth commission had an amnesty committee that could grant amnesty to perpetrators of human rights violations (McGregor 2001). Although the granting of amnesty was a calculated concession in order to maximise justice for victims within the available political space, many perpetrators were far from contrite.

A considerable degree of integration between truth and justice was also designed for Rwanda and East Timor. As is discussed in greater detail below, in Rwanda, Gacaca tribunals (in which perpetrators of all but the most serious offences appear before a community tribunal, which can require him/her to make reparations or can impose prison sentences of up to 30 years) have been integrated within the national criminal justice system. Concessions in sentence are given for full and free confessions. Similarly, in East Timor, perpetrator statements before the truth commission/CAVR are first evaluated and then dealt with by one of two routes. The case may be referred to (a) a Community Reconciliation Process, in which amnesty is available for lesser offences if there is admission of guilt and performance of an act of reconciliation or (b) in the case of serious criminal offences, these are referred to the Office of the General Prosecutor. However, while there may be benefits to a coordinated concurrent operation as demonstrated by the East Timorese model, the uncoordinated concurrent operation of truth commissions and courts can be counterproductive (Evenson 2004: 755). Again, as was previously discussed, the Sierra Leone experience, which saw both a Special Court

---

[76] The original Healing Through Remembering Report recommended that "...all organisations and institutions that have been engaged in the conflict, including the British and Irish States, the political parties and Loyalist and Republican paramilitaries, should honestly and publicly acknowledge responsibility for past political violence due to their acts of omission and commission" (Healing Through Remembering 2002: 50).

and a Truth and Reconciliation Commission established simultaneously, led to some confusion between the institutions.

Where an amnesty is already in existence before a commission begins its work (Chile, Peru, Sierra Leone), there is sometimes concern, either that perpetrators will not participate, or that the truth commission will in effect serve as a "poor relation" to the normal criminal justice process. In practice, however, truth commissions occur in a context where the likelihood of successful prosecutions may be actually quite small for political, evidential or other practical reasons. Although it is true that more perpetrators may participate if offered an enticing "carrot" such as guaranteed freedom from future prosecution, it is questionable whether such self-interested participation will necessarily result in more honest and accurate confession/testimony. Indeed, even without the incentive of an amnesty, just as criminals may confess to ordinary crimes despite the consequences and the protestations of their lawyers, individuals who have perpetrated serious human rights violations may feel the need to unburden themselves (Schabas 2004).

(ix) What happens after a commission?

Hayner (2001) has noted that some level of disappointment is not uncommon as a truth commission comes to an end. To avoid this, there is a responsibility on those involved to manage public expectations carefully and to have provisions in place which ensure that recommendations made by the commission are implemented. For example, truth commissions regularly recommend comprehensive reparations programmes for victims (e.g. Chile, Guatemala, South Africa, Peru, Ghana), but their recommendations are often wholly or partially ignored (De Greiff 2006). Indeed the failure of the South African government to implement punctually the SATRC's extensive reparations recommendations has been widely criticised and, for some observers, has negated, at least in part, the positive advances the Commission had achieved (e.g. Daly 2003; Hamber 2006; McLaughlin 2002).

A sensitivity to the risk of non-implementation has been reflected in increasingly sophisticated truth commission design. For example, the Moroccan IER was empowered to grant reparations directly to victims, while the government of Sierra Leone is obligated by statute to implement the recommendations of the TRC.[77] In effect, informed by the experience of previous commissions, where much of the political and organisational energy went into the establishment and running of a commission and in particular the delivery of the report, there is now a much greater awareness of the need for follow up if the report is to have a real transformative effect on the society in question.

Conclusion

Given the over twenty years of history in the design and implementation of truth commissions, there is a wealth of academic and policy literature on this topic. No commentator would claim that any society should adopt a "one size fits all" approach to such institutions. Rather, a society such as Northern Ireland (and the other jurisdictions affected by the conflict in and about Northern Ireland) must adopt a bespoke approach to the establishment of a truth commission or similar institution. Ultimately, all of these issues – whether perpetrators may be identified, whether a commission can operate publicly, its powers, remit, the role of amnesty, etc. – will be the subject of political negotiations. If any such institution is to have widespread legitimacy and subsequently function effectively, it is important that such negotiations do not remain the exclusive preserve of political elites (ICTJ 2004). As with truth commissions elsewhere, the precise shape of any truth commission in the local context is likely to be framed by the realities of the transitional context in which it is located. If the limitations of the process are recognised, planned, and taken into account, there is still the opportunity to conduct a truth-seeking process with significant impact, influence, and importance.

3. Lustration: administrative investigation and institutional reform

A further international model for the management of transition that has sometimes been associated with the process of truth recovery is what is commonly referred to as "lustration". Lustration is a focus on the exploration of (a) the role of state structures and institutions in creating and sustaining cultures of violence; and (b) an investigation into the records of state officials and the removal of perpetrators of human rights abuse from public office (Ellis 1996; Boed 1999). In transitional terms, "lustration" means "circumventing the need to resort to criminal process by disqualifying or removing officeholders of the previous regime and by keeping them from holding office in the new state" (Barkan 2000: 115). It is an approach that has been associated most with former communist regimes, and the terminology of "lustration" has to an extent fallen out of international favour for this context-specific connotation. Although contemporary discussions tend to rely more on the more comprehensive and less loaded language of "institutional reform" or "vetting", in the

---

[77] "The Government shall faithfully and timeously implement the recommendations of the report that are directed to state bodies and encourage or facilitate the implementation of any recommendations that may be directed to others", Section 17 Truth and Reconciliation Commission Act 2000.

context of Northern Ireland lustration remains of significance and interest in the jurisdiction no doubt due in part to the fact that no such process occurred here.

Lustration procedures to date have been extremely varied in reach, breadth, and ambition. In Lithuania, all citizens who had collaborated with the KGB had to report to a special commission. In Albania, candidates for public office were required to obtain a clearance certificate. In Poland, admission of previous collaboration with the secret police did not automatically bar a public official from office; concealing collaboration, on the other hand, incurred a ban of ten years on holding public office (Los 1995; Letki 2002). Perhaps the best known lustration cases amongst the former communist states are the experiences of the former East Germany and Czechoslovakia.

In East Germany, the secret police (Stasi) had more than 90,000 full-time staff and a much larger number of unofficial collaborators. They kept files on more than six million German citizens (and others), noting the minutiae of their lives in forensic detail for evidence of political dissent or rebellion. As part of an official process of Aufarbeitung – reckoning with/working through the Communist past - the Stasi Records Act 1992 opened the entire Stasi archives to the German public. All citizens were entitled to see their own files, and in the first two years nearly two million people applied to do so. Records of MPs, all elected bodies, and public employees were vetted, and led to dismissal if Stasi collaboration was discovered. Re-employment in the state sector was not permitted. The release of Stasi files was managed by the Gauck Authority. More than 3,000 people were employed to process the millions of requests and manage the 120 miles of archival material. As the Authority Chair, Joachim Gauck, has noted, the East German parliament's intention was to return the former rulers' instruments of knowledge to those it had ruled and oppressed (Gauck 1994). He goes on to argue, however, that the process was underpinned not by a desire for vengeance but rather a desire to rebuild public trust in state institutions, and suggests:

> any foreign reader who thinks that our way of coming to terms with the past is too strict and too organized must realize a simple truth: only in such a distinctively German way can a dictatorship set up on the German model be destroyed (Gauck 1994: 276).[78]

The removal of former communist officials from public office was a priority in many post-Soviet states, but was particularly prominent in the transitional strategy of Czechoslovakia (and, subsequently, the Czech Republic). Their policy excluded all officers and agents of the communist security forces and all party officials from district level upwards from around 9,000 public posts. Under the Czechoslovakian Lustration Law (Act No. 451/1991), persons who held certain state or Communist Party positions between 1948-1989, or who were deemed to have "consciously collaborated" with the State Security during that period, could not seek employment in certain posts for a period of five years (later extended by an additional four). These "excluded" posts included high-ranking governmental, military, and judicial positions but also extended to vacancies within state-run media, financial, commercial, and academic institutions. Act No. 451/1991 required persons who held or wished to hold identified public office positions in Czechoslovakia to prove that they had not collaborated with the communist state security apparatus (Kritz 1995: 533-593).

Between 1991 and 1998 a total of 303,504 screenings took place in Czechoslovakia, of which 15,166 resulted in positive certificates (Williams 2003). However, numbers alone fail to indicate deeper problems in the design of the Czech lustration process. For example, determinations of collaboration were made solely on the basis of information contained in the files of the Czech secret police, many of which had been destroyed prior to the Parliamentary investigation. The nature of intelligence-gathering made it likely that those named in files were low-level agents or collaborators rather than high-level policy directors, who tend to be those in control of the files. Appeal could be made from a finding of collaboration to the Czech national courts and the higher standard of legal proof for corroboration made this a successful process for more than 80% of appellants (David 2003; David & Choi 2005; Williams 2003).

Although lustration is historically closely associated with Eastern European post-communist states, procedures for vetting of employment and other records for recruitment to public office have been implemented in many states and continue to form part of institutional reform procedures worldwide. For example, in El Salvador, the records of high-ranking military officials were examined and those who could be credibly accused of serious crimes were named. Although there was no automatic sanction, all of those identified eventually left office, although some did so on a full pension (Rosenberg 1999: 348). The first order made by the Coalition Provisional Authority (CPA) in Iraq, was for an extensive process of "De-Ba'athification of Iraqi Society" (Order No. 1, May 16, 2003). The Ba'ath Party had been the political bedrock upon which the Saddam Hussein regime was based. At a practical level, this order decimated the state institutions of all their qualified personnel, including people whose party affiliation was largely meaningless (not uncommon in a

---

[78] For further discussion on the German experience see Miller (1998).

state where membership of the Ba'ath party was effectively a precondition for career advancement).[79] Eventually, in November 2003, the CPA transferred authority for de-Ba'athification to the Iraqi Governing Council. At this point, broadly defined possible exemptions were made where it would be "in the interests of Iraqi people" or it would be "fundamentally unfair" not to allow re-employment (Farhang 2004).

While the lustration processes in former communist regimes are interesting, their relevance to the Northern Ireland debate on truth recovery is at first glance less obvious than other themes in this report. At a political level, there are some interesting academic discussions concerning the organisational culture of elements of state structure as essentially unionist in nature.[80] However, there has certainly been no party political dominance of state institutions in Northern Ireland in the last thirty years on a par with the Communist Party in Eastern Europe, or the Ba'ath Party in Iraq. With regard to the more obvious elements of the state infrastructure that might have been subject to some form of lustration-style review, to explore possible involvement of personnel in human rights abuses (e.g. the police, prison service, security services, military, and areas of the civil service involved in security policy), the position is more mixed.

From a legalistic perspective, all such agencies have been subject to rule of law throughout the conflict in and about Northern Ireland. That said, formal legalism has arguably not prevented de facto cultures of impunity from developing, in particular agencies at different junctures of the conflict in and about Northern Ireland, most notably in the intelligence services and elements of the police involved in collusive activities with loyalist paramilitaries (e.g. Cory 2004; O'Brien 2005) or, indeed, in the prison service during the era of the hunger-strikes and no-wash protests (e.g. McEvoy 2001). For an agency such as the police, some would argue that the Patten Reforms and, in particular, the centrality of human rights discourse to the transformation of the RUC to the PSNI, were designed at least in part to create a culture wherein those who may have been involved in human rights abuses would take an early retirement package rather than subscribe to the new ethos (e.g. Mulcahy 2005). Within the prison service, while many of the most notorious abuses happened a long time ago, there has been no similar process of transformation. While the Criminal Justice Review did reflect on the ethos and culture of the system, given that it was primarily written by the civil servants who were then tasked with its implementation, it is perhaps unsurprising that there was no apparent consideration of the appropriateness or otherwise of a lustration process for those who had worked in the criminal justice system during the conflict in and about Northern Ireland. Similarly, attempts through legal mechanisms such as the Bloody Sunday Tribunal to hold members of the British Army accountable have been met by such dogged resistance (Hegarty 2003, 2004) that a willingness to consider some formal lustration measures would be unlikely.

To summarise, some eight years after the conclusion of the Agreement, the opportunity for a serious discussion on lustration as a mechanism for institutional accountability and transformation would appear to have passed. The absence of such a process does, however, lend weight to arguments advanced below with regard to the need for other truth-recovery techniques to ensure that institutional accountability is on the agenda when the design and mandate of any such mechanisms are being considered.

4. Commissions of historical clarification
This model of truth recovery obviously overlaps considerably with a truth commission approach. Such historical commissions are also generally established in the wake of social or political conflict, although they may be set up many years afterwards. They, too, are designed to establish truth as a means for building a more secure and tenable future between affected communities. The primary differences between such historical commissions and truth commissions are, therefore, more in terms of shades of emphasis, rather than clear and finite distinctions. Historical clarification commissions tend to view their role as primarily historical and educative rather than legal; they tend to have less legal powers of compulsion; they tend not to look at individual cases but rather to examine archival material and take witness testimony to arrive at broader social and political narratives of the past; their aim is thus often to seek an agreed historical narrative rather than to hold individual perpetrators accountable; and finally, while such commissions often include some form of reparations or ameliorative programmes designed to assist victims, the focus upon agreeing collective social responsibility for past wrongs means that there is less emphasis on the individual healing of victims. A couple of examples of such "historical commissions" might be useful for illustrative purposes.

---

[79] One American Special Forces Officer was quoted as saying, "Does Bremer [head of the CPA] realize that there are four hundred thousand of these guys out there and they all have guns? They all have to feed their families". "These guys ran the country, and you polarize them. So did these decisions contribute to the insurgency? Unequivocally, yes. And we have to ask ourselves: How well did we really know how to run Iraq? Zero" (cited in Anderson 2004).
[80] See e.g. Ellison & Smyth (2000) and Mulcahy (2005) with regard to the RUC; Livingstone, McEvoy, Rebouche & Mageean (2006) with regard to the courts and criminal justice system; and McEvoy & White (1998) with regard to the civil service.

Between 1942-1945, more than 120,000 Japanese-Americans were forced to leave their homes and were interned in relocation camps in US territory. The entire population of Alaska's Aleutian Islands was also forcibly removed from their native islands and interned in mainland camps. For years, the history of these events was largely absent from the American national consciousness (Nagata 1993). Almost forty years later, in 1980, a Congressional Commission on Wartime Relocation and Internment of Civilians (CWRIC) was established. The CWRIC was mandated to investigate the political circumstances giving rise to the order for internment, the way in which the order was implemented, and the impact it had on those who were interned. For three years the CWRIC conducted research and held public hearings throughout the United States and Alaska and produced a final report with recommendations in 1983. The CWRIC declared in its summary that these actions were:

> ...not justified by military necessity, and the decisions that followed from it - exclusion, detention, the ending of detention and the ending of exclusion - were not founded upon military considerations. The broad historical causes that shaped these decisions were race prejudice, war hysteria, and a failure of political leadership (CWRIC 1997: 459).

The Civil Liberties Act 1988 which established a small reparations programme also stated that Congress, on behalf of the nation, apologises to Americans of Japanese ancestry for their wrongful incarceration. In 1990 President George Bush followed this up with a letter of apology to each Japanese American[81] (Hayashi 2004).

Canada has also undergone a similar, albeit broader and more far-reaching, process. In 1996 a Canadian Royal Commission on Aboriginal Affairs reported on a range of issues including the over-representation of aboriginal peoples in the Canadian criminal justice system, social and economic exclusion, and the need for more equitable governance structures which respected the rights and traditions of such peoples. The Commission had been established upon the recommendation of former Chief Justice Brian Dickson who had himself been asked by the then-prime minister to report on whether such a Commission was necessary. Justice Dickson recommended that the terms of reference should be broad, and thus the Commission had a mandate to "deal with an accumulation of literally centuries of injustice". The Commission held extensive consultations, visiting 96 communities, held 178 days of hearings, heard evidence from 2,067 people, and accumulated more than 76,000 pages of testimony. It traces, albeit briefly, the turbulent history of the relationship between settlers and indigenous peoples from the origins of the country. The Commission quite candidly acknowledged the history of discrimination, exclusion, attempted assimilation, and treaty-breaking which had characterised the relationship between indigenous people and Canadian federal and regional governance structures.[82] It also made direct connections between the historical context and current levels of indigenous poverty and social exclusion. The entire last volume of the Royal Commission's five-volume report to the federal government was dedicated to the Commission's recommendations for resolution of these issues, including investment, education, land reform, governance, and other issues (Manuel & Schabas 2005).[83]

Historical commissions have also been initiated by civil societies or church groups where, for example, there is state opposition to such truth-recovery initiatives (discussed further below). The Armenian people and the vast majority of contemporary historians claim that, during and after the First World War, up to 1.5 million Armenians were systematically slaughtered by Ottoman Turks in massacres and forced deportations. The Turkish government claims instead that while several hundred thousand Armenians did indeed die, this was the result of hunger and disease. Fifteen nations officially recognise that the events of this period were genocide – the UK and the US are not among them. A legal analysis prepared for the International Centre for Transitional Justice (ICTJ), while not addressing the substantive question of whether those events constituted genocide, determined that the Genocide Convention 1948 would apply to the events of this time (ICTJ 2004). A Turkish Armenian Reconciliation Commission (TARC) composed of civil society representatives from both countries was established in July 2001 and concluded its deliberations in April 2004.[84] The TARC Terms of

---

[81] This letter included the statement that "A monetary sum and words alone cannot restore lost years or erase painful memories; neither can they fully convey our Nation's resolve to rectify injustice and to uphold the rights of individuals. We can never fully right the wrongs of the past. But we can take a clear stand for justice and recognize that serious injustices were done to Japanese Americans during World War II".

[82] As Commission co-chair René Dussault said at the launch of the report: "Settler governments, imbued with the certainty of an imperial age, sought dominion over this land and believed it was their duty to remake Aboriginal peoples and societies in their own image, thereby, conveniently, removing opposition to that dominion. We cannot escape the fact that we have built a great liberal democracy in part through the dispossession of Aboriginal people and the imposition of our cultural norms... Canadians are now embarrassed by the arrogance that runs through our history and by the acts of state suppression that it gave rise to...In order to break free of the structure of dependence which has bred so much deprivation and despondency, Aboriginal people must have the opportunity and resources to exercise responsibility themselves, to re-establish themselves as peoples, to build institutions consistent with their values". See http://www.ainc-inac.gc.ca/ch/rcap/spch_e.html

[83] See http://www.ainc-inac.gc.ca/ch/rcap/sg/sgmm_e.html

Reference contains measured goals, including the promotion of "mutual understanding and good will" and the construction of more cooperative relationships between Turks and Armenians. The TARC indicates its intention to circulate its recommendations to "interested governments" in the near future, but there is no mention of an imminent public dissemination.

Although these events occurred almost a century ago, the issue remains intensely political in relations between Turkey and Armenia. In 2004, on the 90th anniversary of the killings, hundreds of thousands of Armenians visited the national state memorial to the genocide.[85] It appears highly unlikely that an official truth commission would gain the support and cooperation of the Turkish government. In September 2004, the Turkish government adopted a new Penal Code providing for sentences of up to ten years imprisonment for Turkish citizens who confirm the occurrence of the Armenian genocide. Internationally recognised writer Orhan Pamuk has been charged under the new Penal Code for stating in an interview that "Thirty-thousand Kurds were killed here, one million Armenians as well. And almost no one talks about it. Therefore, I do".[86] Pamuk's charge was followed less than a week later by the cancellation by court order of a major international academic conference on the genocide claim (*BBC News*, 22 September 2005). That this occurred in the same month as EU accession talks began further illustrates how strongly Turkey feels about this matter - and how unlikely a free and open "truth debate" is.

All of these examples of historical truth recovery speak to a number of themes which are relevant to the debate in Northern Ireland. The first is that, in certain societies with turbulent or violent histories, there may come a time even decades later when it is considered timely for a frank approach to truth recovery concerning unpalatable periods in history. In the case of Japanese-American internees and the Royal Commission on Aboriginal Peoples, these were events or histories which appeared (very broadly) to offend against the national sensibilities of the political elites in America and Canada respectively. Even in jurisdictions where state structures or such political elites set their faces against such a process (such as in the attitudes of the Turkish state to the Armenian massacres), political or moral energy may be mobilised in other civil society or church initiatives "from below" that are willing to engage in such processes despite official "top down" opposition. Indeed, perceived weaknesses of the state-sanctioned Commission on Historical Clarification in Guatemala contributed directly to the establishment of a church-based initiative in the local communities most affected by the violence (discussed in greater detail below). In contexts where it is deemed impossible or inappropriate to establish a modern-day truth commission with associated strong legal and investigative powers, it may still be possible to achieve some shared understanding of the past through an agreed and independent historical commission without such powers. It is true that such a commission would be unlikely to meet the needs of individual victims or indeed to hold individual perpetrators accountable.

5. Drawing a line under the past – the "do nothing" model

In all societies emerging from conflict, there will inevitably be those who argue that a line should be drawn under the past and that, in effect, organised efforts at truth recovery should not be attempted. Although for illustrative purposes this is a concept which the HTR Sub Group sometimes referred to as the "do nothing model", as is discussed in greater detail below, this term may be somewhat misleading. For example, in some transitional settings such as Northern Ireland, there may be already a range of initiatives aimed at truth recovery that will continue regardless of whether or not a central institution such as a truth commission is established. In others, as discussed above, the notion of doing nothing became synonymous with conscious efforts to introduce amnesties in places like Chile and Uruguay which were designed to ensure that no truth-recovery initiatives would ever be established and that nothing would or could be done in the future. It may be accurate, therefore, to think of the "do nothing" alternative more in terms of "do nothing new" by way of a truth-recovery option.

The arguments advanced in post-conflict societies by those who would argue that the past is best left alone may be grouped under a number of themes. Hayner (2001: 185) has suggested four common elements to the public discourses in such contexts which mitigate against the establishment of formal truth-recovery mechanisms. These are:

Fear of negative consequences – the view that violence may increase or could return if old atrocities are revisited.

Lack of political interest – little or no political interest by the political leadership in truth-seeking and a lack of significant non-governmental actors pushing them to do so.

84 See the TARC website at http://www.tarc.info/index.html
85 "Armenians Remember Mass Killings", *BBC News*, 24 April 2004.
86 "Conference Sparks Protest", *The Guardian*, 17 September 2005.

Other urgent priorities – a focus on the demands of survival or post-conflict reconstruction and a concurrent lack of basic institutional structures to support a truth-seeking process in contexts where there has been widespread destruction during the conflict.

Alternative mechanisms or preferences – indigenous nation characteristics may make truth-seeking unnecessary or undesirable, such as unofficial community-based mechanisms that respond to the recent violence or a culture that eschews confronting conflict directly (Hayner 2001: 186).

While Hayner's list is not comprehensive, it does suggest some of the basic themes that characterise the debate amongst those opposed to the establishment of formal mechanisms of truth recovery. From such a perspective, such initiatives may be characterised as unnecessary or unhelpful; as politically destabilising; as unlikely to succeed in their own terms (e.g. in assisting with individual or national reconciliation); as unacceptable trade-offs with justice (e.g. the punishment of those guilty of atrocities through the criminal justice system); as sources for continued conflict concerning competing claims for historical validity and justification, and so forth (discussed in great detail in the relevant section on Northern Ireland below). Again, it may be useful to consider a couple of international examples for illustrative purposes.[87]

For 16 years, Mozambique endured a bloody and violent political conflict. Between 1975 and 1992, one million civilians (more than 5% of the national population) were killed and many thousands were tortured and mutilated in Mozambique (Graybill 2004: 1125). Although technically a civil war between a Marxist government and right-wing guerrillas, the conflict was complicated by both the practical and moral support of outside actors, most notoriously of the guerrilla faction (Renamo) by the right-wing governments of (originally) Rhodesia and subsequently by the apartheid regime in South Africa. Despite the scale of the atrocities, there was little apparent energy for truth recovery following the cessation of hostilities. Ten days after the peace accord was signed, the government declared a general amnesty that would cover acts committed by both sides. Powerful figures in each party which had emerged from the fighting factions feared opening up to public inquiry abuses of political opponents for fear opponents would charge them with similar crimes, thus creating a broad constituency for silence or, as Graybill (2004) describes it, a deliberate choosing of amnesia. Part of the rationale for the absence of demands for truth was thus both practical and political, a fear that conflict might return and a new political class with little interest in its past misdeeds being revisited (Hayner 2001). Part of it was also cultural. The notion of "speaking out" is largely foreign to Mozambicans, since to recall the troubled past is often believed to open the space for malevolent forces to intervene (Green & Honwana 1999). Where local healing and reconciliation efforts have occurred, these have been left largely in the hands of local traditional healers called curandeiros, who are responsible for "defusing the cultures of violence the war had wrought" (Nordstrom 1997: 232).

The Spanish example is also of considerable interest for discussions on the Northern Ireland context and is worth exploring in some detail. The Spanish Civil War (1936-1939) followed a military coup led by General Francisco Franco against the republican government. Over 500,000 people were killed, Franco's forces arranged the executions of 100,000 republican prisoners, and another 35,000 republicans died in concentration camps in the years that followed the war. Franco ruled Spain until his death in 1975. Republicans, too, were responsible for civil war atrocities, although on nothing like the same scale (Beevor 2001).

As part of the complex negotiations which led to the creation of a Spanish democracy under the tutelage of King Juan Carlos II, a far-reaching amnesty law was passed as part of those political negotiations. A largely unspoken consensus emerged amongst the political elites in Spain that the past was best left alone (Blakeley 2005).[88] In many small rural communities affected directly by atrocities, disappearances, and mass graves, people's fear of the return of totalitarianism prevented them from speaking out.[89] This apparent consensus about drawing a line under the past amongst the political classes, as well as those most directly affected, became known as what Madelaine Davis (2005) has referred to as the post-Franco "Pacto del Olvido" – the pact

---

[87] Namibia is also occasionally cited in the older literature as an example of a post conflict society which has also left its past behind without a truth-recovery process. However, in 1995, the publication of a book by Pastor Siegfried Groth, Namibia, *The Wall of Silence*, which detailed violence and human rights abuses committed by South West African People's Organisation (SWAPO – the current government, then guerrilla liberation movement) during the struggle for Namibian independence, sparked a huge debate. The narrative drew on Groth's personal recollections and the stories of ordinary Namibians to detail a period of intense conflict and suffering. The book was not well received by SWAPO with the president condemning the book on national TV. Followings its publication, SWAPO victims mobilised to form 'Breaking the Wall of Silence' (BWS), a NGO lobbying for victim recognition and accountability for the past (Dobell 1997). Other non-governmental transitional justice initiatives in Namibia include a list of Namibia's "Missing Persons", compiled by church groups. Demands from parliamentary members and the Council of Churches of Namibia, to establish a truth commission have been adamantly opposed by the Namibian president. In short, Namibia might therefore be better described as a jurisdiction which, although there was little apparent debate on truth recovery for almost twenty years, a debate has emerged and is being strongly resisted by the ruling political elites.

of forgetting. For many years, in other jurisdictions where truth-recovery mechanisms were being discussed, Spain was often referred to as an example of a successful "do nothing" approach, a functioning and largely successful democracy which emerged without examining the extreme violence of its civil war and totalitarian regime past (Kritz 1995).

However, over the last five years, a movement for remembrance has emerged in Spain, focused upon the campaign to recover the estimated 30,000 unidentified bodies of those who disappeared between 1936 and 1977. The process has been driven by civil society rather than politicians.[90] Civil society organisations have undertaken museum and documentation initiatives, forensic exhumations of mass graves, artistic processes, and international lobbying, as well as enlisted the support of prominent human rights NGOs such as Amnesty International (Davis 2005). The momentum behind the debate concerning the uncovering of truth has been variously attributed to the consolidation of democracy in Spain, the commemoration of a number of important civil war anniversaries and the 25th anniversary of the death of Franco, the prominence of Spain in promoting international human rights law,[91] and the publicity surrounding the recent excavation of mass graves.[92] Lagging some way behind civil society pressures, the political context in Spain has also changed. In 2004 the Partido Popular (PP) was replaced as the governing party of Spain[93] by a Socialist-led government supported by a number of the regional parties. While they have faced criticism that their belated conversion to the cause of truth recovery is motivated at least in part by the potential for embarrassing their primary political opponents (Portillo 2005), the Socialist government has nonetheless recently appointed a commission to explore avenues to provide truth and reparation for the victims of the Franco regime.

The Mozambican and Spanish examples are instructive for a number of reasons. In both contexts, fear for the instability of the nascent post-conflict political accommodations was crucial in the apparent consensus which emerged that a formal truth-recovery process could not be accommodated. In the case of Mozambique, this was further complicated by some fairly specific cultural tendencies. In the Spanish context, early concerns regarding the fragility of the post-Franco democracy (reinforced by the failed coup attempt of 1981) amongst the political elites, as well as both physical and political fears in local communities, sustained the pact of silence. In both instances, however, truth recovery has arguably emerged in other forms. In Mozambique, the emphasis upon the role of traditional and localised forms of victim healing and resettlement of combatants could be framed as a culturally specific form of reconciliation which inevitably involves personal and communal truth-telling. In Spain, admittedly in a context where no-one seriously believes that democracy is any longer under threat, the pressures from below on truth recovery have eventually led to the establishment of a commission to explore the relevant options. As Golob (2002) has observed, pacts of amnesia are not necessarily forever and even "successful" transition pacts sometimes have to be renegotiated or amended.

6. The "bottom-up" model: community and civil society-based truth recovery

Much of the analysis in the transitional justice literature has tended to focus on different types of institutional mechanisms designed to attain truth recovery, in effect a "top-down" approach, which views state, quasi-state or in some instances supra-state structures as the preferred mechanism to achieve such ends. Such measures in conflict transformation are both understandable and self-evidently necessary. They are reflective of what James C. Scott has referred to as "seeing like a state" (Scott 2001), a perspective that the governance

88 It should be noted, however, that some attempts to recover historical memory were made in the early years of the transition, but this process came to an end with the attempted military coup of 1981 and the subsequent belief that the new Spanish democracy would not be able to withstand coming face-to-face with the past (Miller 2003). Aguilar notes that although nothing similar to the truth commissions of Latin America took place in Spain, a few private initiatives were undertaken, but they all fell foul of the 1977 Amnesty Law (2001: 114).

89 Reviews of the testimony of many families of the disappeared highlights the prevalence of fear as a silencing factor in many such communities. Many people in small towns and villages have always known of the existence, and often the exact location, of mass graves close to their homes, but never dared to speak of this knowledge until recently (Davis 2005).

90 In 2002, the Association for the Recovery of Historical Memory (ARMH) appeared before the UN Working Group on Forced Disappearances asking it to press Spain to fulfil its obligations under international law in order to bring to an end the ongoing discriminatory treatment against civil war victims and their descendants. The UN Working Group sent a recommendation to the Spanish government requesting that it investigate the disappearance of at least two republicans shot after the Civil War. The ARMH, in collaboration with the Abraham Lincoln Brigade Veterans' Association, also appeared before the United Nations High Commission for Human Rights.

91 The arrest in London of former Chilean dictator, General Pinochet in 1998, instigated by Spanish magistrate Baltasar Garzón, was a critical moment in international human rights law and re-kindled the possibility of holding to account those who had been thought to have evaded justice for human rights abuses. However, the incongruity of a foreign dictator being held to account by following Spanish enquiries, whilst its own past was not investigated, provoked some considerable discomfort in Spain (Blakely 2005).

92 Between October 2000 and the end of August 2003 the national newspaper El País had documented the location and excavation of approximately 26 mass graves.

93 The PP emerged as the primary Francoista party in the late1970s, and indeed contains many amongst its members who are the direct descendants of prominent members of the Franco regime.

of change can be best effected by the capacity of central state structures to deliver complex social or political outcomes. However, a concurrent "bottom-up" focus on the dynamics of truth recovery at grass roots/community level has emerged.[94]

Perhaps the best known such initiative was the work of the Recovery of Historical Memory Project or the Proyecto de Recuperación de la Memoria Histórica (REMHI) in Guatemala. This project, which operated between 1995 and 1998, emerged from activists within the Catholic Church. It is of particular interest since it predated and then operated in tandem with a more traditional Commission for Historical Clarification (CEH) in Guatemala which had been established under the auspices of the UN as part of the peace accord. This latter body was established in the context of an already far-reaching amnesty agreed as part of the peace pact. The CEH was criticised for its unrealistically short period of operation (6-12 months in which to investigate human rights abuses over a 36-year period), its lack of legal powers of search and seizure or subpoena, its inability to name perpetrators and "individualise responsibility";[95] and for the inability for much of the information gathered by the CEH to be used in future prosecutions (Smith 2001; Quinn 2003). For a number of commentators the parallel existence of the "bottom-up" REMHI process was a useful corrective to the weaknesses of the "top-down" CEH, and actually strengthened the final product of the latter.[96]

Six hundred volunteers worked on the REMHI project to collect more than 5,000 testimonies and document 55,021 human rights violations, and it was supported by more than 70 different churches and NGOs worldwide (Cabrera 1998). The majority of REMHI volunteers were from indigenous communities, which enabled REMHI to gather testimony from the most rural areas of Guatemala (Ballengee 1999). REMHI published a 1,400 page report in 1998 *(Guatemala: Never Again! Catholic Church documentation of war crimes and terrorism of 1960-1996)*. Similar to the CEH, the REMHI project attributed the vast majority of the violence to state forces and argued that the levels of counter-insurgency violence constituted genocide. The CEH report boldly recorded that the violence was a result of racism, structural violence, and antidemocratic institutions (CEH 1999). Both processes were held in private, without public hearings.

The REMHI interviewers went to great lengths to create interviews that were not only information-gathering tools but also sought to look at the context and impact of individual acts of violence. These were qualitative interviews which were "...structured to be emotionally and psychologically supportive of the deponent" (Hayner 2001: 84). That said, some of the victims and others involved paid a high price for their testimony to either REMHI or the CEH, with many being threatened subsequently; a number disappeared or were killed, and some others were publicly lynched (Godoy 2002: 651). Two days after the publication of the REMHI report, the project's General Coordinator, Monsignor Gerardi, was murdered, allegedly by members of a special intelligence unit who had been heavily criticised in the report for their involvement in atrocities (Asson 2003). Both reports tried to go beyond documenting the past. Each offered a list of recommendations to provide for reparations, respect, and economic justice. The REMHI report called for the demilitarisation of daily life and curtailments of the armed forces, intelligence services, and civil patrols. It called for land reform and economic and social reparations for victims. Unlike the CEH report, the REMHI report did name some individuals who were involved in committing acts of brutality and violence.[97] In addition, the substantial documentation of the REMHI report (and arguably elements of the CEH report not covered by the terms of the amnesty) is, of course, a source of information for possible trials in the future (Hayner 2001).

A similar high-profile community-based initiative that involves micro-level truth recovery is the now well-documented Gacaca process in Rwanda. Following the massacres of hundreds of thousands of Tutsi by their Hutu neighbours (estimates generally vary between 800,000 and 1,000,000 fatalities), Rwanda has witnessed attempts to deal with such massive violations at the supra-national, national, and local levels. At the supra-national level, as was discussed above, in 1995 the UN established the International Criminal Tribunal for

---

[94] Such a view has become increasingly prevalent in the parallel literature on post conflict economies and development studies promoted by the World Bank although it has yet to permeate much of discussion concerning crime and justice (see e.g. Collier, Elliott, Hegre, Hoeffler, Reynol-Querol, & Sambanis 2003)

[95] The Guatemalan military had observed the operation of the Truth Commission in El Salvador 6 years previously and were determined that the Guatemalan version would not "name names" (Crandall 2004).

[96] For example, Crandall (2004) suggests that despite the limitations of the CEH mandate, the Commission managed to produce a stronger report than was expected by many. She argues that the lack of individual naming allowed for a greater focus upon the institutional and systemic causes of the violence. In addition, she contends that the fact that the Commission was able to draw upon the experience of those who had worked for the REMHI project and that it reported in a political context wherein many NGOs (energised by the work of the REMHI project) were lobbying for greater accountability and openness meant that the Commission's mandate was stretched to the limit.

[97] The furthest the CEH report went was to state that the massive human rights violations "...occurred with the knowledge or by the order of the highest authorities of the State" (CEH 1999: 38). However, as Hayner (2001: 124-125) argues, even that (together with the other evidence detailed) was considered by some of the NGOs as sufficient to bring charges against those who headed the government during the worst periods of violence.

Rwanda, which began hearing cases in 1997 and has to date delivered 19 judgements involving 25 individuals. The tribunal has ruled on the most serious of cases, including those who planned and incited the genocide, and has a current annual budget of $256,000,000 (ICTR 2005). In addition, the national courts of Rwanda have from 1996 to the present date managed to prosecute several thousands of those involved in the genocide (PRI 2004). However, in 2005 almost 90,000 prisoners remain incarcerated awaiting trial, many of whom have been in custody for the best part of a decade. Recognising the social and financial burden of maintaining such high numbers of prisoners on remand, but loath simply to amnesty those who had been involved in such atrocious acts, in 2001 the Rwandan government passed legislation designed to make use of traditional village justice structures to process more speedily those charged with lower-level involvement in the genocide. After a number of years in an experimental phase, the process became fully operational in 2005.

Gacaca was viewed as something of a halfway house between formal criminal prosecution and a truth commission process (Drumbl 2000, 2001). Commentators have variously attributed the inspiration for Gacaca as deriving in part from the truth and reconciliation experiences of other jurisdictions such as South Africa, and in part the longstanding informal traditions of informal or alternative dispute resolution in African legal tradition (Daly 2002). The term "Gacaca" is derived from the word for lawn, referring to the fact that members of the Gacaca sit on the grass when listening to and considering matters before them. In Gacaca proceedings, respected community figures are elected to serve as "judges", and the proceedings are designed to involve the entire community in the process. The Gacaca courts are empowered to hear cases relating to the charges including murder, serious assaults or property offences, but not those involved in leadership or planning positions, who are dealt with by the formal courts. Gacaca proceedings are empowered to give custodial sentences. However, given that many of the suspects have already served lengthy periods in custody, the proceedings also include considerable emphasis upon perpetrators confessing fully the truth as to their own involvement (and those of other perpetrators) and engaging in acts of public or community service designed to recompense victims and affected communities (Harrell 2003).

The Gacaca proceedings have provoked considerable controversy. Initially, many international human rights groups expressed fair trial concerns at the dangers inherent in locally trained community representatives potentially giving lengthy sentences, concerns which were only partially assuaged by the subsequent decision of the Rwandan government to include appeal proceedings at every level (Tully 2003). At a logistical level, a further feature has only recently become apparent. The proceedings were designed to reach speedy "closure" for the proceedings against the estimated 100,000 genocidaires involved. However, because the Gacaca process encourages those charged to name their accomplices, the numbers have grown exponentially. In 2005 the head of the Gacaca system announced that 1,000,000 Rwandans would now be tried in the revised village-based system. There are a total of 7,000,000 Rwandans, but as many were either too young to have participated in the genocide, or were not living there at the time, this amounts to charging a staggering one third of the adult population with genocide related charges (Schabas 2005). Finally, others have argued that the traditional restorative focus of Gacaca dispute resolution techniques with Rwanda would be corroded by the subject matter of proceedings forced to deal with the realities of genocide by machete, and that the hearings risk becoming little more than sites of localised vengeance (Corey & Joireman 2004).

In some senses, therefore, the development of community-based truth recovery may be viewed as an organic development of the existing indigenous community tradition. Often during conflicts, powerful community-based structures (or indeed structures run by paramilitary or guerrilla groups themselves) or other organisations in civil society may emerge which challenge the legitimacy or effectiveness of state structures operating within such communities (e.g. Merry & Milner 1993; McEvoy & Mika 2002; Roche 2002). In some such communities, local non-state organisations may have assumed responsibility for the delivery of a wide variety of services, strong social networks may emerge to support the efforts of combatants or victims of the conflict, and human rights and other NGOs may appear that focus on the abuses of the state and/or other combatant groups. In sum, vibrant community-based structures are often a tangible by-product of a conflict wherein the state is challenged. After the conflict, in a context where there is often a similar lack of confidence in either the capacity or political will of state structures to engage in meaningful truth recovery, it is perhaps unsurprising that such community-based organisations may also wish to take on the responsibility themselves to engage in micro-level truth finding.

As is detailed below, Northern Ireland has quite an extensive experience of local community initiatives designed to recover truth in circumstances where there was little belief in the state's interest or willingness to take the lead in such a process.[98] As was outlined above, in both Guatemala and Rwanda the emergence of community-based structures (focused at least in part upon truth recovery) occurred in a context where there were similar questions of either political will or capacity for traditional "top-down" structures to deliver. Both, however, have operated more or less in tandem with such top-down processes and indeed, to some extent, have made up for the weaknesses of the CEH in Guatemala and the system of international and national prosecutions with regard to Rwanda. However, the extent to which such community-based initiatives can prove effective without a corresponding state-led initiative will be explored in more detail below.

7. Apology and acknowledgement

Although it arguably falls well short of real truth recovery, formal apologies by those who have been involved in conflict have been described by some commentators as a particular version of truth commission. At the very least, such apologies may serve as a form of acknowledgement to the victims of a conflict that certain actions, or indeed inactions, were wrong or illegitimate (Cunningham 1999; Healing Through Remembering 2006b; Nobles 2003). For example, Gibney and Roxstrom argue that the state apology may "...serve[s] as a special kind of truth commission in the sense that it has become the Western states' vehicle for acknowledging their own involvement (or, in the case of Rwanda, non-involvement) in some of the world's horrors" (2001: 937-8). Although Gibney and Roxstrom's focus is on intra-state or transnational apologies from one nation to another, the benchmarks they advance to give greater meaning to apologies are arguably of broader applicability. Gibney and Roxstrom (2001) argue that apologies may operate as a more meaningful truth model if: (a) the apology is properly publicised; (b) it engages with the actions of perpetrators and the effects upon victims ; (c) it recognises the role of ritual, and, therefore, that an apology should be solemn and accompanied by ceremony; (d) it includes an explanation of what the apology is for and an explanation or attempt to understand why the events apologised for occurred; (e) it is not a mere dictation/acknowledgement of wrong done, but an active request for forgiveness; and (f) an apology should be a promise to change behaviour if it is not to be seen as hypocritical (Gibney & Roxstrom 2001: 926-936).

There have been quite a number of official apologies in recent years. Prominent examples include Japanese Emperor Akihito's apology to Britain for World War II (1998); Queen Elizabeth II's "sorrow" for the so-called Boer War in South Africa (1999); the Australian Prime Minster's "regret" to indigenous Australians for land theft (1999); Pope John Paul II's acknowledgement of the existence of Israel and promise that the Vatican would "never again" tolerate persecution of Jews (March 2000); Netherlands Prime Minister Wim Kok's apology for the failure of Holland to receive Roma, Jews, and Indonesians fleeing the Nazis in 1945 (March 2000); and the previously discussed apologies in the US and Canada to Japanese-Americans and First Nation Peoples respectively. During Bill Clinton's Presidency, the United States issued a number of high-profile apologies. It issued an unequivocal apology to the citizenry of Guatemala and Greece for its Cold War actions in supporting military juntas and systematic human rights abuses; a general apology was issued in Uganda for US support of unjust regimes worldwide (1998); and a quasi-apology was issued in Rwanda for failure to intervene to prevent the genocide (1998). Britain, too, has offered "expressions of regret" with regard to the Irish Potato Famine – indicating that those who governed in London at the time failed their people (Gibney & Roxstrom 2001). While the federal Australian government has to date refused to apologise, a number of individual states and parliaments within Australia have instigated a "National Sorry Day"– on 26 May – intended to acknowledge the wrongs visited on aboriginal peoples and provide an opportunity to contemplate the reconciliation of indigenous and non-indigenous Australian communities (Brooks 1999).

Often, the demands for a formal apology from the contemporary leadership and subsequent follow-through in the form of reparations become a major focus of campaigns designed to highlight unpalatable truths of past conflicts.[99] For example, the issue of sexual slavery has become a major campaign in different parts of Asia. Forced prostitution and sexual slavery between 1932-1945 happened to tens, probably hundreds, of thousands of women in Japanese-occupied countries (China, Indonesia, Japan, North and South Korea, Malaysia, the Philippines, Singapore, Taiwan, Thailand, East Timor, and Vietnam). From the outset, there was a national and international failure to recognise the suffering of these women. The International Military Tribunal for the Far East did not recognise sexual slavery as a war crime and the Japanese Government remained silent until 1992, when the Prime Minister's Office acknowledged "moral, but not legal" responsibility for the so-called "comfort women". The Government failed to follow up on this statement or to make reparations or genuine acknowledgement other than through a private fund from which many qualifying recipients have rejected sums offered. The Japanese government followed its half-hearted and evasive apology to victims with a diplomatically useful apology to the South Korean government. Duggen notes that the Japanese government's

---

[98] The best known example internationally of a local truth-recovery initiative operating within a context of a lack of any similar state initiative is probably the work of the Ardoyne Commemoration Project here in Northern Ireland which is discussed in more detail below. For another interesting example see the Greensboro Truth and Reconciliation Project established in Greensboro North Carolina to investigate the deaths of five people and injuries to ten others carried out by members of the Ku Klux Klan and American Nazi Party in 1979 of people gathered for a lawful "death to the Klan" rally and conference. See http://www.gtcrp.org/context.asp

[99] "When it comes to the past that is past, however, an era with just a few survivors, the trend has shown it more desirable in the international order of things not to hold trials against ghost regimes but to have living national leaders articulate apology in new narratives and through cash payment. National leaders have in effect become culpable points of reference for the behaviour of their countries' past or almost past inhabitants" (Duggen 2002: 81).

1993 public apology for waging a war of aggression "sufficed to make the South Korean government guarantee Japan it would never officially support the efforts of the Korean sex slaves to receive an apology and compensation" (Duggen 2002: 82).

Apology is sometimes portrayed as a basic minimum in terms of truth seeking (Hayner 2001). Certainly, if a state or particular institutions of a state or non-state entities, such as paramilitary organisations, are unwilling to acknowledge at a very basic level the harms committed, they are unlikely to cooperate fully with an extensive investigation which uncovers even less palatable details (Healing Through Remembering 2002). However, formal apologies are arguably most useful when accompanied by or in the wake of other, more detailed mechanisms of truth recovery. Apology can operate as a political and moral statement and reinforcement of universal norms. For example, when the Chilean Rettig Commission presented its final report, President Aylwin made a powerful apology on national television. Such a formal process involving the different protagonists to a conflict may well be necessary to underscore the closure of a conflict and the beginning of a real process of national reconciliation.

In the Northern Ireland context, the notion of apology has had something of a controversial history. There have been different forms of apology from the different protagonists to the conflict. The Combined Loyalist Military Command included a state of apology to the "innocent victims" of the loyalist paramilitary campaign.[100] The IRA did not offer an apology as part of the ceasefire statement, although they did offer a more fulsome statement at the anniversary of the Bloody Friday bombings some eight years after the original cessation.[101] Both republican and loyalist paramilitaries have also apologised for specific incidents both during and after the conflict in and about Northern Ireland.[102] The British government has apologised for specific events, including the imprisonment of the Guildford Four and Maguire Seven who were wrongly convicted and imprisoned for the Guildford and Woolwich pub bombings respectively.[103] However, in each instance there has been criticism of the wording of the apology statements, concerns that they did not go far enough or, as evidenced by the careful wording in each, an eye to the difficulties with regard to internal constituencies lest it appear that apologies might be deemed as delegitimising all of the actions carried out by either paramilitary or state forces. As is suggested elsewhere (HET 2006), it may well be that apology more generally may have to follow on from an intense process of internal discussion and negotiation amongst all of the armed actors as part of a broader process of acknowledgement.

---

[100] "In all sincerity, we offer to the loved ones of all innocent victims over the past twenty years, abject and true remorse. No words of ours will compensate for the intolerable suffering they have undergone during the conflict. Let us firmly resolve to respect our differing views of freedom, culture and aspiration and never again permit our political circumstances to degenerate into bloody warfare." Combined Loyalist Military Command Statement, 13 October 1994.
http://cain.ulst.ac.uk/events/peace/docs/clmc131094.htm

[101] "Sunday 21 July marks the 30th anniversary of an IRA operation in Belfast in 1972 which resulted in nine people being killed and many more injured. While it was not our intention to injure or kill non-combatants, the reality is that on this and on a number of other occasions, that was the consequence of our actions. It is therefore appropriate on the anniversary of this tragic event, that we address all of the deaths and injuries of non-combatants caused by us. We offer our sincere apologies and condolences to their families. There have been fatalities amongst combatants on all sides. We also acknowledge the grief and pain of their relatives. The future will not be found in denying collective failures and mistakes or closing minds and hearts to the plight of those who have been hurt. That includes all of the victims of the conflict, combatants and non-combatants. It will not be achieved by creating a hierarchy of victims in which some are deemed more or less worthy than others. The process of conflict resolution requires the equal acknowledgement of the grief and loss of others. On this anniversary, we are endeavouring to fulfil this responsibility to those we have hurt... We remain totally committed to the peace process and to dealing with the challenges and difficulties which this presents. This includes the acceptance of past mistakes and of the hurt and pain we have caused to others" Statement Issued by the IRA, BBC News Website, 16 July 2002.
See http://news.bbc.co.uk/1/hi/northern_ireland/2132113.stm

[102] For example, in April 2006 the IRA apologised to the family of Newry man Eugene McQuaid who was killed in an IRA bomb in 1974. At the time Mr McQuaid was wrongly accused by the security forces of having been an IRA man who was killed by his own bomb when it detonated prematurely. After being requested to conduct an investigation by the McQuaid family the IRA issued a statement admitting that they had failed to acknowledge at the time of his death that he was not a member of the IRA, an admission which would have saved the family considerable heartache when such allegations emerged in the press. The statement continued: "Our investigation has found that an IRA operation was in place on the day aimed at a British army patrol that was known to travel that particular stretch of road regularly. Eugene McQuaid was killed when the bomb detonated prematurely. Eugene McQuaid was not a member of the IRA. He was not involved in the IRA operation...The IRA offers its sincere apologies to the McQuaid family for the death of Eugene and for the heartache and trauma which our actions have caused." "IRA Sorry for Death of Man in Explosion," *Daily Ireland*, 13 April 2006.

[103] "'The Guildford and Woolwich bombings killed seven people and injured over 100. Their loss, the loss suffered by their families, will never go away. But it serves no one for the wrong people to be convicted for such an awful crime... It is a matter of great regret when anyone suffers a miscarriage of justice,' Blair said in Wednesday's statement. 'I recognize the trauma that the conviction caused the Conlon and Maguire families and the stigma which wrongly attaches to them to this day. I am very sorry that they were subject to such an ordeal and such an injustice. That's why I am making this apology today. They deserve to be completely and publicly exonerated.'" Statement from Prime Minister Tony Blair, 9 February 2005.
See http://cain.ulst.ac.uk/issues/politics/docs/pmo/tb090205.htm

8. Internal organisational investigation

The final model discussed by the HTR Sub Group was a process wherein organisations or institutions involved in the conflict establish and run a mechanism that is designed to achieve truth recovery. As is explored in the HTR paper on Acknowledgement (Healing Through Remembering 2006b), such a process might entail trawling through historical archives if they exist, interviewing surviving personnel who were active in the period in question, and compiling some form of organisational or institutional account of their role during the conflict. The difficulties concerning quality control, objectivity, victim confidence, and so forth raised by such an approach are discussed in some detail in the relevant section below, concerning the potential of such a model in the Northern Ireland context. At this juncture, however, it might be useful to use the best-known international example of such an approach in order to illuminate better some of the relevant issues.

The only prominent non-state party in a conflict to have conducted thorough investigations of its own actions is the African National Congress in relation to its struggle against the apartheid regime. In three different enquiries – the Stuart Commission (1984), the Skweyiya Commission (1992), and the Motsuenyane Commission (1994) – the ANC comprehensively explored allegations of abusive activities and internment conditions in its camps. Indeed, despite their non-state character, the Skweyiya and Motsuenyane commissions are identified by Hayner as truth commissions in their own right (2001).

The Skweyiya Commission (1992) was established to conduct "a full and thorough investigation" of allegations of abuse at ANC detention camps.[104] The commission had three commissioners, two of whom were ANC members. A final report was produced after seven months, describing widespread torture and abuse within ANC camps. The Skweyiya Report did not name perpetrators, but did provide sufficient identifying characteristics to enable the South African media to recognise those responsible and publish their names. Geula (2000) suggests the decision not to name perpetrators was in deference to Nelson Mandela's assumption of collective responsibility for the actions of the ANC leadership. The Commission recommended medical and psychological assistance be given to witnesses who had appeared before it, and also that monetary compensation be given to "all witnesses who had suffered maltreatment while being detained in ANC camps" (1992: O (ii)).

The Skweyiya Commission was criticised for its perceived ANC bias and for failing to allow persons accused of perpetrating human rights abuses to defend themselves (Hayner 2001: 64). In 1993, then-ANC President Nelson Mandela appointed a second commission of inquiry to re-examine conditions in the camps. The Motsuenyane Commission improved upon the Skweyiya model: it had three commissioners – one American, one South African, and one Zimbabwean – who were not ANC members and were widely perceived as independent. It conducted its proceedings in a court-like manner, with public hearings. "Defendants" were allowed legal representation and the right to cross-examine witnesses. This second commission published a report in 1994, which confirmed the findings of the Skweyiya report: serious human rights abuses in detention camps over a sustained period. In another distinction from the first process, the Motsuenyane Report published the names of perpetrators.

The ANC accepted the findings of the commission, but noted the need for further action: "We regard the Skweyiya and Motsuenyane Commission Reports as a first step in a process of national disclosure of all violations of human rights from all sides" (ANC 1993 cited in Hayner 2001: 64). Indeed, the contribution of the Skweyiya and Motsuenyane commissions was recognised by the SATRC in its Final Report.[105] Clearly, the publication of an effective admission of guilt raises questions regarding prosecution by the state criminal justice system. In the case of the ANC, commanders accepted responsibility before the publication of the first report. In particular, Mandela refused to individualise accountability, taking collective responsibility for all his troops (Geula 2000).

---

[104] As Hayner (2001: 60) notes, the ANC did not establish these commissions entirely of its own volition. In 1991 a group of former ANC detainees (all were members who have been accused of being state agents and held in ANC camps) had established a "Returned Exiles Committee" and began to focus international and local media attention on their allegations of having been abused in the camps.

[105] "The Commission [TRC] recognises that it is able to make some very detailed observations and findings about the abuse of human rights in the military camps of the ANC owing to the fact that the ANC had earlier initiated a number of its own enquiries...The Motsuenyane enquiry, in particular, was a public and independent enquiry to which anyone could bring evidence about such abuses, and a significant number of individuals did so. This enquiry is, in fact, recognised in some of the international literature as a truth commission in its own right...The Commission believes that this was an unprecedented step for a liberation movement to take, and that the ANC should be commended for setting a high standard in this regard. It regrets that it did not receive the same level of co-operation from other structures and organisations in the compiling of this report. Much of the detail contained in the section that follows comes from the ANC's own enquiries and submissions to the Commission" (South African Truth and Reconciliation Commission 1998, Vol. II Ch. IV, para 3-5).

This example is particularly interesting in relation to the ANC's construction of its conduct throughout the SATRC process as a just war and a legitimate struggle. The ANC did, however, acknowledge comparatively early on that even just causes could lead to abuses of power and crimes (Leman-Langlois 2002). This did not diminish in any way their view of the anti-apartheid struggle. As former Justice Minister Dullah Omar has argued, "in the same way that we honour and salute those who fought against Nazism, we honour and salute our freedom fighters" (quoted in Leman-Langlois 2002: 85). Nonetheless, the ANC's early initiatives with regard to acknowledging their own misdeeds did provide that organisation with considerable moral credibility in the period leading up to and during the work of the SATRC proper.[106]

More broadly, the South African experience suggests that such internal organisational investigations may have some role to play in the broader process of truth recovery. Arguably, the credibility of the Motsuenyane Commission in particular underlined the crucial role of some form of independent oversight function by non-organisational members. As one would expect, the decision by that commission to name names was controversial amongst elements of the ANC, but it also certainly enhanced public confidence in the proceedings.

Conclusion

As noted previously, the HTR Sub Group on Truth Recovery and Acknowledgement explored the complexity and range of options on truth recovery in order to better inform the debate on the conflict in and about Northern Ireland. In no sense does the Sub Group advocate simplistic or mechanistic transpositions from one jurisdiction to another. Any truth-recovery process must be tailored to the particular needs of the context in which it will operate. Nonetheless, the Sub Group is persuaded that there are themes, issues, and experiences from the international context that are of relevance to our emerging debate. On the basis of analysis of that international context, the Sub Group has opted to put forward five options which were ultimately chosen as the most appropriate with regard to the debate on truth recovery concerning the conflict in and about Northern Ireland. However, before exploring those options in greater detail, Chapter Three offers a brief overview of the range of truth-recovery style initiatives which have already been completed, are ongoing, or are due to take place here regardless of whether an agreement can be reached on the establishment of a formal mechanism.

---

[106] Some of the sheen was subsequently taken from that credibility when the ANC first took the TRC to court just prior to publication of the report seeking to prevent publication of sections which were critical of its actions, and then when some senior members of the ANC criticised the report for equating their actions with those of the apartheid oppressors (Boraine 2000: 306-333).

CHAPTER THREE

Truth-recovery initiatives regarding the conflict in and about Northern Ireland

Introduction

Unlike some of the peace accords discussed in the last chapter, the 1998 Agreement (also known as the Good Friday Agreement or Belfast Agreement, hereafter the Agreement) in Northern Ireland did not include a mechanism such as a truth process designed to deal with the past. However, as Christine Bell (2003) has argued, the Agreement did contain a number of mechanisms which might be described as piecemeal elements of an approach to the past. The elements of the Agreement relating to the release of paramilitary prisoners (McEvoy 2001, ch10), the provision of services to victims (Hamber and Wilson 2003), the establishment of the Patten Commission to decide on the future shape of a policing service for the jurisdiction (Mulcahy 2005) – these and other measures certainly addressed past consequences of the conflict, albeit not necessarily in an entirely holistic fashion. As will be detailed below, discussions concerning truth recovery nonetheless have been a persistent theme in the intervening years in a variety of academic and policy discussions. This chapter draws upon this broad range of sources in order to underline the range and styles of truth recovery which have gone on either in Northern Ireland or the Republic despite the absence of a formal truth-recovery process from the Agreement.

There have been many initiatives in Northern Ireland with a bearing on truth recovery. These include legal inquiries, cases before local and international courts, policing initiatives, different types of community- and victim-led processes, and a range of other activities. In some instances, the sheer breadth of truth-seeking activities discussed speaks at least in part to a number of institutional failings during the conflict. For example, the collusion of elements of the security forces with paramilitaries, a prosecution service that failed to charge or prosecute serious offenders even when there was overwhelming evidence against them, the failure in some cases of the judiciary to exclude confessions which had been obtained through torture, their reluctance in some cases to find guilty members of the security forces who had been in clear breach of international human rights standards, or the inability or unwillingness in some instances of the police to conduct effective investigations into controversial killings – these and other failings have often forced victims of violence and their families to resort to different strategies designed to compel reluctant institutions towards truth recovery. In other instances, such as the years of pressure which sought to have the IRA admit to what they knew regarding the whereabouts of the remains of those who were killed and those who disappeared in the 1970s, it was the obduracy of paramilitary organisations which compelled those affected towards public mobilisation in search of truth. In both contexts, whether those seeking truth had been affected by state or paramilitary violence, the creativity and persistence of their efforts (often over many years) is often what stands out in reviewing the range of initiatives discussed below.

Public inquiries

In their recent review of official inquiries in Northern Ireland, Rolston and Scraton (2005) detail the plethora of such initiatives during the period of the conflict in and about Northern Ireland. While there have been only three full-scale such inquiries under the 1921 Tribunal of Inquiry (Evidence) Act,[107] these authors document a further 23 different styles of inquiry into different aspects of state policy concerning the conflict. Most of those inquiries dealt with the ways in which the criminal justice system and police and military responded to the campaigns of political violence.[108] As Rolston and Scraton (2005: 558) argue, with the possible exceptions of the Scarman and Cameron Inquiries, frequently the terms of reference were deliberately narrow; they avoided obvious and objective conclusions which might show the security forces in a bad light and delayed reporting to mute criticism.

Rather than examine all of these inquiries, we have chosen to focus on the most recent and arguably those most germane (in the sense that they have occurred in a transitional context rather than during the conflict in and about Northern Ireland) in assessing the insights such inquiries may offer to the broader process of truth recovery.

---

[107] The Saville Tribunal into Bloody Sunday, the Scarman Inquiry into the violence and civil disturbances of 1969, and the Widgery Inquiry also into Bloody Sunday. As is discussed below, the precise legal basis for the establishment of the most recent public inquiries has been a matter of some controversy.

[108] For example, internment, interrogation, rules of evidence, proscription of paramilitary organisations, the abolition of jury trials and amendment of rules of evidence, and the ending of political status led to nine inquiries: Compton, Parker, Diplock, Gardiner, Shackleton, Bennett, Jellicoe, Baker and Colville.

Bloody Sunday

The events of Bloody Sunday have received much scholarly and journalistic analysis.[109] On 29 January, 1998, British Prime Minister Tony Blair announced the establishment of a public inquiry into the events of Bloody Sunday in 1972, when 13 civilians were killed and a further 13 injured (one of whom subsequently died) by members of the parachute regiment of the British Army. The original inquiry, chaired by Lord Widgery, which was established immediately after the killings, had largely exonerated the Army as well as concluding that there was "strong suspicion" that a number of those killed had been nail-bombers or handling weapons prior to their deaths (Widgery 1972, Conclusion 10). These findings had been discredited over a twenty-six year campaign (McCann 1992; Mullan 1997; Walsh 2000). In 1992, the then-Prime Minister, John Major sent a letter to John Hume as MP for the area indicating that "at the time that they were shot" those killed should be regarded as innocent of any allegation that they were handling weapons or nail-bombs. In announcing the inquiry, Mr Blair paid tribute to the families' campaign to overturn the Widgery Tribunal findings and emphasised that the purpose of this fresh inquiry was to seek the truth and reach closure rather than punish those involved.[110] The inquiry was established on the basis that a range of new evidence as well as advancement in forensics and other relevant scientific techniques meant that the events should be looked at afresh.[111]

The Tribunal, chaired by Lord Saville of Newdigate and assisted by two international judges, was established under the Tribunal of Inquiry (Evidence) Act 1921, which gives it the same legal powers to compel the production of evidence and the attendance of witnesses as a High Court. The terms of reference for the Tribunal were to inquire

> ...into a definite matter of urgent public importance, namely the events on Sunday, January 30, 1972, which led to loss of life in connection with the procession in Londonderry on that day, taking account of any new information relevant to events on that day.[112]

The Tribunal website further notes the duty of the Tribunal and its staff as "to seek the truth about what happened on Bloody Sunday. That duty, which is the object of the Inquiry, is to be carried out with fairness, thoroughness and impartiality."[113]

The Tribunal opened on 3 April 1999. Hearings commenced in March 2000 and the final witness did not give evidence until January 2005.[114] Statements were taken from around 2,500 people, 921 of whom gave oral evidence.[115] Soldiers who gave evidence did so in London, following a Court of Appeal ruling that it would be unsafe for them to give evidence in Derry/Londonderry.[116] Additional security protections included permission for some witnesses to give evidence anonymously and a determination that all soldiers whose identity was not already clearly in the public domain would not be identified in the course of the inquiry's proceedings unless the Tribunal directed or ruled otherwise. Further incentive for witness cooperation was given in a ruling by

---

[109] See e.g. McCann (1992), McClean (1997), O'Brien (2002), Pringle & Jacobson (2000), Walsh (2000), Hayes & Campbell (2003) and Hegarty (2004).

[110] "Let me make it clear that the aim of the inquiry is not to accuse individuals or institutions, or to invite fresh recriminations, but to establish the truth about what happened on that day, so far as that can be achieved at 26 years' distance. It will not be easy, and we are all well aware that there were particularly difficult circumstances in Northern Ireland at that time. Bloody Sunday was a tragic day for all concerned. We must all wish that it had never happened. Our concern now is simply to establish the truth, and to close this painful chapter once and for all. Like the Hon. Member for Foyle [John Hume], members of the families of the victims have conducted a long campaign to that end. I have heard some of their remarks over recent years and have been struck by their dignity. Most do not want recrimination; they do not want revenge; but they want the truth. I believe that it is in everyone's interests that the truth be established and told. That is also the way forward to the necessary reconciliation that will be such an important part of building a secure future for the people of Northern Ireland" (Tony Blair, Hansard, Commons Debates, Jan. 29, 1998, at Col 503).

[111] "The time scale within which Lord Widgery produced his report meant that he was not able to consider all the evidence that might have been available. For example, he did not receive any evidence from the wounded who were still in hospital, and he did not consider individually substantial numbers of eye-witness accounts provided to his inquiry in the early part of March 1972. Since the report was published, much new material has come to light about the events of that day. That material includes new eye-witness accounts, new interpretation of ballistic material and new medical evidence. Last year, the families of those killed provided the previous government with a new dossier on the events of Bloody Sunday. The Irish Government also sent this government a detailed assessment that analysed the new material and Lord Widgery's findings in the light of all the material available" (Tony Blair, Hansard, Commons Debates, Jan. 29, 1998, at Col 502).

[112] http://www.bloody-sunday-inquiry.org.uk/index.htm

[113] http://www.bloody-sunday-inquiry.org.uk/index2.asp?p=7

[114] http://www.birw.org/bsireports/100_120/Witness%20X.html

[115] Broken down by occupation, oral testimony was gathered from: 505 civilians; 9 experts and forensic scientists; 49 members of the media (including photographers); 245 members of the military; 34 paramilitaries or former paramilitaries; 39 politicians and civil servants (including intelligence officers); 7 priests; 33 members of the RUC.

[116] *R v Lord Saville*, ex parte A, [1999] 4, All ER 860.

the Attorney General that any evidence provided to the Tribunal by a witness could not be used to incriminate that witness in any subsequent criminal proceedings. Although the protection against self-incrimination may have been influential in persuading witnesses to give honest evidence before the Inquiry, (e.g. Hegarty 2004: 230) it does not preclude all further criminal action, since, for example, evidence provided by other witnesses could still be used in a criminal court case.[117] It appears that the Tribunal Final Report is likely to be published in 2007.

The attempt at uncovering the truth concerning the events of Bloody Sunday arguably holds lessons for a broader contemporary truth process. The manifest inadequacies of the original Widgery Tribunal (see Walsh 2000; Hegarty 2003) are a textbook example of how a discredited truth-recovery mechanism which fails to command the confidence of those most affected by the events may not only fail to contribute to the healing of those victims affected but may actually exacerbate their hurt. The Widgery Tribunal, memorably described by Bishop Edward Daly (2000) as "the second atrocity", was, for a generation of nationalists and republicans, an orchestrated cover-up by the British establishment of the murder of innocent civilians by members of the Army. In no small part because of the contempt and insincerity of the Widgery Tribunal, Bloody Sunday holds a "place in Irish history as a formative moment which not only claimed fourteen lives but also hardened attitudes, increased paramilitary recruitment, helped generate more violence, and convulsed Anglo-Irish relations" (McKittrick & McVea 2000: 77).

As regards the Saville Inquiry, although it is difficult to assess before the actual publication of the report, the manner in which the inquiry was conducted holds lessons for truth recovery. The Saville Inquiry is the largest and most complex public inquiry in British legal history, and the sheer volume of information it has generated stands testament to its thoroughness. In addition, the powers under the 1921 Act to compel production of evidence and cooperation have facilitated the uncovering of an impressive array of evidence and the appearance of many high-ranking political and military figures before the Tribunal (including former Prime Minister Ted Heath) – all of which speak directly to its capacity for greater truth recovery. In addition, notwithstanding the controversial decisions to hold part of the inquiry in London in order to assuage the fear of military witnesses for their security, the Tribunal held their deliberations in public and asserted the importance of such a process in order to maximise public confidence.[118] Daily updates of Tribunal proceedings were made on the Bloody Sunday Inquiry website.

The weaknesses of the Bloody Sunday Tribunal have been more prominent in commentary. Chief amongst such criticisms has been the issue of cost, and legitimately so. In November 2005 the government estimated that the total cost of the Tribunal would be in the region of £163 million, approximately half of which was spent on legal fees.[119] Subsequent press speculation has suggested that this may in fact be something of a conservative estimate.[120] To put such figures in perspective, most past truth commissions have operated on around US $5million or less: less than 2% of the cost of the Bloody Sunday Tribunal. Even one of the most ambitious, the South African Truth Commission which had a staff of 350, still only cost US $18 million per year during its time of operation (Freeman & Hayner 2003).

A large part of the phenomenal expense of the Saville Inquiry was the legal fees, which came close to reaching £86 million.[121] The high level of IT provision and the decision to move the Tribunal to London for a period added to the costs, as did defending against the six legal challenges made to the Tribunal in its early years of operation.[122] Despite the self-professed desire of the Tribunal to adopt an inquisitorial approach, by far the

---

[117] http://www.bloody-sunday-inquiry.org.uk/
[118] "...the statute under which we are acting allows us to exclude the public or any portion of the public from any part of the proceedings, if we consider it would be in the public interest to us do so, but we shall need very strong grounds indeed to take that course..." (Bloody Sunday Tribunal Opening Statement, 3 April 1998). For a critical perspective on the effect on public confidence with regard to the decision to move parts of the Tribunal to London, see Hegarty (2004).
[119] Costs can be broken down as follows: £85,246,000 on legal fees, £14,954,000 on accommodation, £3,217,000 on transportation, £12,836,000 on IT costs, £7,534,000 on hiring halls, £39,213,000 on other costs including salary costs for Tribunal members and Inquiry staff, witness expenses, expert witnesses, office services and security, telecommunications, a police investigation and other miscellaneous office expenditure and fees (House of Commons Debates, 8 November 2005).
[120] The most extravagant of these appeared in the *Daily Telegraph* which suggested that the Inquiry might cost as much as £400 million. "Bloody Sunday: Full inquiry, cost £400m. July 7 bombs: No inquiry, 'too expensive'", *Daily Telegraph*, 5 July 2006.
[121] The breakdown of the total £85,743,724 legal fees is as follows: payments made by the NIO to lawyers: £56,363,009, of which Counsel for Inquiry received £18,458,924; Solicitors for witness statements £12,609,388; families' senior counsel £5,352,479; NICRA senior counsel £507,359; families' junior counsel £5,257,484; NICRA junior counsel £230,151; families' solicitors £14,016,967; NICRA solicitors £436,125; other legal representatives £12,539,645. The Ministry of Defence covered a further £29,380,715 of legal fees, paid as follows: Armed Forces senior counsel £11,022,993; Ministry of Defence senior counsel £235,145; Armed Forces junior counsel £8,344,340; Ministry of Defence junior counsel £15,883,000; Armed Forces solicitors £9,762,354 (Hansard, 25th February 2004. col. 495 W.
Available at http://www.publications.parliament.uk/pa/cm200304/cmhansrd/vo040225/text/40225w19.htm
[122] L. Blom Cooper "The Cost of Bloody Sunday", *The Observer*, 20 January 2002.

biggest contributing factor to the spiralling costs was the adversarial and legalistic character which quickly evolved in the conduct of the Inquiry.

The 1921 Act requires that witnesses be treated "fairly" and the definition of fairness is laid down in the Salmon Principles, which include that any witness should be afforded a lawyer by the public purse and that those lawyers should be able to cross-examine on issues which may affect their client. According to Hegarty (2004: 240), while few of the civilian witnesses were represented in this fashion at the actual Tribunal (they were not deemed "interested parties" by the Tribunal and were therefore not afforded counsel although they were given legal assistance in the preparation of their statements), all of the military witnesses were deemed "interested parties" and were represented by counsel paid for by the Ministry of Defence. Given the seriousness of the allegations levelled against the soldiers, it is hardly surprising that they were so regarded and sought representation by counsel. However, the presence of so many lawyers, with many of them working for the military, arguably created the worst of both worlds. It inevitably slowed the process, gave it an extremely legalistic ethos much like that of a courtroom, and (given the disparity in representation between civilian and military witnesses) arguably created two tiers of witnesses.[123] Such a perception was augmented by the view, expressed by a number of counsel for families at the inquiry and some commentators, that senior members of the political and military establishment were treated much more softly than civilian witnesses (McCann 2005).[124] Any similar perception in a broader truth-recovery process of partiality as between protagonists or witnesses would be quite disastrous.

The Cory Collusion Inquiries and the Inquiries Act 2005

Largely as a result of the sustained campaigns by the families of Patrick Finucane, Rosemary Nelson, Robert Hamill, and Billy Wright and human rights NGOs who supported them, the issue of collusion between paramilitaries and the security forces rose to the top of the political agenda in the negotiations regarding the implementation of the Agreement.[125] During the Weston Park negotiations in 2001, the British and Irish governments agreed to appoint a judge of international standing to investigate allegations of state collusion with terrorists in the deaths of Pat Finucane, Rosemary Nelson, Robert Hamill, Billy Wright, Chief Superintendent Breen, Superintendent Buchanan, and Lord Justice and Lady Gibson (O'Brien 2005). It was agreed that "in the event that a Public Inquiry is recommended in any case, the relevant Government will implement that recommendation."[126]

Former Canadian Supreme Court judge, the Honourable Justice Peter Cory, was appointed in May 2002. Cory delivered his reports on the Finucane, Nelson, Hamill, and Wright cases to the British government on 7

---

123 Hegarty (2004: 241) recounts an interesting exchange between Lord Saville and a civilian witness concerning precisely this point. In responding to the witness, Lord Saville said "...there are plenty of barristers in this room acting for the interested parties, the families and so on who I am sure would be the first to raise the matter with us if they felt we had not treated the citizens of this city properly". In responding one of the Counsel for the families pointed out (correctly) that he had not been instructed by nor would they be able to defend such civilian witnesses. Michael Mansfield QC acting for a number of families summed up "we do not represent witnesses other than the families we are personally responsible for".

124 For example Eamon McCann details how former Prime Minister Edward Heath refused to answer over 50 questions put to him, variously describing questions as "silly", "imaginary", "irrelevant", "disgraceful" etc. McCann also accuses Lord Saville of persistently interrupting examining counsel in order to protect Mr Heath and of showing no such similar instincts when civilian witnesses were being probed by Army barristers. See also E. McCann "Saville Too Soft on Heath", *Irish News*, 27 January 2003. Michael Lavery QC, the senior lawyer in question who was cross examining Mr Heath on behalf of a number of the families, took the highly unusual step of addressing this question directly to the inquiry. Lavery pointed to the large number of refusals to answer by Mr Heath and the failure by the Tribunal to prevent Mr Heath abusing counsel, continuing "...I have to say that the latitude that this witness has been given is completely outside my experience" (Inquiry transcript, 21 January 2003, p100, lines 11-16).

125 Space does not permit exploring the full details of each of these cases. However, some of the details concerning the Finucane case are worth reproducing as an example of the complexity of the debate concerning security force/paramilitary collusion. Pat Finucane was a lawyer who was murdered by the loyalist Ulster Defence Association in 1989. During interrogations of loyalist suspects, RUC officers consistently urged loyalists to kill him, alleging wrongly that he was a member of the IRA. Less than a month prior to the murder, Conservative Junior Minister Douglas Hogg announced in the House of Commons that "there are in Northern Ireland a number of solicitors who are unduly sympathetic to the IRA." Hogg later acknowledged that this statement was based on a Special Branch briefing. The intelligence which led to Finucane's murder was co-ordinated by Brian Nelson, a UDA member and Army's Force Research Unit agent. The principal weapon was supplied by another RUC Special Branch agent, William Stobie. Ken Barrett, one of the prime actors convicted of the murder in 2004, was also an RUC informer. When Brian Nelson was arrested in 1990 and faced 34 charges including two counts of murder (after speculation that he would expose the Army's role in open court), counsel for the Attorney General told the court that after "a rigorous examination of the interests of justice", fifteen charges were to be dropped including the two murders. As discussed below, these facts have been the subject of three investigations by the former Chief of the Metropolitan Police Sir John Stevens and an independent report by Judge Cory, both of whom found that collusion had taken place (see CAJ 1999; British Irish Rights Watch 2000; Stevens 2003; Lawyers Committee for Human Rights 2003; Cory 2004; O'Brien 2005).

126 Para 19 at http://cain.ulst.ac.uk/events/peace/docs/bi010801.htm

October 2003, and on the Breen, Buchanan, and Gibson cases to the Irish government at the same time. In all but the Gibson case, Cory found material that could be found to constitute collusion and recommended public inquiries.[127] The Irish government published Cory's report immediately and established a state inquiry into the deaths of Chief Superintendent Breen and Superintendent Buchanan in compliance with Cory's recommendations.

Cory's reports on the killings of Finucane, Hamill, Nelson, and Wright were only made public by the British government in April 2004 after some intense political pressure, not least from Justice Cory himself. In all four cases, Cory concluded that there was sufficient evidence of state collusion in the killings to warrant the holding of a public inquiry and, indeed, that these cases may even illustrate the rare situation where an inquiry would "be of greater benefit to the community than prosecutions". A prompt inquiry was deemed necessary to reflect the status of the Weston Park agreement: "the failure to hold a public inquiry as quickly as it is reasonably possible to do so [...] could be seen as a cynical breach of faith which could have unfortunate consequences for the peace accord".[128]

During his inquiries, Cory had no power to subpoena or compel evidence. The effects of this were noted by Cory in, for example, his inability to access documents held by the Criminal Injuries Compensation Authority that may have been of relevance to the Robert Hamill inquiry.[129] To prevent similar restrictions on other investigations, Cory outlined the basic standards necessary for a credible public inquiry, that is:

- An independent commissioner or panel of commissioners;
- Powers to compel cooperation and production of evidence;
- Ability to select its own counsel and to engage investigators;
- Holding hearings in public where possible; and
- Findings and recommendations made public.

Allaying fears that all public inquiries necessitate the haemorrhage of public funding that the Bloody Sunday Tribunal incurred, Cory also made clear in his reports that public inquiries "are not designed, and should not be considered, as a means of enriching the legal profession" and inquiry time and counsel costs can be easily and reasonably controlled with a modicum of forethought.[130]

Following publication of the Cory Report, the British government announced that public inquiries would be established into the cases of Hamill, Nelson, and Wright, but that ongoing criminal prosecutions would have to be concluded in relation to the killing of Pat Finucane before inquiry procedures were announced for that case. The way for the Finucane inquiry was cleared with the conviction of UDA man and Special Branch informer Ken Barrett in September 2004.[131] The Wright, Hamill, and Nelson inquiries were established with powers of subpoena equal to those of the Bloody Sunday Tribunal.[132]

Cory protested that a public inquiry could be conducted alongside the Finucane prosecution case but, instead of following his recommendations, the government introduced new legislation under which it said the Pat Finucane inquiry would be established. On 7 April 2005 – less than a week after the publication of the Cory reports and on the final day of session before Parliament closed – the government replaced the Tribunals of Enquiry (Evidence) Act 1921 under which the Bloody Sunday Tribunal was established (which, as was noted above, gives tribunals of inquiry established under it the same evidential power as the High Court) with the Inquiries Act 2005, which effectively allows Executive control over all aspects of a public inquiry.

For tribunals established under the Inquiries Act 2005, Ministers control appointment and dismissal of an inquiry panel; set the temporal and substantive terms of inquiry; control inquiry funding; and control access to evidence and dissemination of inquiry findings (or omission of evidence from a final report). These controls diverge radically from Justice Cory's minimum basic standards for a public inquiry.

This legislation has been opposed by many organisations and institutions, including the Joint Committee on Human Rights;[133] Amnesty International;[134] the Northern Ireland Human Rights Commission; British Irish

---

[127] Justice Cory defined collusion as the state security services "ignoring or turning a blind eye to the wrongful acts of their servants or agents or supplying information to assist them in their wrongful acts or encouraging them to commit wrongful acts" (Cory 2004: 21).
[128] Cory (2004) at 1.296 (re Finucane); 2.256 (re Hamill); 3.226 (re Wright); 4.244 (re Nelson).
[129] Cory (2004) at 2.250.
[130] Cory (2004) at 1.305; 2.265; 3.231; 4.254
[131] "Finucane's Killer Jailed Amid Clamour for Inquiry", *The Guardian*, 17 September 2004.
[132] The Billy Wright Inquiry was established under the Prison Act (Northern Ireland) Act 1953. The Robert Hamill and Rosemary Nelson Inquiries were established under the Police (Northern Ireland) Act 1998.

Rights Watch; the Committee on the Administration of Justice;[135] the Committee on International Human Rights of the Association of the Bar of the City of New York;[136] and the relatives of the victims. Judge Cory criticised the injustice to victims and families of changing the "ground rules" in a way which could not have been anticipated at Weston Park, particularly as "the proposed new Act would make a meaningful inquiry impossible".[137] This was a view strongly endorsed by Lord Saville, the current chair of the Bloody Sunday Tribunal.[138]

Despite these public protests, and reassurances to the contrary during the original parliamentary debates, the government "converted" the Billy Wright Inquiry into an inquiry under the new legislation on 23 November 2005 and the Hamill Inquiry in March 2006. In December 2005 the government also announced that the public hearings for both the Nelson and Wright inquiries scheduled for Spring 2006 would be delayed by up to a year because of the volume of evidence to be considered in both cases.[139] The Finucane family has continued to insist that they will not take part in an inquiry established under the terms outlined in the Inquiries Act.[140]

Independent Commission of Inquiry into the Dublin and Monaghan Bombings
The struggle for truth has not just been confined to victims and families victims of the conflict in the jurisdiction of Northern Ireland. The Dublin and Monaghan bombings of 1974 killed 33 people and injured 250, marking these attacks as the largest loss of life in a single day of this conflict in and about Northern Ireland in the last forty years, including the Omagh bombing. The inadequate police investigation at the time and significant circumstantial evidence of state collusion (between British military intelligence and the Ulster Volunteer Force who carried out the bombings) sustained survivors' determination to see a public investigation instituted (Mullan 2001). The organisation Justice for the Forgotten was formed by families and victims of the bombings, because: "Closure will only come once we have been told the truth and nothing but the truth. Truth will only be established when the British Government and the Irish Government deal openly and honestly with our grievance".[141]

Following the campaign by victims group Justice for the Forgotten and others, on 19 December 1999 the Independent Commission of Inquiry into the Dublin and Monaghan Bombings was established to undertake a thorough examination, fact-finding, and assessment of the bombings. The Inquiry was subsequently directed to investigate a number of other incidents, including the shooting of Brid Carr (1974), the bombing of Kay's Tavern in Dundalk (1975), and the killing of Seamus Ludlow (1976). The Inquiry was initially chaired by departing Chief Justice Liam Hamilton, who was forced to resign due to ill-health and succeeded by former Supreme Court Judge the Hon. Henry Barron in October 2000.

The *Report into the Dublin and Monaghan Bombings* was presented to An Taoiseach on 29 October 2003 and published three weeks later. The Barron Report recognised that collusion between state security forces and paramilitary organisations had occurred in the Republic of Ireland but found there was not sufficient evidence of collusion in these particular attacks to reach a finding that the bombings were anything other than the solo work of loyalist paramilitaries. This conclusion was heavily criticised. A sub-committee was then established to report on the report and determine whether the Inquiry had fulfilled its terms of reference.[142] The sub-committee reported back in early 2005, concluding that a Public Tribunal of Inquiry with full statutory powers should be established to provide closure to the investigation.

---

[133] The Joint Committee concluded that several provisions of the Bill may not be compliant with Article 2 of the European Convention on Human Rights in that they would inhibit an effective investigation into cases involving deaths.
[134] Amnesty International called for potential appointees to decline appointment to inquiries under the act and called for the repeal of the Inquiries Act, as did Geraldine Finucane, wife of murdered solicitor Pat Finucane.
See http://www.serve.com/pfc/pf/inqubill/ai050420.html
[135] CAJ decried such parliamentary "sleight of hand" as contrary to the goals of justice and truth.
[136] The New York Bar Association submitted an 18-page commentary on the legislation in its initial draft form, see http://www.abcny.org/pdf/report/ABCNY_Inquiries_Bill.pdf
[137] Letter by The Hon. Peter Cory to US Congressional Committee, Tuesday 15 March 2005.
[138] In a strongly worded letter to Baroness Ashton, minister in the department of constitutional affairs, Lord Saville argued that the corrosion of the powers of a Tribunal Chairman previously established under the 1921 Act "...makes a very serious inroad into the independence of any inquiry; and is likely to damage or destroy public confidence in the inquiry and its findings, especially in any case where the conduct of the authorities may be in question... As a judge, I must tell you that I would not be prepared to be appointed as a member of an inquiry that was subject to a provision of this kind", quoted in "Finucane Widow Urges Judges to Shun Inquiry", *The Guardian*, 14 April 2005,
[139] "New Inquires Set Back as Nelson Delayed for a Year", *Irish News*, 12 December 2005.
[140] "Family Reject Legislation", Press Release, 26 November 2004. Available at http://www.serve.com/pfc/pf/inqubill/041126pf.html
[141] Statement of Dublin/Monaghan Bombing Families and Wounded, 19 September 1998.
[142] The Joint Committee on Justice, Equality, Defence and Women's Rights (Sub-committee on the Barron Report) Interim Report on the Report of the Independent Commission of Inquiry into the Dublin and Monaghan Bombings (Interim Barron Report 2003).

The Report describes obstructive and uncooperative behaviour from the Northern Ireland Office and Ministry of Defence during the course of the Inquiry. Barron is philosophical about the methods but does not seek to disguise their impact: "While the Inquiry fully understands the position taken by the British Government on these matters, it must be said that the scope of this report is limited as a result" (Barron 2003: 22). The second report further noted that lack of cooperation from the British authorities had been the primary impediment to the first Barron Inquiry, and "the Sub-Committee met with the same difficulty" (Joint Committee 2005: 6).[143] The sub-committee recommended that, if further cooperation from the British authorities was not forthcoming, the British government should be brought before the European Court of Human Rights (ECHR) requiring it to institute a proper investigation into the events (Joint Committee 2005: 77). The Irish government established another Commission of Investigation with Mr Patrick MacEntee SC as the sole member. That Commission was tasked with investigating why the Gardai investigation into the bombings was wound down in 1974 and why certain leads which appeared to suggest the involvement of British intelligence were not properly followed up (MacEntee 2006). In early 2006, when Mr MacEntee was due to complete his final report, he announced that some important additional cooperation had been forthcoming from individuals with links to British intelligence and that this had delayed his reporting.[144] The families and victims continue with their campaign.

Conclusion

While families and human rights NGOs have often campaigned relentlessly for the establishment of independent public inquiries, this was often in a context wherein they saw few other viable options rather than because they had complete confidence in the capacity of such bodies to uncover the whole truth. There remains a considerable degree of cynicism concerning the reasons for establishing such inquiries. As Angela Hegarty has argued, "...on many occasions, public inquiries are employed by governments not as a tool to find truth and establish accountability for human rights violations, but as a way of deflecting criticism and avoiding blame" (Hegarty 2003: 1159). Similarly, Rolston and Scraton contend that, historically, such inquiries were not established in Northern Ireland to restore confidence in the rule of law, "but rather to give that appearance to a British and international audience" (2005: 558). The prohibitive costs associated with the Bloody Sunday Inquiry and the lengthy delays in the beginnings of the public aspects of the Wright and Nelson cases added to such scepticism. Finally, the introduction of the much-criticised Inquiries Act on the final day of the last parliament to deal with the Finucane case (and any future inquiries) has probably fatally undermined the capacity of the public inquiry as a vehicle of truth recovery, at least under the terms of that piece of legislation.

Legal challenges as truth recovery

For a number of years, families and campaigning organisations have attempted to use legal challenges and the ensuing publicity which often surrounds high-profile cases as vehicles to either uncover hidden truths and/or apply political or moral pressure to individuals or organisations who may be in possession of relevant information. These have taken two broad forms: (i) challenges based on the provisions of the European Convention on Human Rights, focused in particular on the right to life, and (ii) civil actions and private prosecutions brought against the alleged perpetrators.

The "Right to Life" Cases under the European Convention on Human Rights

The European Convention on Human Rights, which was incorporated into United Kingdom domestic law with the passage of the Human Rights Act 1998, has formed the basis of a number of legal challenges aimed at truth recovery. Most prominent of these have been the series of "right to life" cases which have been ruled upon by the ECHR.

The "right to life" provision contained in Article 2 of the ECHR is obviously one of the most fundamental rights contained in the Convention (Mowbray 2004).[145] In a number of Northern Ireland cases, the UK government has been found to be in breach of this right. Thus, for example, in a 1995 judgement, the ECHR ruled the Article 2 right to life had been breached by UK state security forces who shot dead three unarmed IRA members (Farrell, McCann, and Savage) on an active bombing mission in Gibraltar in 1988.[146] In this case and in the subsequent case, the European Court "safeguarded its stance that whether the deceased is an ordinary

---

143 Joint Committee on Justice, Equality, Defence and Women's Rights, Final Report on the Report of the Independent Commission of Inquiry into the Dublin Bombings of 1972 and 1973 (February 2005) at 6.

144 "Further Extension for Bombings Probe", *RTE News*, 28 February 2006. Available at http://www.rte.ie/news/2006/0228/barron.html

145 Article 2 provides that: (i) everyone's right to life shall be protected by law. No one shall be deprived of his life intentionally save in the execution of a sentence of a court following his conviction of a crime for which this penalty is provided by law; (ii) deprivation of life shall not be regarded as inflicted in contravention of this article when it results from the use of force which is no more than absolutely necessary: (a) in defence of any person from unlawful violence; (b) in order to effect a lawful arrest or to prevent escape of a person lawfully detained; and (c) in action lawfully taken for the purpose of quelling a riot or insurrection.

146 *McCann and others v the UK* 18984/91 [1995] ECHR 31 (27 September 1995).

citizen or a member of a paramilitary organisation, a substantive measure of life protection is due to them" (Ní Aoláin 2002: 578). However, in recognition of their illegal activities, the ECHR declined to award any damages to the applicants.

More recently, so-called "procedural" aspects to that right have been ruled on by the ECHR. Following a line of reasoning developed in a number of Turkish cases, in the joined cases of *Jordan*,[147] *McKerr*,[148] *Kelly*,[149] and *Shanaghan* v. *United Kingdom*,[150] the Court found that an effective investigation was a necessary component of the right to life. The Court ruled that the United Kingdom (UK) had violated Article 2 because it had not properly investigated the killings of twelve individuals, some of them killed by the police, some by the army, and one killed by loyalist paramilitaries in circumstances which strongly suggested collusion (Bell & Keenan 2005).[151] The Shanaghan ruling was particularly significant, as this was the first time that the possible state collusion with terrorists in unlawful killing was acknowledged in a legal forum (Ní Aoláin 2002).

The British government had contended that an amalgam of a number of factors (including the police investigation, review by the Director of Public Prosecutions, the inquest system, and the possibility of civil proceedings) cumulatively satisfied the procedural requirement of Article 2. The European Court of Human Rights accepted that a combination of such remedies could satisfy Article 2. However, it found that they had not in these cases. The Court determined that an investigation had to be capable of leading to a determination of whether the force used in such circumstances was or was not justified in the circumstances and to the identification and punishment of those responsible.[152] In 2003 the Court came to a similar decision with regard to the death of Pat Finucane.[153]

Following the Courts' judgements, the UK government was obliged to engage with the Committee of Ministers of the Council of Europe (which has responsibility for the implementation of the judgments of the Court) to determine the steps the government had to take to meet the terms of the judgment. In September 2002, the UK Government presented the Committee with a "package of measures" outlining the steps it had taken to implement the judgments of the Court in the principal cases under consideration so as to ensure that future investigations would comply with Article 2.

In February 2005, the Committee of Ministers produced its response to the "package of measures".[154] The Committee noted steps being taken, including: the establishment of the Police Ombudsman's Office; arrangements allowing for the "calling in" of other police forces to investigate deaths; the establishment of the Serious Crimes Review Team (now the Historical Enquiries Team); the option for families to judicial review

---

[147] *Jordan v UK* (No. 24746/94).

[148] *McKerr v UK* (No. 28883/95).

[149] *Kelly and others v UK* (No. 30054/96).

[150] *Shanaghan v UK* (No 37715/97).

[151] In *Jordan*, the applicant's son was killed when a member of the RUC who was pursuing his car opened fire as Jordan tried to escape. Jordan was an IRA member, but unarmed at the time. In *Kelly*, the applicant's son, together with seven other armed IRA members and a civilian, was killed by SAS soldiers located around a police station which the IRA was attacking. In *McKerr*, the applicant's father, together with two other companions, was shot dead by undercover RUC officers - they were members of the IRA, but unarmed at the time. In *Shanaghan*, the deceased who was not a member of the IRA, but who had claimed that he had been the subject of ongoing police harassment, including the threat of death, was shot dead by a masked gunman shortly after the police informed him that his personal details had fallen into the hands of loyalist paramilitaries and in circumstances which suggested official involvement in the murder.

[152] The Court criticised inadequacies at each stage in the process regarding the investigation of these controversial killings. These included: (a) a lack of independence in the police investigation of officers suspected of malpractice; (b) a lack of public scrutiny of the work of the DPP and a failure by the latter to supply reasons to the families regarding decisions not to prosecute; and (c) weaknesses in the Inquest system including the fact that state witnesses could not be compelled to attend, the fact that the range of possible verdicts did not include one which was capable of leading to a prosecution, the lack of availability of legal aid to families, the non-disclosure of witness statements prior to inquests, the usage of Public Interest Immunity Certificates which prevented examination of central issues, delays in the proceedings, and the failure to effect prompt investigation into the allegation of collusion on the states own initiative (Bell & Keenan 2005: 74).

[153] The court held that Article 2 had been violated in the *Finucane* case because: (a) the lack of an independent police investigation which "raised serious doubts as to the thoroughness or effectiveness with which the possibility of collusion had been pursued"; (b) the failures of the Inquest to "address serious and legitimate concerns" with regard to collusion meant that it could not be regarded as having constituted an effective investigation; (c) the three Stevens Inquiries (discussed below) did not constitute an effective investigation since two had not been directly focused on the Finucane killing and the third, while specifically concerned with the murder, took place some 10 years after the event, and thus could not be regarded as having been carried out "promptly and expeditiously" as required under the relevant case law; (d) the fact that the Director of Public Prosecutions was not required to give reasons for his decisions not to prosecute relevant individuals and no possibility of challenge to such decisions by way of judicial review meant that "no information had been provided to reassure the applicant and the public that the rule of law had been respected"; and (e) in conclusion, there had been a failure to provide a prompt and effective investigation into the allegations of collusion by security personnel. (*Finucane v. the United Kingdom* (application no. 29178/95) July 2003).

of decisions not to prosecute; new practices relating to the verdicts of coroners' juries at inquests and developments regarding disclosure at inquests; legal aid for inquests; measures to give effect to recommendations following reviews of the coroners' system; and the Inquiries Act. The Committee welcomed the Government's intention to address the issues arising from the Court judgments but considered that "certain general measures remain to be taken and that further information and clarifications are outstanding with regard to a number of other measures, including, where appropriate, information on the impact of these measures in practice". Interestingly, one issue which has arisen but which the government has strongly resisted is the suggestion that the cases which were the subject of the judgements from the Court should now be reopened for Article 2-compliant investigation. Despite the opposition from the government, this remains a live issue for the Committee of Ministers.

Some families have attempted to compel such an Article 2-compliant re-opening of the investigation into the death of their loved ones. Thus, in *Re McKerr* an application for judicial review was brought on foot of the ECHR judgement in which a son of the deceased sought to compel the Secretary of State to order an Article 2 ECHR-compliant investigation into his father's death in 1982. The applicant also sought damages, as well as a declaration that he had a continuing right to an investigation and that the Secretary of State was in breach of Article 2 ECHR and Section 6 of the Human Rights Act for so long as he failed to order a full investigation. The application was first dismissed by the High Court in Northern Ireland, which considered that the earlier award of damages by the European Court of Human Rights had compensated the applicant for the violation of Article 2 ECHR and that the violation had at that stage ceased. However, the Northern Ireland Court of Appeal overturned that decision and made a declaration that the applicant had a continuing right to an investigation.[155] The Secretary of State in turn appealed to the House of Lords, where the central question was whether the Human Rights Act – which came into force on 2 October 2000[156] – could have retrospective effect such as would allow it to apply to a death that predated the Act's coming into force by, in this instance, 18 years.

The House of Lords decided that the Government was not obligated to reopen investigations into the death of McKerr (and, by extension, of other similar cases). This finding was based on the reasoning that (i) there was no such obligation under domestic law, because the events concerned occurred before the incorporation of the European Convention on Human Rights into UK domestic law; and (ii) there was no obligation under the European system as the violation of Article 2 determined by the ECHR was not a continuing violation and therefore would not be remedied by opening a new investigation.[157] Essentially, this ruling means that, while an initial violation occurred concerning the failure to investigate independently and expeditiously, this violation was not ongoing and there is no obligation to investigate retrospectively because the events happened before the ECHR was incorporated into domestic law. As Anthony and Mageean (2006) argue, the logic of the House of Lords in the *McKerr* judgement was somewhat undermined by two other House of Lords judgements concerning right to life issues in two cases which were unrelated to the conflict in and about Northern Ireland (*Sacker* and *Middleton*) delivered on the same day.[158]

This inconsistency has, however, since caused significant difficulty in the lower courts, where the choice has been between distinguishing or following *McKerr*. For example, in *Re Jordan's Application*, (another of the families who had successfully taken their case to the ECHR) the Northern Ireland Court initially chose to distinguish *McKerr* when holding that an incomplete inquest into the death of Pearse Jordan should be conducted in the light of *Sacker* and *Middleton*.[159] In effect, the argument here was that the inquest had begun, but never been properly completed, and that there the re-opening of this inquest "falls to be completed subsequent to the commencement of the Human Rights Act".[160] In contrast, the Northern Ireland Court of Appeal adopted the opposite approach in *Re McGaughey and Grew's Application*.[161]

[154] Council of Europe (2005) Action of the Security Forces (case of *McKerr v UK* and five similar cases). Measures taken or envisaged to ensure compliance with the judgements of the European Court of Human Rights in the cases against the United Kingdom listed in Appendix III (Adopted by the Committee of Ministers on 23 February 2005 at the 941st meeting of the Ministers' Deputies). Interim Resolution Res DH (2005) 20.
[155] *Re McKerr's Application* [2003] NICA 1.
[156] SI 2000/1851.
[157] *Re McKerr* [2004] N.I. 212
[158] In *R (Sacker) v West Yorkshire Coroner* [2004] 1 WLR 796 and *R (Middleton) v West Somerset Coroner* [2004] 2 WLR 800 (also right to life cases) deaths had also occurred prior to incorporation of the ECHR but the Coroners Inquests were being held for the first time after the date of incorporation. The corresponding issue for the House of Lords was whether the governing legislation should be interpreted in the light of the ECHR (as per section 3 of the Human Rights Act) so as to ensure consistency with Article 2. Their Lordships held that it should, and stated that compliance could be achieved by a slight re-reading of the relevant provisions – in essence, giving the Human Rights Act retrospective effect in these non-Northern Ireland cases.
[159] *Re Jordan's Application* [2004] NICA 29 & [2004] NICA 30.
[160] [2004] NICA 29, para 13 (Girvan J).
[161] [2005] NICA 1.

This was an appeal against a decision of the High Court that held that the Chief Constable of the PSNI was under a continuing duty by virtue of section 8 of the Coroner's Act (Northern Ireland) 1959 and Article 2 of the ECHR to provide the coroner with police documents relevant to an inquest into the deaths of the applicant's sons. These deaths had also occurred before incorporation of the ECHR in 2000.[162] In allowing the appeal, the Court of Appeal considered at length the Court's earlier decision in *Jordan* before concluding that it had been wrong to distinguish *McKerr*. Kerr LCJ stated that because the deaths involved had occurred before the Human Rights Act came into force the relevant sections of the ECHR did not apply. Kerr LCJ thus concluded by referring to Lord Hoffman's opinion in *McKerr*: "Lord Hoffman put it bluntly, 'Either the Act applies to death before 2 October 2000, or it does not'. He held that it did not".[163]

In sum, families who have sought to utilise the mechanisms of the European Convention on Human Rights as a form of truth recovery with regard to what happened to their loved ones have had mixed results. Certainly the findings of violations of Article 2 in the *McCann* and *Jordan et al* cases were highly significant and have led to major changes to the system for the investigation of controversial deaths. However, as evidenced by their efforts before the local courts to re-open investigations which would now be Article 2-compliant (e.g. in terms of investigation by an external police agency, availability of evidence, reasons for non-prosecution, an inquest system capable of leading to charges etc.), these families could not appear to have made substantial progress. The firm rejection by the House of Lords in *McKerr* and now the Northern Ireland Court of Appeal judgement in *McGaughey and Grew* appear to rule out the further usage of the Convention as a vehicle of truth recovery before the local courts in cases of controversial killings which occurred before incorporation.

Civil actions and private prosecutions

In a number of prominent cases, victims or their families have been involved in taking civil actions or attempting to bring a private prosecution against individuals who were alleged to have been involved in violent acts against their loved ones. Often, such actions have been framed as "an attempt to get at the truth" as well as seeking justice for what has happened.

One significant reason to initiate civil suit is as a precursor to petitioning the ECHR. In order for a case to be admissible before the ECHR, it must first be shown that all domestic remedies have been exhausted, including, where appropriate, civil action. Thus, for example, in 1992, Geraldine Finucane filed suit for damages against the Ministry of Defence and Brian Nelson,[164] alleging that her husband Patrick Finucane was killed by or with the connivance of the Ministry of Defence and that Brian Nelson was an army agent. The process of document request and delivery dragged out over the next six years, during which some truth was uncovered – that is, in the admission that Nelson was a British agent – but other information was withheld and obfuscated and the interminable length of reply to information requests suggested that the Ministry of Defence was stalling as a deliberate ploy.[165] With no conclusion to the case in sight, Geraldine Finucane took the case to the ECHR.

Many other families affected by the conflict have similarly sued or attempted to sue for damages those responsible for the death or injuries inflicted. However, the capacity of a law suit for damages to serve as a vehicle for truth recovery is somewhat limited. As evidenced by the civil action taken by Geraldine Finucane, a civil action arguably gives much greater scope for obfuscation, delay and obstruction than a criminal trial, for example, if those responsible for the actions were state actors, the agency responsible may well seek to apply for a public interest immunity certificate. While such a course of action is also available at a criminal trial, in the latter circumstances the trial judge would at least review whether such a certificate was warranted. No such check is available in civil proceedings. In addition, it is important to bear in mind that a civil action is primarily designed as a mechanism to achieve damages rather than necessarily uncover truth. For many families affected, the availability of legal aid for such actions was and is a crucial advantage to such proceedings. However, if a reasonable offer of damages is made by the respondent individual or organisation, and rejected by the family who are seeking truth recovery, legal aid funding may be withdrawn. Similarly, if those responsible for the death or injury in question are members of a non-state paramilitary organisation, and therefore in some instances may have few assets from which to pay out, legal aid may not be granted where there is little realistic chance of recovery of damages.[166]

Beyond civil actions for damages, other families have attempted to use the method of private prosecution both as a mechanism for truth recovery (and to ensure some form of justice) and as a related method to generate

---

[162] *Re McCaughey and Grew's Application* [2004] NIQB 2
[163] [2005] NICA 1, para 44.
[164] *Finucane v Ministry of Defence* (Unreported – Northern Ireland).
[165] Decision as to the Admissibility of Application no. 29178/95 by *Geraldine Finucane v the United Kingdom*, ECHR (2 July 2002).
[166] For a useful critique of the capacity of civil proceedings to uncover truth see submission by the Committee on the Administration of Justice (CAJ) to the ECHR in the *Jordan et al* cases – copy available at CAJ office.

publicity concerning their case. Perhaps the best known such action has been the efforts of the families of victims of the Omagh bombing in which 29 people were killed and more than 200 injured in 1998. In 2002, backed by a number of major celebrities including Sir Bob Geldoff and a number of British and Irish newspapers, they formed the Omagh Victims Civil and Legal Action Group to initiate a civil action against five individuals and the Real IRA who planted the bomb.[167] The estimated cost of the action was put at £1.6-2million. In 2003 the government announced that it would contribute £800,000 towards the cost of the case. However, after the legal basis for that grant was successfully judicially reviewed by one of the defendants to the civil action, in December 2005 the government passed the Legal Aid (Northern Ireland) Order which offered a firmer basis for the granting of legal aid in exceptional cases such as Omagh.[168] Writs for damages were served to a total value of £10 million, but the real value of this action is largely symbolic – it is highly unlikely that any of the individual defendants has sufficient assets for an award of that magnitude. In a separate case, media reports have also suggested that the family of Robert McCartney would take a private civil action against the IRA if ongoing criminal investigations and prosecution did not bear fruit.[169]

At first blush, private prosecutions may appear an obvious resource for families seeking truth. The resort to such legal avenues is often in a context when the prosecution authorities (in the case of Northern Ireland the Public Prosecution Service (PPS), formerly known as the Department of Public Prosecutions) has arrived at a view that they either cannot or will not bring a prosecution. The process can be initiated by the victim, in contrast to criminal prosecution, which must be decided by the PPS. As evidenced by the Omagh case and the possibility of a similar action by the McCartney family, such civil suits can raise the public profile of a case by forcing it onto the media and political agenda. Notwithstanding these advantages, the obstacles to successful truth recovery via this route remain formidable.

Most obvious is the prohibitive cost of such an action. Even with the highest possible public profile and levels of public sympathy and new legislation introduced to facilitate statutory funding, the Omagh families have struggled to raise the huge monies required to fund their action. It is debatable whether less high-profile or, indeed, less universally sympathetic cases would prove able to raise the necessary resources. In addition, while families may initiate a private prosecution, such a process is always likely to be taken over at any stage by the PPS or equivalent body in other jurisdictions.[170] While the prosecuting authorities may continue with prosecution, they may also decide not to proceed, thus in effect removing ownership and control over the proceedings. For these reasons, as with civil actions aimed at securing damages, the capacity of the courts as a vehicle for truth recovery in such instances are considerably muted.

Conclusion

The use of law to uncover truth is an obvious route for those affected by past acts of violence (Teitel 2000). The resort to law may be viewed as an attempt to fix historical meaning, to shape how events or individuals are remembered as part of a broader process of what Osiel has described as "mastering the past" (Osiel 1997: 192). Whether it is through the public or performative aspects of legal hearings, or law's emphasis upon recording a definitive account as to "what actually happened", legal processes are often imbued with considerable practical and symbolic importance in broader efforts to uncover and acknowledge unpalatable historical truths (Sarat 1999). However, factors such as cost, time, and the ceding of victim "ownership" over the process all mitigate against legal challenges as vehicles of truth recovery. Indeed, in some instances at least, it could be argued that such challenges before the court have been options of last resort, borne out of a sense of exasperation at the lack of availability of other less legalistic avenues of truth recovery. It also means

---

[167] http://news.bbc.co.uk/1/hi/northern_ireland/1832747.stm

[168] http://news.bbc.co.uk/1/hi/northern_ireland/3135907.stm See House of Lords Debate, 5 December 2005, Col. 482 at http://www.publications.parliament.uk/pa/ld199900/ldhansrd/pdvn/lds05/text/51205-22.htm

[169] In 2005 a majority of members of the European Parliament voted in favour of European Union financial support for a possible McCartney family civil action in the event of the failure of the criminal investigation. "MEPs Back McCartney Justice Fight", *BBC News*, 10 May 2005 . The case concerned Robert McCartney who was killed after a bar fight by alleged members of the IRA who also removed or destroyed forensic and other evidence from the scene. Subsequent police investigations of the murder were hampered by a reluctance of witnesses to give evidence, amidst widespread allegations of intimidation by those involved. The controversy concerning the case was heightened when the IRA offered to shoot those involved, an offer declined by the McCartney family. The McCartney family have continued to campaign for prosecutions to be brought against those they believe responsible for their brother's death. See http://news.bbc.co.uk/1/hi/northern_ireland/4533029.stm and http://en.wikipedia.org/wiki/Robert_McCartney_(murder victim).

[170] As the Crown Prosecution Service for England & Wales makes clear, "The CPS will take over and discontinue a private prosecution when (a) There is so little evidence that there is no case to answer; or (b) The prosecution falls far below the public interest test in the Code for Crown Prosecutors; or (c) The prosecution is likely to damage the interests of justice. The CPS will take over and continue a prosecution when the case in an important or difficult one that merits a public prosecution, i.e. only if the case passes the two tests in the Code, i.e. there is sufficient evidence and a prosecution is in the public interest", see http://www.cps.gov.uk/publications/communications/fs-privatepros.html. The criteria is the same for the PPS in Northern Ireland.

that, for those families whose cases do not lend themselves to legal challenge, or do not have the necessary campaigning or political support structures, their need for truth recovery is left largely unanswered.[171]

Policing initiatives

A further range of initiatives that can arguably be described as forms of truth recovery in Northern Ireland have emanated from the policing community. Aside from normal criminal investigations, and the plethora of inquiry reports into allegations of police malpractice in interrogations and public order policing discussed above, there have been a number of important police-led inquiries in this area. Much of the most damaging information forthcoming from these inquiries has concerned agents acting outside the law, their actions being either directed or covered up after the fact by their handlers, information and intelligence not being shared with investigating officers, and allegations of sub-standard police investigation of violent acts for political, intelligence or operation reasons. The most significant of the developments from this quarter have arguably been the Stalker/Sampson Inquiry, the Stevens Inquires, the Patten Commission, the work of the Police Ombudsman and, most recently, the establishment of the Historical Enquiries Team. Each is discussed below.

The Stalker/Sampson Inquiries

The Stalker/Sampson Inquiry is probably one of the most controversial police investigations conducted during the conflict in and about Northern Ireland. In a one-month period in 1982, a unit of the RUC known as E4A, which had been trained by the SAS, was involved in the killings of six unarmed individuals (five of whom were republican paramilitaries) in three separate incidents. Four RUC officers were ultimately charged with murder as a result of these incidents, but all were acquitted (Taylor 1987). The presiding judge at one of the trials, Lord Justice Gibson, sparked further controversy when he appeared to praise the officers who killed three of the men.[172] It also emerged from evidence presented at the trials that senior RUC officers had provided the officers involved in the shooting with a fabricated cover story - that the encounter arose from a random patrol rather than directed surveillance – which had been presented to the investigating RUC Criminal Investigation Department (CID) officers. The reason stated for these concocted stories was in order to protect a republican informer (Ellison & Smyth 2000).

The public outcry in response to the acquittals, the comments of Lord Justice Gibson, and the details of the cover-up in relation to the circumstances of the killings led to the appointment of John Stalker, Deputy Chief Constable of the Greater Manchester Police, to examine the circumstances of the killings. Stalker issued an apparently critical interim report which recommended 11 prosecutions and asked for and was refused a copy of an audio tape of one of the killings which MI5 had secretly recorded (Lashmar 2003). Shortly afterwards, he was removed from the investigation following allegations of professional misconduct, including that he had had an inappropriate friendship with a Manchester businessman Kevin Taylor, a man allegedly connected to a Manchester criminal gang (Lashmar 2003). Stalker was replaced by Colin Sampson (Chief Constable of West Yorkshire Constabulary), who was tasked with completing the investigation as well as conducting the investigation into Stalker himself. In early 1988, the British government acknowledged that the Stalker/Sampson Inquiry in Northern Ireland had produced prima-facie evidence of a conspiracy to pervert the course of justice by RUC men, but announced that no criminal proceedings would take place. The British government then appointed yet another senior British police officer, Charles Kelly, the Chief Constable of Staffordshire, to investigate the RUC. The Attorney General, Sir Patrick Mayhew, concluded that, despite the evidence suggesting a conspiracy to pervert the course of justice, it would not be in the public interest to prosecute the officers involved (Mulcahy 2005). In 1989, 18 RUC officers were reprimanded and one cautioned by the Chief Constable for their actions. Two superintendents involved in the cover-up retired on health grounds (Taylor 1987; Ellison & Smith 2000). The Stalker/Sampson Report has remained unpublished, despite continued political pressure and a number of judicial hearings which sought to compel its publication.[173]

---

171 As the Chief Constable Sir Hugh Orde has argued: "A failure to engage in this difficult territory [the past] leaves the legal route as the only current way forward. As a result a grievance process has emerged that flows from an initial demand (by families, lawyers, interest groups, or special rapporteurs), through organisational resistance (as the service checks out the legal position), resort to law (ranging from judicial review to Strasbourg), media campaigns and use of champions (National and International), towards some low level promise to review old papers, as a minimum final response, through formal re-investigations (independent or in-force), to government involvement and full blown public enquiries in a small number of cases. This approach is unsatisfactory. It lends itself to a survival of the fittest phenomenon since it delivers results for those high profile cases which stay the course or attract the most media or political attention" (Orde 2005: 3).

172 "I wish to make it clear that having heard the entire Crown's case, I regard each of the accused of being absolutely blameless in this matter. That finding should be put on the record as well as my own commendation as to their courage and determination in bringing these three men to justice, in this case, to the final court of justice" (quoted in Cory 2004: 11).

173 For example, in the long running "right to life" cases discussed above which related to the events investigated by Stalker and Sampson, lawyers for the families had sought to compel publication of the reports. In 1994 after a number of false starts to the inquests, the Coroner indicated his view that such publication was in the public interest to see whether any further relevant evidence had come to light. The Secretary of State responded by issuing a "public interest immunity certificate" stating that disclosure of the Stalker/Sampson Report would cause serious damage to the public interest and the Coroner abandoned the re-opened inquest. See *Re McKerr*, House of Lords judgement, 12 March 2004, [2004] UKHL 12.

Stalker subsequently claimed that while he could not definitely claim the existence of a shoot to kill policy, "The circumstances of those shootings pointed to a police inclination, if not a policy, to shoot suspects dead without warning rather than to arrest them" (Stalker 1988: 253). He also remained adamant that he had been removed from the investigation because it would have caused huge political embarrassment and led to a number of resignations, an allegation vehemently denied by the then-Chief Constable of the RUC, Sir John Hermon (1997). Sampson's report into Stalker's own conduct ultimately found that he had infringed a number of minor rules about using police staff cars but exonerated him from the more serious charges and he was permitted to return to his post in Manchester. However, Stalker concluded that he could no longer work with the then-Chief Constable James Anderton and retired in 1987. Kevin Taylor, the businessman with the alleged links to Manchester gangland criminals, sued the Greater Manchester Police for malicious prosecution and agreed an out of court settlement reputed to be around £1 million in 1995 (Lashmar 2003).

Given that the Stalker/Sampson Report has never been published, it is difficult to assess its significance as a vehicle for truth recovery. Publication of the report has been a constant demand of human rights groups and nationalist politicians for almost two decades now. Indeed, in a context where collusion allegations between loyalist paramilitaries and the security forces have become increasingly accepted as a fact, the existence or otherwise of "a shoot to kill" policy against republican suspects may seem somewhat less controversial than it did in 1982. It is certainly arguable that the report's continued significance is due at least to the circumstances surrounding Mr Stalker's removal from the inquiry and to the prolonged efforts by the government to keep its content out of the public domain.[174] That said, that same dogged determination to keep the report and its interim predecessor hidden is likely to suggest, for some commentators at least, that there must indeed be information contained in those documents which is highly significant to the broader process of truth recovery.

The Stevens Inquiries

Although the Stevens Inquiries have, to some extent, been superseded by the Cory Inquiries it is useful to acknowledge briefly that they too have played an important, and at times controversial, role in the process of truth recovery in Northern Ireland. The first of the Stevens Inquiries took place in 1989, shortly after the murder of defence solicitor Pat Finucane as well as Catholic man Laurence Maginn, both of whom the organisation responsible (the UDA) claimed were members of the IRA. In order to back up their claims that they were targeting active republicans, loyalists began to paste and pin up copies of security force documents around Belfast and leak them to the media (Amnesty International 1994). John Stevens (later Sir John) was called in to investigate the leaks of these security force documents to loyalist paramilitaries.

As a result of this inquiry, 94 people were arrested, of whom 59 were charged and 44 convicted. Approximately 30 of those arrested were UDR officers, of whom several were charged (Mulcahy 2005). No RUC officers were charged, although a report was submitted to the Director of Public Prosecutions (DPP) concerning two officers against whom no actions were taken (Ryder 2000). By 1990, the Stevens team had identified Army agent Brian Nelson as a key suspect and planned to arrest him and others in a dawn raid. However, officers from the team returned to their secure investigation HQ hours before the planned arrests to find their office on fire, and that fire alarms, telephones, and heat-sensitive intruder alarms were not working at the headquarters. The fire destroyed many of their files, although others had been copied and moved to England. Brian Nelson fled Northern Ireland, but was eventually apprehended after he decided to try to return to Belfast.[175] Stevens was ultimately unable to trace the origins of many of the documents found in possession of the loyalists or to determine the numbers of files which had been copied. Nonetheless, in the summary of the report published in 1990, he concluded that collusion "is restricted to a small number of individuals and is neither widespread nor institutionalised" (RUC 1990: 6).

In 1993, Sir John was called back into Northern Ireland by the DPP to, in the words of the then-Chief Constable Sir Hugh Annseley, "tie up some loose ends" regarding his first investigation. No summary of this second inquiry was published, and no-one was charged, although it appears that both RUC officers and army handlers were reported to the DPP (British Irish Rights Watch 2003).

Following publication of a British Irish Rights Watch Report (1999), which included detailed allegations concerning the roles of military intelligence (the Force Research Unit or FRU), the police (Special Branch), and the secret intelligence service (MI5) in the murders of Patrick Finucane and several others, Sir John was called in to conduct his third inquiry. The terms of reference were to investigate the British Irish Rights Watch

---

[174] For example, according to journalist and former police authority member Chris Ryder (2000: 491), while the police were under instructions to provide the Patten Commission with all the materials they required, including the sensitive files concerning the cases reviewed by Stalker and Sampson, they too did not see either the 18 volume interim report by Stalker or the final Stalker/ Sampson Report.

[175] http://news.bbc.co.uk/1/hi/northern_ireland/2954383.stm

allegations, but also to review the investigation into the murder of Pat Finucane in its entirety. In the published summary of that investigation, Stevens came to a number of hard-hitting conclusions. He found that he had been obstructed in his previous inquiries; that Nelson had been warned of his impending arrest by his army handlers; that the fire in the previous Stevens office was "a deliberate act of arson" which was never properly investigated; that the murder of Pat Finucane and a Protestant civilian Brian Lambert (killed by loyalists who thought he was a Catholic) could have been prevented; and that both murders resulted from collusion (Stevens 2003).[176]

Full versions of the first and third Stevens Inquiries have never been published, and none of the second Inquiry. While the findings outlined in the summary of the third Inquiry were damning enough, as with the Stalker/Sampson Inquiry, it is likely that the full findings of each of them would be of considerable interest to any broader truth-recovery process. With regard to the third Stevens Inquiry, this third police investigation was seen by some prominent campaigners as a delaying tactic designed to alleviate pressure for a more far-reaching public inquiry into the Finucane murder (e.g. British Irish Rights Watch 2003). As is discussed below, this tension between comparatively narrow police-led investigation and broader truth-recovery initiatives is a theme of much broader relevance.

The Patten Commission
Clifford Shearing, a prominent member of the Independent Commission on Policing for Northern Ireland (the Patten Commission), has rightly pointed out that their work was not envisaged as a "Commission of Inquiry" into past policing events in Northern Ireland, but rather a forward-looking body designed to achieve a new beginning and a new direction in policing in the jurisdiction (Shearing 2000: 387). Despite that focus, which is clear in the report itself (Patten 1999), the process of conducting the work of the Commission inevitably focused on the events of the past and is worth noting for current purposes.

The Commission sought the views of the public on their experience of policing in the jurisdiction through an extensive advertising campaign. They sent out 130 letters to political parties, churches, non-governmental organisations, and others known to have a particular interest in policing. They held numerous collective and individual private meetings with a number of people – clerics, politicians, civil liberties groups, community and youth workers, editors, academics, and others – and visited every police sub-division, other police stations, headquarters departments, and met individual police officers. They held a series of open meetings in every District Council area in Northern Ireland, most of which were conducted in November and December of 1998. In all, more than 10,000 people attended the public meetings, with over 1,000 speaking. In addition, about 450 further written submissions were handed in at these meetings, most of them on forms distributed by the Commission for this purpose, so that the total number of individual written submissions received was approximately 2,500. Consultants were engaged to conduct a focus-group study, involving eight focus groups selected from different traditions and backgrounds, and a number of research studies and surveys were commissioned – all designed to inform the deliberations of the Commissioners (Patten 1999: 11).

Although the report itself eschewed much overt analysis of the impact of these hearings and submissions, a number of the Commission members have subsequently spoken of the impact of that method of working. In effect, they heard two parallel and competing historical narratives. One of these focused on a history of bravery, sacrifice, and professionalism in the face of paramilitary violence – the other on sectarianism, unaccountability, and partiality (Mulcahy 2005). Both were, from the perspectives of those who gave oral accounts or who made their submission, true accounts of their own experiences of policing. In effect, the Patten Commission provided a platform upon which people could tell their story of policing. While the report has been criticised for its failure to analyse these accounts in depth (Tomlinson & Hillyard 2000), the actual process of the Commission conducting its work, and the undoubted power of some of those public hearings for any who witnessed them, does have both a practical and symbolic bearing on the broader debate concerning truth recovery in the jurisdiction.

Office of the Police Ombudsman for Northern Ireland [177]
Another major institution which has taken on an important role in the area of truth recovery has been the Office of the Police Ombudsman (OPONI). Established under the Police (Northern Ireland) Act 1998, it became operational in November 2000. The office currently has 125 staff and an annual expenditure of £7,750,000

---

[176] "Collusion is evidenced in many ways. This ranges from the wilful failure to keep records, the absence of accountability, the withholding of intelligence and evidence, through to the extreme of agents being involved in murder... My three Enquiries have found all these elements of collusion to be present. The co-ordination, dissemination and sharing of intelligence were poor. Informants and agents were allowed to operate without effective control and to participate in terrorist crimes. Nationalists were known to be targeted but were not properly warned or protected. Crucial information was withheld from Senior Investigating Officers. Important evidence was neither exploited nor preserved" (Stevens 2003: 16).
[177] www.policeombudsman.org

(OPONI 2005a: 68). As well as investigating individual complaints against police officers with regard to alleged criminal acts or breaches of the police code of conduct, the OPONI can also conduct investigations into "trends and patterns" of policing. In addition, the Police Ombudsman can also "call herself in" to investigate policing matters even when no formal complaint has been received, if it is deemed desirable "in the public interest", and she may also at her discretion publish reports into major policing operations.[178] As is discussed below, these various powers of the OPONI have been deployed in reviewing a number of recent and historical policing investigations, with important consequences for the broader process of truth recovery.

Some of the most controversial work of the OPONI has involved investigations and reports on incidents which the families affected suggest have involved informers or agents in illegal activities. Often, the suggestion put forward by those affected is that this has resulted in either intelligence information not being properly shared by Special Branch with investigating officers or, more generally, in investigations which have not been properly carried out.

For example, in the case of Eoin Morley, a republican activist in the Irish People's Liberation Organisation (IPLO) who was shot dead by the Provisional IRA in 1990, his family asked the OPONI to investigate the killing, alleging that the police had not conducted a proper investigation and that they had done so in order to cover up the actions of a police agent. The OPONI confirmed that ten separate pieces of relevant intelligence information held by the Special Branch were not passed to the Investigating Officers. The Ombudsman concluded that "this is one of many occasions on which intelligence held at Special Branch headquarters, which was relevant to investigation of the most serious of crimes, was not transmitted to those who were carrying out those investigations". The OPONI also concluded that the standard of the actual investigation fell short and that the police failed to conduct a proper and thorough investigation into the murder. With regard to the allegation that a known suspect was protected by the police, while there was nothing in the file to suggest that they (the police) had sought to protect this suspect, the Ombudsman decided that the frequent practice of the RUC Special Branch not to disseminate information inevitably led to the suspicions that individuals were being protected and that, therefore, this complaint was partially substantiated. The OPONI rejected the claim that the murder was set up at the instigation of the police to initiate an IPLO/IRA feud (OPONI 2005b).

Also well known is the OPONI investigation into the murder of a prominent member of the Gaelic Athletic Association (GAA), Mr Sean Brown, in Bellaghy, County Derry. Mr Brown was abducted, forced into the boot of his car, driven to Randalstown, shot dead, and had his vehicle set alight. The murder occurred between 23.30 and 23.45 on 12 May 1997. His wife alleged to the OPONI that the investigation into his murder had not been "efficiently and properly carried out", that the police had not kept the family up to date with the investigation, and that there was "no earnest effort" to identify the person who murdered Mr Brown.

The OPONI found that indeed the investigation into the murder of Mr Brown had not been "efficiently and effectively carried out". Significant failures were identified in the investigation including: the failure to carry out a proper search for witnesses or to follow up on one important witness who had identified himself to the police; the failure to identify and to deal properly with all the available forensic evidential opportunities, including cigarette butts which were found close to the burnt-out car; the failure to identify vehicles passing through Toomebridge in a northward direction prior to 22:30 hours on the night of the murder where their registration would have been noted as they passed the police station; and inadequate enquiries into "a convoy of vehicles" which passed through Toomebridge between 22:30 hours and 22:47 hours on the night of the murder. The police only checked vehicles for a total of two minutes either side of the period between 23.30 and 23.45 when the murder was known to have been committed, a decision described by the OPONI as "wholly inadequate." In addition, the OPONI found that Special Branch had failed to pass a significant amount of relevant and available intelligence to the Murder Investigation Team. There was no audit trail as to who was responsible for the passage of material from Special Branch to the Murder Investigation Team. Also, highly significant documentation was not available for the OPONI to review. Most importantly, the policy file which recorded all significant decisions in the course of the murder inquiry and the reasons behind such decisions was missing from the file, and this was described as having had "massive consequences" for the OPONI investigation. As the report outlines:

---

[178] As well as those cases detailed below, the Police Ombudsman has also investigated the death of Mr Sammy Devenny in 1969 who died a few days after he and a number of his children were assaulted by RUC officers in his home. Although the office of the Police Ombudsman did not review the original events, the were able to make known the results of an external police investigation by a senior member of the Metropolitan Police which had been scathing of the original RUC investigation and which had never been imparted to the family (OPONI 2001a).

failure to access and review the Policy File has seriously impeded enquiries undertaken by the Police Ombudsman, particularly in relation to issues such as family liaison, forensic strategies, receipt and handling of intelligence and any strategy relating to the arrest of identified suspects. It has also effectively prevented the allocation of responsibility for individual decisions made by senior officers (OPONI 2004: 11).

The OPONI concluded by also partially upholding the complaint that the family had not been sufficiently kept up to date during the conduct of the investigation and fully upheld the charge that no earnest efforts had been made to apprehend the killers of Sean Brown (OPONI 2004: 15).

Perhaps the most publicised of what might be described as truth recovery-style investigations was that carried out by the Office of the Ombudsman into the Omagh bombing. The investigation concerned allegations by a police informer that the police had received prior warning from him of the dissident-republican bomb plan which resulted in the deaths of 29 people and two unborn children and injuries to over 250 people at Omagh. The main thrust of newspaper allegations was that the police had failed to act on this prior warning in order to protect the identity of the informant. Although the Ombudsman's report concluded that it was unlikely that the bomb could have been prevented, it was highly critical of the use of intelligence by police officers.

The report found in this case, too, that significant intelligence information held by the RUC Special Branch was not shared with either the original Omagh investigating team or a subsequent internal police review of the investigation (OPONI 2001b: 11). It also included a strongly worded criticism of former Chief Constable Ronnie Flanagan and other senior officers.[179] Mr Flanagan expressed outrage at the report's comments and stated that, if the allegations that the RUC had failed to take the bomb threat seriously or had pursued the investigation with insufficient rigour were proved true, he would resign and "publicly commit suicide".[180] The then-Secretary of State, Peter Mandelson, and Prof. Des Rea, Chair of the Policing Board, as well as a number of unionist politicians also intervened in support of the Chief Constable and in criticising the Ombudsman (Mulcahy 2005: 176). Following the report and subsequent backlash, new protocols were introduced with regard to future reports concerning communication channels which, according to Deputy Chief Constable Paul Leighton, dramatically improved relations between the two institutions in recent years (NIAC 2005: Ev 55).

The considerable legal powers of the office of the Police Ombudsman in terms of compelling witnesses as well as capacity to access relevant files including intelligence information, and the apparent dogged persistence with which that office has gone about its work, have made it quite a powerful tool of truth recovery in the field of policing. It has been useful in, for example, making available information at its disposal to other truth-recovery initiatives such as the Cory Inquiries. Of course, its remit remains limited to the actions of the police. It has no powers to investigate the actions of other state agencies (such as the intelligence services or military) or of the paramilitary organisations, which were responsible for the greatest number of deaths in the conflict in and about Northern Ireland. In addition, while it has been announced that the Ombudsman will have responsibility for investigating the 48 deaths caused by the RUC before 1998, rather than the Historical Enquiries Team or HET (discussed below), some human rights organisations have voiced concerns both that extra resources will be needed and that the affected families may not benefit from the high degree of involvement and ownership promoted by the HET in the cases under their remit.[181] That said, regardless of whether there is a broader initiative in the jurisdiction, the work of the OPONI will remain of central importance in the process of truth recovery concerning those who were killed by the RUC.

The Historical Enquiries Team
In March 2005, the Secretary of State announced £32 million of funding to establish a department within the Police Service of Northern Ireland (PSNI) to examine unsolved cases of conflict-related murder which

---

[179] "The Police Ombudsman has concluded, with great sadness that the judgement and leadership of the Chief Constable and ACC Crime have been seriously flawed. As a result of that, the chances of detaining and convicting the Omagh Bombers have been significantly reduced. The victims, their families, the people of Omagh and officers of the RUC have been let down by defective leadership, poor judgement and a lack of urgency. This should not have been the response to an incident which resulted in the death of twenty-nine people and two unborn children" (OPONI 2001b: 12).

[180] "Omagh Bomb Report 'Grossly Unfair'", BBC News Website, 12 December 2001.
http://news.bbc.co.uk/1/hi/northern_ireland/1707299.stm

[181] Paul O'Connor, Pat Finucane Centre, quoted in "RUC is Outside Killing Probe", *Daily Ireland*, 24 January 2006. In the same article a spokesperson from the Police Service of Northern Ireland (PSNI) explained how it is envisaged that the two organisations will relate to one another. "The Ombudsman has jurisdiction over police officers and HET has provided it with details of 48 killings carried out by police officers. HET will review all other deaths. The relationship between HET and OPONI is one of ongoing liaison through a structured process, which includes a protocol and memorandum of understanding. This ensures that both agencies can progress their independent and important work in a complementary fashion, especially in any cases where a process of parallel review may be necessary."

occurred between 1968 and the signing of the Agreement in 1998. The HET will have a staff of 80-100 people and is likely to take four to six years to complete its work. It began its work on 20 January 2006.

The HET was set up by the Chief Constable of the PSNI, Hugh Orde, in consultation with the Northern Ireland Office (NIO). Mr Orde had begun to seek support from the NIO for this initiative in September 2004.[182] Mr Orde, who previously worked on the Stevens Inquiry before becoming PSNI Chief Constable, appointed an officer who had worked with him on the Stevens team (Dave Cox, a retired senior officer from the Metropolitan Police) to head up the HET. Although originally envisaged as answering to Assistant Chief Constable Sam Kincaid (Orde 2005), it has since been agreed that the team will instead report directly to the Chief Constable. The original remit of the HET has also been broadened from reviewing the 2,000 "unsolved murders" of the conflict to a total of 3,268 cases. The stated grounds for this expansion to include cases where individuals had in fact been convicted is that, even in such cases, there may be others involved in such murders who avoided arrest.[183]

As part of the PSNI, the HET comes within the criminal justice system, and investigations will therefore be conducted to criminal standards of burden of proof. Where appropriate, cases will be passed to the Public Prosecution Service for further action. However, while the historical enquiries process may lead to prosecutions, much of the surrounding language on the initiative from the police has focused largely on its "families-centred focus" and desire to assist with "resolution".[184] For its part, the government, too, has emphasised this initiative as a process designed to assist with "closure" rather than on the potential of large numbers of prosecutions.[185]

The HET will have assessment, review, evidence-gathering and investigative capabilities. It will have two distinct Review and Investigation Teams. One will be staffed exclusively by externally seconded officers from other police services and An Garda Síochána. This team will deal with those specific cases where independence is essential (e.g. where there are allegations of collusion or involvement of the security forces) and "where sections of the community or individuals are not yet comfortable working with the Police Service of Northern Ireland" (HET 2006: 5). The other will be made up of members of the PSNI and will process the remainder of cases, supported by the intelligence and analytical staff. In effect, therefore, it will be for the families affected by the events to determine which personnel should be tasked with the investigation of their individual case.

The process of case examination will involve a number of phases including: the collection and assessment of existing records and evidential exhibits; review to determine whether any further investigation or evidential opportunities exist; where it is deemed appropriate, reinvestigation of issues which emerge in the review process; and finally, judicial proceedings "where possible in appropriate cases, or, alternatively, resolution" (HET 2006: 3). In order to assist with relations between the HET and affected families and those who provide them with assistance and support, a system of different styles of liaison will also be established. These include a Help Desk and the appointment of Individual Case Officers when the cases are due to be reviewed who will maintain contact and update people as the process develops, "whether this involves court hearings or a meeting to explain what has been done and why the case can go no further" (HET 2006: 6). The HET will also establish a number of Group Liaison Officers who will be tasked with maintaining relations with victim-support groups, NGOs, trade unions or other representative bodies. If families wish, they can conduct their dealings with the HET solely through these intermediaries. The stated principle that will guide the nature of the information imparted by the HET is described as "maximum permissible disclosure"– a policy of "telling as much as we can no matter how difficult that may be" (HET 2006: 6).

---

[182] PSNI Press Release, "New Police Historical Enquiries Team", see
http://www.psni.police.uk/index/media_centre/press_releases/pg_press_releases_2006/pr_2006_january/pr-police-historical-enquiries-team.htm

[183] "Nationalist Groups Sceptical on £30 Million Inquiry Team", *Irish News* 20 January 2006.

[184] "I have met fathers and mothers, brothers and sisters, sons and daughters – people from all sides who struggle with questions about the deaths of their relatives. Often they just ask how or why, believing that these details will bring, if not some level of comfort, at least a measure of knowledge and understanding. They are simply looking for someone to tell them the story of how their relatives died...Families will sit at the heart of all of our enquiries. We have a simple message. We do care. And we will work in a determined and genuine way to achieve our objective of bringing a measure of resolution for as many people as possible" (Introduction from the Chief Constable, HET 2006:1).

[185] "The Government, through the provision of additional funding to set up the Historical Enquiries Team, is committed to addressing unanswered questions for as many families of victims as possible. I do not underestimate the challenges that lie ahead for the Team in investigating this complex and sensitive work. I believe the efforts in meeting these challenges will be of vital importance as we continue to move the peace process forward and assist those who have been most directly affected to reach some understanding and closure on the past". Comments from Secretary of State for Northern Ireland Peter Hain, in "Hain Welcomes the Formal Launch of the Historical Enquiries Team", NIO Press Release, 20 January 2006. See http://www.nio.gov.uk/media-detail.htm?newsID=12696

Given that the HET has only recently commenced its work, it is impossible to comment authoritatively at this juncture on its potential as a vehicle of truth recovery. It is undoubtedly a Herculean task of police historical investigation, and without real historical precedent on such a scale. The scale of the financial and personnel commitment, the efforts at trying to maximise independence for events which may touch upon the police themselves, and the considerable outreach efforts from the HET themselves to date all suggest a serious effort is being made with this initiative. Of course, it is in the interest of the PSNI to seek to maximise public confidence in the bona fides of its commitment to real truth recovery – an initiative that enjoyed the confidence of only one side of the community would be ultimately self-defeating. Indeed, the Chief Constable has made it clear that he views such a process as necessary if the past is not to continue to undermine the changes wrought by the Patten reforms.[186] He has also been explicit that the HET initiative should not be seen as either an alternative to such a broader truth-recovery process or as an attempt by the security forces to avoid taking responsibility for their own misdeeds.[187] Whether it can secure sufficient trust and confidence to fulfil its laudable ambition as a police contribution to bring a measure of resolution for as many people as possible remains to be seen.

Conclusion
Many of the skills required for effective truth recovery are synonymous with effective professional policing. Investigation expertise, the capacity to garner and evaluate intelligence information, access to forensic expertise, legal powers to seize documents, arrest and interrogate suspects – these and other technical attributes traditionally associated with policing are precisely those which are often utilised in truth-recovery processes. However, the police themselves in any transitional setting will inevitably be one of the institutions that will be a focus of any such broader process. Even if investigations into police or security force malpractice are conducted by police officers from outside the jurisdiction, and as we have seen in Northern Ireland such investigations can be and have been highly critical, they are still comparatively narrow and legalistic in their focus. They do not generally investigate broader issues of causes, context or extent. They are usually carried out largely in private and much of the information gathered has (at least traditionally) never been made available to the public. As Chief Constable Sir Hugh Orde has made clear with regard to the work of the HET, even the most effective and well-resourced professional police investigation of past events is in no way a substitute for a broader societal truth-recovery process.

The "On The Runs" Legislation
In November 2005, in the wake of the IRA statement regarding the end to its armed campaign and the decommissioning of its weapons, the British government published the Northern Ireland (Offences) Bill, which has commonly become known as the "On The Runs" Legislation. The Bill was designed to give effect to commitments given in the Weston Park negotiations of 2001, wherein the two governments had promised to introduce legislation regarding those individuals who were suspected of paramilitary offences but who had not been tried or convicted by virtue of the fact that they were "on the run".[188] The Irish government proposed to deal with the issue by virtue of a Presidential pardon.[189] The British government's Bill contained provisions designed to deal with individuals who might be charged in the future, or who had been charged and convicted but who had subsequently escaped from prison. The logic of the Bill was that, since all such individuals would

[186] "From a policing perspective, I have some compelling reasons for insisting that we deal with the past in order to facilitate movement forward. In simple terms, the past has the potential to destroy all the effort and real change policing has delivered in the post-Patten world. Firstly, in practical terms the sheer volume of unsolved crime would incrementally lead to the increased deployment of current resources to chase old cases, at the direct expense of day to day demands. As I have said previously we are funded to police the present, not the past. In the broader context, revisiting old cases in an unstructured way over a prolonged time period would mean regularly surfacing old accusations and old suspicions and will detract from progress and reforms made in policing and investigation methods in recent years. I am opposed to a piecemeal approach to history; we need a comprehensive strategy" (Orde 2005: 2).
[187] "...it is important to emphasise that this work must not be seen as some alternative to a wider truth commission. Neither should it be dismissed as an effort by police to avoid independent examination of its own activities or as a means of avoiding difficult questions for the security forces. Rather it should be viewed as a significant contribution to a broader process to address the past" (Orde 2005: 5).
[188] "Both Governments also recognise that there is an issue to be addressed, with the completion of the early release scheme, about supporters of organisations now on cease-fire against whom there are outstanding prosecutions, and in some cases extradition proceedings, for offences committed before 10 April 1998. Such people would, if convicted, stand to benefit from the early release scheme. The Governments accept that it would be a natural development of the scheme for such prosecutions not to be pursued and will as soon as possible, and in any event before the end of the year, take such steps as are necessary in their jurisdictions to resolve this difficulty so that those concerned are no longer pursued" (Weston Park Proposals 2001: para. 20, Available at http://www.pixunlimited.co.uk/sys-files/Guardian/documents/2001/08/01/westonpark.pdf). These proposals were then firmed up in a 2003 commitment to introduce legislation "in the context of acts of completion." Those proposals included provision for the establishment of a body to consider eligibility for the scheme and a special tribunal to hear the cases (NIO 2003).
[189] An Taoiseach, Bertie Ahern, told the Dáil that a special board would be created to deal with the eligibility of individuals, and that the issue would be decided by the Cabinet before going to the President, Mary McAleese (RTE News, 23 November 2005, at http://www.rte.ie/news/2005/1123/northpolitics.html).

have benefited from the early release provisions of the Agreement had they been in the jurisdiction, their continued potential for arrest and conviction was an "anomaly" which needed to be rectified.[190] The legislation would have enabled the award of exemption from prosecution certificates for politically related offences committed pre-Agreement in Northern Ireland. The government also included a provision in the draft Bill that those who had been guilty of "offences committed in the course of efforts to combat terrorism" would also be eligible for the exemption (NI Offences Bill Explanatory Note 2005: 1-2).[191]

The draft legislation was severely criticised from a broad range of quarters. Unionist politicians, the SDLP, liberals, conservatives, and some back-bench labour MPs reacted angrily to what the *News Letter* described as this "squalid" piece of legislation.[192] The major focus of unionists and conservatives was the "get out of jail free card" for republican suspects and the equating of those suspected of paramilitary offences with the actions of the security forces. For the SDLP, the primary point of attack was that the Bill meant that those in the security forces who had been guilty of collusion and other illegal acts would now never be held accountable by the courts and that loyalists who had not decommissioned any weapons might benefit. The Bill was also criticised by a large number of victim groups and human rights organisations for these and other features. For example, a number of groups criticised specific provisions in the Bill, including: the lack of international involvement in the proposed tribunal which would issue the exemptions; the failure to involve relatives or impose an obligation to provide information to relatives; the grant of potential anonymity for offenders applying for certification; and the potentially excessive powers granted to the Executive in appointment, control of evidence, and control of information dissemination.[193] Finally after Sinn Féin also formally withdrew its support for the Bill, the British government relented and the legislation was shelved in January 2006. However, the Secretary of State for Northern Ireland indicated in shelving the legislation that the issue would still have to be tackled.[194]

The experience of the "On The Runs" Legislation is instructive in terms of the debate concerning truth recovery for a number of reasons.

First, at the political level, it speaks to the central importance of both judging the political context and maximising the potential political consensus in taking forward any controversial policy initiative. The attempt at dealing with the "anomaly" of the "on the runs" occurred in a very different political context from the early release provisions of the Agreement. Those difficult measures occurred as part of broader historical package which involved pain for all sides and ultimately garnered the acquiescence, at least, of all of the major political parties in Northern Ireland with the exception of the DUP. While few can realistically dispute the fact that the IRA decommissioning and declaration were at least highly significant, the British government's move gave all the appearance of a side-deal with only one group of the political actors - in this case Sinn Féin. Implacable opposition from all of the other political parties would suggest that, in both content and timing, the initiative was misjudged.

Secondly, the British government singularly failed to achieve the support of any of the community, victims or human rights groups most directly affected by the initiative on the ground. While Ministers did meet with a number of victims groups relatively late in the process, there was a singular failing to seek to build any grassroots constituency that would support the move in the face of the inevitable political opposition. Thus, a basic lesson from this debacle would be to ensure that efforts at the macro level to maximise political consensus on truth recovery must be matched by concurrent efforts in the community sector designed to optimise ownership and involvement at that level, too.

---

[190] Secretary of State for Northern Ireland Peter Hain, House of Commons Debates, 11 January 2006 at col. 267.
[191] "The original draft did not apply to members of the security forces at all. I took the view that, leaving aside the question of whether the Bill is right or wrong in principle, if we were to proceed with legislation that we believed to be essential, it would be entirely wrong for members of the security forces in the course of their duty to find themselves [interruption] ...Members of the security forces may have committed a criminal offence in the course of their duty: it has happened in a handful of cases and who knows what might be uncovered in the future? For them to find themselves serving a prison sentence when members of the IRA and loyalist terrorists could be walking free would, I thought, be entirely wrong. That is why I gave members of the security forces—including, in principle, serving soldiers now—the choice of availing themselves of the special procedure. If they found themselves charged—and only if they found themselves charged—with a crime uncovered as a result of historic inquiries, I felt that it would discriminate against them in comparison with the IRA or loyalist terrorists to deny them the opportunity of taking advantage of the provisions" (Secretary of State for Northern Ireland Peter Hain, House of Commons Debate, 25 November 2005, col. 1538). The Bill is available at
http://www.publications.parliament.uk/pa/cm200506/cmbills/081/2006081.htm
[192] "Lords Can Still Smash On-The-Run Legislation" Editorial, *News Letter*, 29 November 2005. For the range of critical political views on the Bill see House of Commons Debate, 25 November 2005. The legislation was also variously described as "grubby", "reprehensible" and "a step too far". "MPs Condemn Grubby Paramilitaries Plan", *The Guardian*, 23 November 2005.
[193] Joint statement from Justice for the Forgotten, Relatives for Justice and the Pat Finucane Centre, 30th November 2005.
[194] "'On-the-Runs' Issue to Remain', says Hain", *RTE News*, 11 January 2006, http://www.rte.ie/news/2006/0112/north.html

Third, while the response from the victims of state violence to the late inclusion of the security forces in the legislation was understandable, the experience would suggest that any process which appears to benefit only the non-state combatant actors will face inevitable opposition (in private at least) from those who represent the interests of the security forces. Whatever the public protestations about "moral equivalency", any truth-recovery initiative that seeks to encourage members of combatant organisations and security forces to come forward is likely to have more chance of success if it is applied equally to both state and non-state actors from the outset.

Victim initiatives

During the conflict in and about Northern Ireland and transition, there have been a number of victim-centred initiatives which have been broadly focused on the issue of truth recovery, or at least of documenting what happened and the consequences of these happenings (e.g. Fay, Morrissey, & Smyth 1999; McKittrick, Kelters, Feeney, Thornton, & McVea 1999; Morrissey & Smyth 2002). In addition, there is already a considerable literature on developments within the victim sector more generally (e.g. Hamber & Wilson 2003; Gilligan 2006).[195] Indeed, HTR (Kelly 2005) itself published an overview of "storytelling" initiatives concerning the conflict in and about Northern Ireland and held a conference on the subject in November 2005.[196] Many of these oral, written, and multimedia storytelling projects involved individual victims and communities who had been most directly affected by the conflict in and about Northern Ireland. As discussed in Chapter Two, there is an inevitable overlap between "personal narrative" notions of truth recovery and different styles of storytelling. Therefore, in part in order not to replicate the audit conducted by the HTR Storytelling Sub Group, the section below does not include an exhaustive list of all victim-centred initiatives which have included elements of truth recovery as part of their work. Rather, it is focused upon two of the prominent developments, the context and workings of which are particularly instructive for the discussions in the next chapter concerning the proposed options for truth recovery regarding the conflict in and about Northern Ireland.

The Bloomfield Report

One of the most prominent victim-centred initiatives which touched upon the area of truth recovery was the report published by the first Victims' Commissioner, Sir Kenneth Bloomfield, who was appointed to the post in 1997. In this pre-Agreement initiative, Bloomfield was mandated

> to examine the feasibility of providing greater recognition for those who have become victims in the last thirty years as a consequence of events in Northern Ireland, recognising that those events have also had appalling repercussions for many people not living in Northern Ireland (Bloomfield 1998: 8).[197]

His findings were published in the 70-page *"We Will Remember Them": Report of the Northern Ireland Victims Commissioner*, also known as the Bloomfield Report (Bloomfield 1998). Bloomfield notes in the report a "special responsibility" to address the needs of those killed or injured "in service of the community" (Bloomfield 1998: 16). The discussion in that report included reference to the significance of storytelling, the views for and against memorials, issues relating to practical help and assistance offered to victims of violence, compensation, memorialisation, and truth (Bloomfield 1998: 36). The Bloomfield Report made a number of recommendations, many of which were focused on service-delivery issues for victims.[198] However, the report stopped short of advocating a truth commission for Northern Ireland, noting that:

> [A] clear approach to truth may demand the corollary of reconciliation. Unhappily, 'truth' can be used as a weapon as well as a shield. If any such device were to have a place in the life of Northern Ireland, it could only be in the context of a wide-ranging political accord (Bloomfield 1998: 38).

---

195 For a useful overview of policy-related developments in the victims sector generally, see Hamber (2004).

196 The definition of storytelling initiatives employed by the Healing Through Remembering Storytelling Sub Group was "A project or process which allows reflection, expression, listening, and possible collection of personal, communal and institutional stories related to the conflict in and about Northern Ireland" (Kelly 2005: 12).

197 The work of the Bloomfield Commission was mirrored in the Irish Republic by a Commission chaired by former Tanaiste John Wilson to examine victim-related issues in the Irish Republic. The Report entitled *A Place and A Name*, called for an annual North-South Day of Remembrance, as well as greater compensation, counselling and advice for victims of the conflict in and about Northern Ireland. In addition, and amongst other recommendations, the report recommends erecting a memorial building in the border area as a tribute to all those from the Republic of Ireland who died or suffered because of the Troubles (Wilson 1999).

198 For example the report led directly to a review "to consider the fitness of purpose of the compensation arrangements in Northern Ireland for the victims of terrorist violence". See the Criminal Injuries Compensation (Northern Ireland) Order 2002 at http://www.opsi.gov.uk/SI/si2002/20020796.htm

The report did go on to comment in its final recommendations that "the possibility of benefiting from some form of Truth and Reconciliation Commission at some stage should not be overlooked" (Bloomfield 1998: 50).

Quite apart from its brief discussion on truth and reconciliation, the workings and recommendations of the Bloomfield Commission are also worth noting, at least in part, as examples of how truth recovery should not be attempted. As Sir Kenneth himself acknowledges in the report, the appointment of the former head of the Northern Ireland Civil Service to chair such a body was always bound to call into question its independence. Despite the inclusive mandate and definition of "victims", only two paragraphs of the report discussed those killed by state violence (Bell 2003: 1102). This, together with the references to the particular needs of security forces and other victims who were killed or injured "in service of the community", have led to charges that the Bloomfield Report encouraged a hierarchy of victims. Some victims' groups whose work focuses mainly on the victims of state violence have argued that they had to fight to be included in the Bloomfield consultation process, while other groups who were the victims of republican violence were actively sought out by the Commission (Rolston 2002). An amalgam of these factors arguably contributed to the strong perception of bias by the nationalist community, which was later found to have impacted in the take-up of funds which had resulted from the Bloomfield Report (Clio Evaluation Consortium 2002).

Any process that is interested in taking forward truth recovery will have to be seen to be independent; to include the views of victims in all of their diversity, not just in its definition but also in its actual working practices; and to ensure that any sense of a hierarchy of victims is to be avoided if the process is not to become mired in political controversy.

The Disappeared
Another key victim initiative was the process established to facilitate the recovery of the remains of individuals murdered and "disappeared" by the IRA between 1972 and 1981. Under the Northern Ireland (Location of Victims' Remains Act) 1999 and the Criminal Justice (Location of Victims' Remains Act) 1999 (in the Irish Republic), the two governments established a commission to assist in the grim task of recovering the bodies of these victims. Despite government protestations to the contrary, this legislation arguably amounted to a de facto amnesty act in both jurisdictions. The respective Acts created effective immunity from prosecution by providing that no evidence gleaned by the commission was admissible in criminal proceedings, that forensic testing could only be carried out to facilitate identification, and that the information could only be passed on to other authorities for the purpose of assisting with locating the remains.[199] In introducing the Bill, the British government emphasised that:

> ...this Bill is designed to help those families [of the disappeared]. Its sole purpose is to bring to an end the suffering they have endured for far too long. They simply want to know what has happened to their loved ones and to give them a decent burial.[200]

Under considerable political pressure with regard to this from families of the victims and their supporters, the IRA leadership had already established an internal investigation.[201] Once the legislation was passed, they returned one body themselves and pointed the authorities to a number of additional sites where digging began, watched over by the anxious families.[202] Ultimately, three more bodies from the nine acknowledged as killed and disappeared by the IRA were recovered, the most recent (of Mrs Jean McConville) by accident in August 2003 after a number of unsuccessful digs at the site indicated by republicans had failed to recover her body.[203] The political and emotional significance of this issue of recovering the dead and affording them a respectful burial should not be underestimated. The Republican Movement is notoriously careful with the language utilised by its spokespersons to describe conflict-related events. Despite numerous examples of lethal attacks on civilians during the conflict in and about Northern Ireland, the issue of the "disappeared" is one of the few actions perpetrated by the IRA during the conflict that has been acknowledged by republican leaders as "a human rights abuse."[204]

---

[199] Northern Ireland (Location of Victims' Remains) Act 1999, ss 3-5 and Criminal Justice (Location of Victims' Remains) Act 1999, s 5. For a critical commentary see Morgan (2002).
[200] Lord Dubbs, House of Lord Debate, 18 May 1999, col. 154.
[201] "In March 1999 the leadership of Óglaigh na hÉireann [IRA] revealed the outcome of an 18 month investigation to locate the graves of nine people executed and buried by the IRA from 1972 to 1981. In initiating that investigation our intention was to do all within our power to redress injustices for which we accept full responsibility and to alleviate the suffering of families, particularly those families who have been unable to properly bury or mourn their relatives" "Text of IRA statement", *An Phoblacht* [Republican News], 4 September 2003.
[202] "The Bloodstained Soil of Ireland Yields First of the Disappeared", *The Independent*, 29 May 1999; "The Mourning Begins: Families can Finally Grieve as IRA Hands Over Bodies", *Irish News*, 29 May 1999; "Families of Terror Victims Await Call: Utter Agony as IRA Begins to Return Bodies After 20 years", *The Guardian*, 29 May 1999; and "War Crimes of the IRA", *The Guardian*, 2 June 1999.
[203] "Family Ends Long Wait to Bury Mother Murdered by the IRA", *The Guardian*, 3 November 2003.
[204] Gerry Adams quoted in *Irish News*, 1 June 1999.

The issue of the "disappeared" is also instructive for discussions on truth recovery for a number of reasons. First, it is illustrative of the political and moral power of victim-focused initiatives in this field, since the campaign of the families and their supporters was directly responsible for the legislative actions of the two governments and the establishment of the IRA investigation. Second, as is outlined above, the respective Acts created de facto amnesties in both jurisdictions, in so far as no evidence acquired as a result of the work of the commission could be used to prosecute those involved. As with other amnesties in British and Irish legal history, this legislation is a useful reminder that such Acts are actually much more common than is sometimes suggested. For example, during the negotiations that led to the Agreement, it was suggested by one prominent unionist politician that the legislation giving effect to the early release of politically motivated prisoners amounted to a de facto amnesty and that such legislation was without precedent in British legal history. In fact, the British Parliament has enacted at least 110 Acts of general pardon or amnesty for different classes of offenders in its history (McEvoy 2001). Third, that the IRA established its own investigative unit to seek to interview those involved and pass on the relevant information is of direct relevance to at least one of the options discussed below, both in terms of the practical challenges of organisational information-seeking so many years after the event, and also in terms of the likely reactions in some quarters as to the bona fides of such "internal" truth-recovery efforts.

"Bottom-up" community initiatives

As in other transitional settings where there has been an absence of confidence in the capacity of state institutions to deliver truth (McEvoy & McGregor 2007 in press). Northern Ireland has seen a range of "bottom-up" truth-recovery initiatives. In such instances, local communities and civil society organisations have taken on the mantle of either attempting truth recovery themselves, or at least raising awareness and the level of debate at local community level about the issues involved in such a process. Again, the initiatives detailed below are not an exhaustive list of all such local processes, but rather a number of illustrative examples which are of relevance to the broader debate. To date, the most prominent of these "bottom-up" attempts at truth recovery have emanated from the nationalist community.

"Bottom-Up" community inquiries into specific events

Community inquiries into specific events have been something of a feature of the conflict in and about Northern Ireland from its very earliest years (Rolston 1996, 2000). Often, such inquiries concerned controversial killings by the security forces or deaths where there was an element of collusion alleged, and therefore little confidence amongst the families or communities affected in the capacity of the police, coroner or prosecution services to deliver an effective or truthful investigation of what had occurred. Often, the actual process involved bringing in outside British or international legal experts to chair proceedings at which local people, witnesses, and others gave evidence, which would then be written up into a report and used as a basis for further campaigning concerning the case.

For example, local community activists were involved in 1971 in establishing an inquiry chaired by prominent British lawyer Lord Gifford and Albie Sachs (later to become a Supreme Court judge in South Africa) into the circumstances surrounding the deaths of Seamus Cusack and George Desmond Beattie in Derry (Gifford 1971). That inquiry addressed the killing of these two men by the Army in disputed circumstances wherein the Army claimed that both were armed at the time, an allegation strongly contested by local witnesses. The Army did not participate in the inquiry. The inquiry took evidence from 24 witnesses, including 18 eye-witnesses, as well as the forensic scientist who examined Beattie's clothes, and the pathologist who conducted the post mortem. The inquiry concluded that "the eye-witnesses made out a massive and compelling case that Cusack was not armed with a rifle at the time he was shot" (para. 49) and "we are satisfied on strong probabilities that he was not the man who was about to throw a bomb, that there is no other evidence to suggest that he was carrying a bomb, or threw a bomb, or used any other such lethal weapon" (para. 103).[205]

Another prominent community-led inquiry was established to investigate the killing of Fergal Caraher, an unarmed member of the IRA who was shot dead at a checkpoint by the British Army in South Armagh in 1990. The soldiers alleged that he and his brother (injured in the shooting) had driven through the checkpoint, an assertion again contradicted by local witnesses. In a context where no prosecutions against the soldiers appeared imminent, local people established the Cullyhanna Justice Group which, with the assistance of the Irish National Congress, established an inquiry in June 1991. The inquiry, which was chaired by Michael Mansfield QC and included jurists from England, France, and the US, produced an 80-page report which suggested that there was sufficient evidence to charge the two soldiers with the murder of Fergal Caraher and attempted murder of his brother Miceál (Mansfield 1992).[206] Shortly afterwards, the two soldiers were charged with murder and attempted murder, but were ultimately acquitted of all charges.

---

[205] Cusack had been taken to Letterkenny hospital rather than Altnagelivin and therefore the post mortem was conducted in the Irish Republic.

A similar community inquiry was instigated by the Castlederg-Aghyaran Justice Group into the killing of Patrick Shanaghan, after his family withdrew from the state inquest five years after his death. Six months later, in September 1996, former US judge Andrew Somers presided over an inquiry which heard 13 witnesses over three days. Somers concluded there was "more than enough evidence to point the finger of collusion. Either the RUC killed Patrick Shanaghan or they ordered his death."[207] In part, this inquiry influenced the selection of Shanaghan's case as one of the four joined Article 2 cases which the ECHR gave judgement on in 2001.[208] Indeed, the ECHR made specific mention of the inquiry in its judgment.[209]

More recently, in 2003, a community hearing was held into the deaths of six individuals shot dead by the British Army in 1973 in one night in the New Lodge area of North Belfast. The New Lodge Six Time for Truth Committee, held the New Lodge Six Community Inquiry "...to establish the full facts and seek justice" (Mullan 2003: 4). Again, a range of prominent British, Irish, and American individuals involved in human rights and civil liberties work (including Don Mullan, Gareth Pierce, Colin Harvey, Eamon McMenamin, Kate Ackester, and Ed Lynch) were involved in hearing submissions from local eye-witnesses. These witnesses alleged that two of the men were killed in a drive-by shooting, and the rest by British troops who opened fire from the military observation post on the top of New Lodge flats and from the direction of Duncairn Gardens. The army claimed that the six men had been killed and one seriously wounded by their troops in a gun battle, while eye-witnesses were again adamant that the men were attacked without provocation, either because they had the misfortune to be out that night, or killed in the process of trying to assist those already shot by the British Army. In a statement read out on behalf of the lawyers involved, Eamon McMenamin stated that they had concluded that:

> ...as a matter of common sense, law, and public policy, we find that the state is responsible for the unlawful killings of each of the New Lodge Six and that the state is responsible for the actions of the individual British soldiers who fired the lethal shots (Mullan 2003: 78).

These and other similar community-led hearings share a number of traits. First, they have emerged in a context where there was a lack of confidence amongst the communities most directly affected in the willingness or capacity of the criminal justice system to deliver truth or accountability. Second, while they have all adopted aspects of legal formalism in terms of their operational procedures, these inquiries have operated without legal powers of discovery or the ability to compel witnesses. Third, building upon local grassroots hard work and organisations, these inquires have generally employed international or British lawyers to chair the proceedings and sought and received assistance from other legal groupings. Thus, while the judges or lawyers who chaired the proceedings may have been sympathetic to the families' desire for truth, many of them are extremely prominent and respected legal practitioners who brought their experience to bear on the conduct of such inquiries and the writing of the final reports. These community inquiries, particularly in recent years, have also received technical and legal assistance from local and international human rights NGOs, which have assisted particularly in framing the discussions within the relevant international human rights standards. Fourth, while the authorities concerned have generally not co-operated with such inquiries (e.g. by giving oral or written evidence), as evidenced by the Shanaghan case in particular, despite their technical and legal limitations, subsequent legal proceedings may draw upon the findings of such inquiries at

---

[206] "We needed to have something independently done, something that would have no influences from the RUC, although we recognised that it would have no power, except for the public power it would have. We went ahead and started to organise it...There was an awful lot of organisation went into it. The first couple of months was trying to find out what our options were and from March on til the Inquiry was held midway through June, it was organisation all of the time, with the last couple of weeks being full time. We targeted anybody – TDs, MPs, priests, nuns, anybody we thought would add any influence to at all – all the human rights groups. We did obviously invite the RUC and the army to participate but they declined. ...So we did get a panel of international jurists from France, Germany, America and England and set it up like a courtroom with terms of reference, solicitors, the witnesses giving their evidence and making their statements open to the public. It was a great success: it was very well attended. There were over 200 observers. It was very well attended" (Margaret Caraher, widow of Fergal Caraher in Rolston 2000: 228).

[207] M. Brown "Judge Slams RUC On Shanaghan Case", *An Phoblacht*, 3 July 1997. Available at http://republican-news.org/archive/1997/July03/index.html

[208] *Jordan, Kelly, McKerr* and *Shanaghan*

[209] "A community inquiry into the circumstances surrounding the murder was organised by family and friends after the conclusion of the inquest in the hope that the whole truth about the murder could be revealed. The inquiry, conducted by the Castlederg-Aghyaran Justice Group and chaired by a retired United States Judge, Andrew Somers, heard thirteen witnesses over the period from 17 to 19 September 1996. The witnesses included family, local residents and friends of the deceased. Evidence was given alleging that police officers had frequently stopped Patrick Shanaghan in the street and issued threats, that the police warned people to keep away from him or they would end up being shot, that police officers made comments to persons in custody before the incident that Patrick Shanaghan would be targeted and, after the incident, claimed that they had him killed. Two witnesses claimed that they had seen Patrick Shanaghan still moving after the shooting had occurred. The Judge concluded that the applicant had been murdered by the British Government and, more specifically, with the collusion of the RUC." *Shanaghan v The United Kingdom* 37715/97 [2001] ECHR 300 (4 May 2001) at para 40.

a later stage. Finally, as with formal legal proceedings, such inquiries provide a platform for further campaigning and mobilisation designed to pressurise those in authority to be more forthcoming with the truth, as well as a vehicle for families to feel that they are doing something in response to the loss of their loved ones.

"Bottom-Up" initiatives designed to raise the truth-recovery debate
There are a number of ongoing initiatives which might be described as having contributed to raising the truth-recovery debate in Northern Ireland, including the various constituent elements of HTR itself. However, perhaps the most significant have been those efforts directed at the republican and loyalist constituencies whose participation, together with the various elements of the security and intelligence services, would obviously be of particular importance to the viability of any truth-recovery process.

Within the republican/nationalist community, Eolas ("information" in Irish) was established as a network of grassroots individuals who had experience in working with victims primarily of state and loyalist violence, former prisoners, and other community and human rights activists. Those involved expressed their frustration at the sporadic but intense focus on the issues of victims and political prisoners and the focus on the arguably less contentious issue of service delivery for victims at an official level (e.g. through the Victims Strategy produced by the Office of the First and Deputy First Minister in 2002), despite the fact that many organisations involved in the area of victims work had stressed that a more far-reaching investigation into the past was required (Eolas 2003). Thus, they convened a three-day residential in 2003 facilitated by an external consultant with considerable international and local experience of truth recovery (Dr Brandon Hamber) and the process culminated in the production of a 35-page *Consultation Paper on Truth and Justice* (Eolas 2003).[210]

That document draws upon some of the relevant international experience of truth recovery, it acknowledges the need for greater understanding of unionist/loyalist views and needs with regard to truth recovery, and sets out a mission and a series of principles and values which should guide any process of truth recovery. It also proposes three overlapping "discussion models" of how truth recovery might be achieved, each of which had a strong investigative dimension. The report concluded that:

> ...full acknowledgement and understanding of the human rights abuses of the past can assist all victims and contribute to building a just future for all. Rather than focusing on individual cases, in our view such a mechanism can only work if it is capable of addressing in any report the 'nature, causes and extent' of the conflict in a comprehensive way (Eolas 2003: 32).

A similar initiative was established in the loyalist community, albeit largely focused upon the Ulster Volunteer Force/Red Hand Commando section of that community. This initiative is the most significant to come from former loyalist combatants concerning the debate on truth recovery. A discussion document emerged from two days of discussion amongst people from a Progressive Unionist Party, UVF, RHC background and a number of community organisations on the question of truth recovery. It is frank about its primary intent to focus the debate within loyalism.[211] In a similar fashion to the Eolas process, it drew upon the international experiences of truth recovery in order to frame the broad range of concerns with regard to truth recovery. The detailed concerns from within loyalism articulated within that document are discussed at some length in the chapter below (under the "Drawing a Line Under the Past" option). However, the document does acknowledge the need to "get the truth out as we see it" in order to counter the demonisation of loyalists and prevent the future teaching of history as being too "one sided". It concludes that, unless a clear answer can be provided to the question "what are the benefits for Loyalism", a truth-recovery process has little chance of success (EPIC 2004: 11).

The loyalist community has been less obviously engaged in truth-seeking discussions and arguably has presented a less coherent victim focus altogether. Loyalist political ex-prisoners are offered a measure of

---

[210] "Eolas seeks to contribute to individual and societal healing and understanding informed by a common narrative of the past. This has driven the organisations and individuals involved in Eolas to examine and explore ways of addressing our past. Essentially we are working in the present through seeking to come to terms with the past. The debate within our own community is, as is the case in the unionist community, uncertain about dealing with the past. Despite the fact that we are most suspicious of the British state, we believe that it is imperative that we do deal with the past. The question of 'how' prevails. Though coming from a single identity context, we seek to be objective and remain conscious of the need for a process to be universal, inclusive and challenging for all of us involved" (Eolas 2003: 2).
[211] "This consultation document is an attempt to provide opportunities for our constituencies to begin debating the issues around truth recovery. We acknowledge that people may experience this document as being inward looking and self reflective. It is. It needs to be. It has to reflect the reality of where our constituency is in its current process of conflict transformation. Our intent is not to alienate others: our intent is to encourage honest and challenging thinking with a constituency and to allow others to respond critically to that thinking" (EPIC 2004: 3).

representation and assistance through EPIC, an organisation formed by ex-combatants from Ulster Volunteer Force (UVF) and Red Hand Commando (RHC), which works to address reintegration problems with former prisoners and paramilitary combatants. EPIC does not seem to have made such a visible a contribution to the truth debate as Eolas.

What is particularly interesting about the Eolas process and the EPIC initiative in particular is the role played by former combatants. As has been argued elsewhere (e.g. Shirlow, Graham, McEvoy, Purvis, & Ó hAdhmaill 2005), former combatants have exercised considerable grassroots leadership in the transition from conflict in Northern Ireland. Essentially, the argument put forward is that such leadership has been exercised militarily (within the paramilitary organisations); politically, in guiding, cajoling and at times "stretching" political constituencies; but also within communities where former combatants who have both inflicted and often been on the receiving end of armed conflict are also those with the most credibility in seeking to transform communal cultures of violence (McEvoy & Ericcson 2006). Given the central role that individual members and paramilitary organisations would have to play in any successful process of truth recovery, it is precisely the leadership capacity of ex-combatants in terms of raising and engaging with a difficult debate such as this which is likely to shape the views of those constituencies.

"Bottom-Up" truth recovery in local communities
As well as the huge range of storytelling work ongoing within local communities in Northern Ireland (Kelly 2005), there have also been a number of community-specific efforts at local truth recovery. The best known process and the one most useful for illustrative purposes is the Ardoyne Commemoration Project (ACP).

The ACP was established at the time of the Bloomfield Report and set out to "reclaim the victims' agenda" by presenting a perspective which the organisers felt was missed by Bloomfield. In particular, it was framed as a direct challenge to the view articulated by the organisers that a "hierarchy of victims" was being propagated by that report and related official discourses. The project identified all the members of the Ardoyne community killed as a direct result of political violence between 1969 and 1998 (99 in all) and went directly to the closest next-of-kin of each victim to request both their testimony and the recommendation of another significant contact who would assist with the project. In this way, a picture was built of victims' lives through the testimony of those closest to them and was published in a 543-page book (Ardoyne Commemoration Project 2002). The project documented 99 deaths and conducted over 300 interviews. Considerable emphasis was placed throughout the process on victim and community ownership of the project. For example, all but one of the committee members were from Ardoyne; the interviewers, transcribers and other volunteers were from the local community; and participants were each given editorial control over their contribution. The importance of this grassroots ownership and involvement was confirmed in a subsequent project evaluation (Lundy & McGovern 2005b).

Other aspects of the way the project was conducted were instructive. For example, considerable debate emerged as to the definition of "victim" and, in particular, whether the project should include ex-state agents and informers. Such intra-community tensions in what might appear from the outside as a homogeneous community were amongst the most difficult and challenging aspects of the process (Ardoyne Commemoration Project 2002). Ultimately, the project opted for an inclusive approach, to include all those people who were killed from that community, in recognition, as one of the organisers said to one researcher "...of the principle that no one has a monopoly on grief and loss" (cited in McGregor 2003: 14).[212] However, as Lundy and McGovern (2005b: 12) point out in their evaluation, the question of inclusivity might present greater difficulty in unionist communities, since some of the victims' organisations there insist on making a distinction between "innocent" victims and "non-innocent" victims.

As to the effects of the process, a number of themes emerge. One of the key issues which comes across strongly in reading the report is the fact that, for many families, the testimonies reflected the first time they had ever spoken about the traumatic events. In many instances, they actually knew little about the circumstances of the death of their loved one (Ardoyne Commemoration Project 2002: 12). For some participants, the act of taking part in the process may have been enough. Others viewed this community-based initiative as either complementary to or preparatory for other more formal truth- or justice-seeking initiatives. The project was regarded as having been particularly effective in creating a vehicle to deal with the legacy of intra-community violence such as long-standing rifts between individuals, families or, indeed, between republicans and the Church. Those involved appear well aware of the limitations of community-

---

[212] "Alongside local participation and control, inclusivity was seen as a key principle in the project's ethos. The definition of a victim arrived at for the book meant that some people who were killed in Ardoyne but were not from Ardoyne (i.e. members of the security forces, non-Ardoyne civilians) were not included. On the other hand all Ardoyne residents who could be identified as such, whether nationalist or unionist, killed by the British Army, loyalist or republican organisations were included, as were people from Ardoyne who were killed elsewhere" (Lundy & McGovern 2005b: 16).

based truth recovery in terms of its ability to access previously hidden documentation or evidence. Nonetheless, in general terms, the prevailing view of community respondents was that the process helped to push the boundaries and made inroads into the prevailing "...culture of silence on previously taboo subjects" (Lundy & McGovern 2005b: xiii).

It would be naive to think that the Ardoyne model could be simply, and without amendment, superimposed on or replicated in other communities affected by the conflict in and about Northern Ireland. Any efforts at community-based truth recovery must be built around the particular strengths and needs of the community in question. That said, the work of the ACP demonstrates that, with sufficient indigenous community skills and energy, and the technical and methodological expertise (either from within or outside the local area), such a process is both possible and of considerable potential benefit to local communities.

Conclusion

This chapter has sought to offer an overview of some of the truth-recovery initiatives which have either been completed or are ongoing with regard to the conflict in and about Northern Ireland. Public inquiries, legal challenges, policing initiatives, the "On The Runs" Legislation, victims' initiatives, and projects that have emerged in local communities are part of a broader range of activities, all of which could be described as having truth recovery as one of their primary tasks. This is not an exhaustive overview.[213] It does, however, underline the fact that regardless of the outcome of discussions of the various options discussed below, forms of truth recovery continue to happen on a daily basis. Chapter Four explores what some of those options might entail in more detail.

---

[213] For example, academic and journalistic research; the release of cabinet papers and other important materials under "the thirty year rule"; and the ever burgeoning number of books, autobiographies, and memoirs written by former paramilitary activists, members of the security forces and intelligence services, and former agents and informers. These and other ongoing activities might all be described as contributing to the broader process of truth recovery.

CHAPTER FOUR

Options for Truth Recovery regarding the conflict in and about Northern Ireland

Introduction

Informed by the lengthy discussions outlined in Chapter One concerning the different international truth-recovery experiences and the range of ongoing or pending initiatives either in or concerning the conflict in and about Northern Ireland, the HTR Sub Group engaged in detailed reflection designed to propose possible options for achieving truth recovery. Eventually it was agreed that a total of five options be proposed. These options are:

(1) "Drawing a Line Under the Past"
(2) Internal Organisational Investigations
(3) Community-Based "Bottom-Up" Truth Recovery
(4) A Truth-Recovery Commission
(5) A Commission of Historical Clarification

In putting forward these options, a number of points should be reiterated.

First, our purpose in this document is to inform the ongoing debate regarding truth recovery and to offer a practical and intellectual framework that may assist in better shaping that debate. One of the strengths of HTR generally, and of the Truth Recovery and Acknowledgement Sub Group in particular, is the breadth and diversity both in its membership and of their views. As with the readership of this document, different members have different preferences between the various options advanced below. However, the Sub Group is in broad agreement that these options reflect different shades of opinion on how this issue may be dealt with and can contribute to a more focused discussion on the relevant themes.

Second, while the options may be regarded as stand-alone models to address truth recovery, this document is not arguing that all are necessarily mutually exclusive. Obviously the option of "drawing a line under the past" and establishing a fully fledged truth-recovery commission are not compatible. On the other hand, it might well be possible to include elements of "bottom-up" truth-recovery initiatives, internal organisational investigations, and a truth-recovery commission as part of an overall truth-recovery process. Many of the thematic discussions concerning the relative strengths and weaknesses of different options may well be relevant to others.

Third, while the focus of discussions on truth recovery tends to narrow on Northern Ireland, it bears repeating that there have been many other individuals, families, and communities in the Republic of Ireland and Great Britain who have been affected by the conflict.[214] In a similar fashion to the management of the peace process more generally, it is important that the two governments continue to recognise that, whichever option or options are ultimately adopted to deal with truth recovery in the future, their remit has to be sufficiently broad to meet those needs in the jurisdictions affected outside Northern Ireland.

Finally, it is important to stress again that the purpose of proposing these options is to stimulate debate and discussion. It is not being claimed that these options offer fully developed practice models with regard to truth recovery. They are designed to be sketches or broad explanatory options to give readers a sense of the distinct ways in which truth recovery may be taken forward. A decision to adopt any or several of these options would obviously require a much closer analysis of their practical outworking.

---

[214] See e.g. Tim Parry and Johnathan Ball Trust (2003) and evidence submitted by the Tim Parry Johnathan Ball Trust to the Northern Ireland Affairs Committee (NIAC 2005: Ev 12).

Option One - "Drawing a Line Under the Past"

Introduction
The HTR Sub Group spent considerable time exploring the opinions of those in Northern Ireland and elsewhere who are of the view that there should not be an organised truth-recovery process concerning the conflict in and about Northern Ireland. This is sometimes referred to as the "do nothing" option.[215] Of course the title "do nothing" is something of a misnomer. As is outlined in Chapter Two, the series of ongoing or planned initiatives will most likely continue regardless "of nothing else being done". In effect, therefore, what the option of "drawing a line under the past" really refers to is a moratorium on truth recovery. In practice, it would entail letting the current initiatives discussed in Chapter Three run their course and establishing no new truth-recovery process or processes.

Rationale
There are a number of sometimes-overlapping arguments advanced by those who would argue for drawing a line under the past with regard to truth recovery. For the sake of brevity, these arguments may be summed up as follows:

Is the conflict in and about Northern Ireland over?
One viewpoint which appears to be shared across the political spectrum with regard to truth recovery is a consensus that any new overarching process in this area cannot take place unless the conflict in and about Northern Ireland can be said to have truly finished. This was a perspective which was repeated again and again between 2003 – 2004, when there appeared considerable governmental energy with regard to such an initiative. For example, it was one of the criteria for truth recovery outlined by former Secretary of State Paul Murphy concerning his visit to South Africa to explore the work of the Truth and Reconciliation Commission there.[216] Brian Feeney, the prominent nationalist commentator and author argued a similar position in 2004 when he stated that

> there have been about 40 truth and reconciliation processes around the world in places like South Africa and Peru. The only time they have worked is when the conflict has definitively come to an end. That is not the case here.[217]

A comparable perspective was also advanced by the loyalist discussion document on truth recovery, where those involved argued that the political situation remained too volatile and that "people in loyalist areas feel their culture and future to be under threat by a 'republican war' carried out by politics and propaganda" (EPIC 2004: 5).

The past is too painful for further truth recovery
Such a perspective would appear to be based on a number of factors. For some, the arguments centre around the destructive potential of "opening up old wounds".[218] Others have framed such a position in the context of the small size of the jurisdiction and the immediacy of the conflict in both rural and urban areas where victims may literally live and work in close proximity to those who killed or injured their loved ones.[219] Still others have argued that the effect of establishing some form of truth commission would be to raise the expectations of families that they might achieve healing or closure only to have those hopes dashed as the process inevitably became yet another side of conflict for the warring sides.[220] Finally, from amongst the ex-combatant constituency, there is a view that for some of those who were involved in acts of violence but who may have long since built new lives for themselves and their families and sought to leave that past behind, the revisiting of past actions may cause considerable personal and familial trauma (EPIC 2004: 8-9). For these and other reasons, some would argue that the past is simply too painful to address through any further truth-recovery process.

---

[215] See e.g. Lee Reynolds' (2003) interesting discussion of the ways in which unionists should respond to calls for a truth-recovery process. For an alternative perspective in the same collection see Watters (2003). See also Unionist Group (2006).

[216] Murphy advanced a number of criteria for truth recovery including that "...the conflict must truly be over. There must be no more additions to *Lost Lives* [a book detailing the casualties of the conflict], no more young people mutilated in 'punishment' attacks by loyalist and republican paramilitaries". "Hearing the Stories of the Troubles is Part of Building a New Society", *The Irish Times*, 2 June 2004.

[217] Quoted in "Truth Process would be Part of Conflict.", *Irish News*, 1 June 2004.

[218] See David Trimble with regard to the Bloody Sunday Inquiry "Opening up old wounds like this is likely to do more harm than good", 29 January 1998 at http://news.bbc.co.uk/1/hi/uk/51740.stm.

[219] "There are probably people who have been victimised and are living in ignorant bliss of who inflicted the harm upon them, and if it happens to be their next door neighbour across the field who set them or their loved one up for assassination or whatever, what sort of consequences would that have?" Evidence from Tom Roberts, Ex-Prisoners Interpretive Centre [EPIC] to the Northern Ireland Affairs Committee (NIAC 2004: 9).

[220] See e.g. Brian Feeney quoted in "Truth Process Would be 'Part of Conflict", *Irish News*, 1 June 2004.

Further truth recovery is unnecessary
There are a number of different shades of opinion to this position. It may be expressed as a sense of exasperation in some loyalist and unionist quarters that, apart from the inquiries into Billy Wright's death and the allegations of Garda collusion in the deaths of RUC officers Breen and Buchanan, much of the other truth-recovery work to date has been focused on grievances emanating from the nationalist community, and that there has been enough of it (Reynolds 2003).[221] For others, at least historically, the "patchwork" approach may have been the most appropriate in a context where there was little apparent political appetite for a more far-reaching truth-recovery process (e.g. Bell 2003). Such a view would suggest that this piecemeal approach to truth recovery was and is in effect a "bespoke" method which emerged organically from the Northern Ireland context and that one should not automatically seek to apply international models to a context where they may not readily fit (McGregor 2003). Still others have argued that the criminal justice system is sufficient to deal with whatever truth recovery is required in the Northern Ireland context.[222]

Truth recovery could be politically destabilising
This is essentially an argument from a political management perspective. It is based on the premise that, in a context where considerable political energies are being expanded in trying to re-establish a devolved administration, in particular one which includes a power-sharing executive with both Sinn Féin and the DUP, a public focus on the misdeeds of the past would prove too destabilising for establishing and maintaining such a fragile political arrangement. For example, such a perspective appeared to underpin the British government's announcement in March 2005 to suspend the nascent consultation process on truth recovery in Northern Ireland. As the former Secretary of State Paul Murphy outlined to the Northern Ireland Affairs Committee in explaining that decision:

> ...there have to be clear signs of political movement for the better for such developments [concerning truth recovery] to occur. If we were to have something along the lines of ... a Truth and Reconciliation Commission we would have to have two things occurring: one is political progress and secondly, consensus on it. I was not convinced that we could get either ... I have not for one second suggested that we have abandoned the idea of going down a wider road on the question of dealing with the past, I am simply saying I did not think this was the time for it and if anything it could be counterproductive...it is something you have to deal with in a better atmosphere and that is an atmosphere of progress rather than stalemate (NIAC 2005: Ev 243).

Truth recovery as a republican Trojan Horse
This is a view expressed in some loyalist and unionist quarters that truth recovery is in reality some form of "republican Trojan Horse" or an attempt to "rewrite" history from a republican perspective. This position again takes a number of overlapping forms. In some manifestations it appears as an expression of the deep suspicion of loyalists of the motives of republicans, their truth-telling record and the concern that they might use any truth-recovery process such as a truth commission as "a stick with which to beat the British state".[223] Such distrust is often accompanied by a eulogising of republican organisational and political skills and a juxtaposition of these attributes with the lack of such skills in the loyalist community.[224] Such a perspective may lead in turn to what Lundy and McGovern (2006) refer to as the articulacy/inarticulacy dichotomy, a self-characterisation amongst loyalists which obviates the need for engagement because of concerns that they would inevitably come off worse in any truth-recovery process.

Truth recovery as the criminalisation of loyalism
A final and related objection to further organised truth recovery is the view, again amongst elements of loyalism, that such a process could contribute further to ongoing efforts at the criminalisation of loyalist political violence, particularly by unionist politicians. Such a concern, which is replicated on other recent research on former loyalist prisoners and combatants (e.g. Shirlow et al. 2005), was forcefully put in the loyalist discussion document on truth recovery. The document argued that:

---

[221] "In the context of Northern Ireland there is little point in having a truth and reconciliation commission. All these various inquiries are doing is reopening the wounds of 30 years of conflict" (Jeffrey Donaldson, Irish News 10 June 2003).
[222] "Whilst truth is necessary to deal with the past and to aid reconciliation by bringing closure for victims, it must be borne in mind that in terms of the past there exists in the United Kingdom a truth recovery process. It has been tried and tested and has evolved through centuries of experience and has afforded society a means by which to learn of the past, to recognise that victims have been wronged, to apply independent arbitration to differing accounts of the past and to arrive at a conclusion as to the accepted truth of historical events. ... In short we have the British Criminal Justice System, it has recently been reviewed and there appears to be new and complete political acceptance of it. It offers the best way of dealing with the past." Evidence from Families Acting for Innocent Relatives [FAIR] presented to the Northern Ireland Affairs Committee, 2005: Ev 184].
[223] "Truth Commission And Amnesty The Last Thing Northern Ireland Needs Says Foster", DUP Press Release, 19 February 2004.
[224] "The republican machine is adept at these things, they are better organised, they are long term organised, so the loyalists see inquiries as one-sided." Evidence from William Smith, Ex-prisoner Interpretative Centre [EPIC] to the Northern Ireland Affairs Committee (NIAC 2005: Ev 10).

The ongoing stigmatisation, criminalisation and even demonisation of loyalist ex-prisoners, especially within unionist circles ('middle unionism'), clearly suggest that it would be madness for any loyalists who have not been successfully prosecuted to expose any of their actions before a truth commission... any 'truth' process that would require individual ex-prisoners or ex-combatants to give public testimony about specific past actions will most likely contribute to the continuing demonisation of these loyalist activists. It is very difficult for them to see any benefit from such a process, and therefore there is very little chance that they will co-operate/participate (EPIC 2004: 7-8).

Genuine truth recovery will never happen
There is, finally, in some quarters a perspective that genuine truth recovery will never happen. For example, from the perspective of some unionists, a truth commission might succeed in unearthing the previous activities of state actors in the conflict, but the non-compellability of the paramilitary organisations would render such a process partial and inoperable.[225] At the other end of the spectrum, some republicans have argued that the increased interest in a broader truth process expressed by the British government in 2003/2004 was deliberately designed to obfuscate rather than illuminate truth.[226]

Discussion
All of these issues and more have been explored in detail over the past year by members of the HTR Truth Recovery and Acknowledgement Sub Group. While it is for readers to decide on the respective merits or demerits of each argument, this document can at least offer an outline of the contours of the debate.

A broad agreement was reached within the Sub Group that, as noted above, the option of "drawing a line under the past" or the "do nothing else" option would mean, that in effect, the ongoing patchwork of processes - the Bloody Sunday Inquiry, the post-Cory inquiries, the work of the Police Ombudsman, the Historical Enquiries Team, the steady release of information concerning former spies and informants and so forth – would continue regardless of any decision to draw a line under the past. The experience of recent years led many in the Sub Group to conclude that "truth will out" or, as one member described it, "...truth appears to be seeping under the doors, through the cracks in the ceiling and down the chimney, no matter how determined the attempts to stem the flow". This image speaks directly to the argument raised above concerning the relationship between truth recovery and political stability. While it might make the already difficult task of establishing and maintaining a devolved administration more demanding, the reality is that truth recovery will continue, albeit in an uneven and unmanaged fashion. Intimate details of neighbours who have been involved in murdering or setting up their neighbour will surface, but without the necessary support structures around the victims affected by such ugly truths.

One effect of the establishment of an overarching truth-recovery process would be to create a structure or structures which would, in effect, manage that process. Locating the responsibility for managing such a process elsewhere would not entirely remove dealing with the past from the political arena, but it could afford local politicians some breathing room to attend to more immediate contemporary concerns while those involved in the truth-recovery process continued with their work.

As for the question of whether further truth recovery would "do more harm than good", this is a perennial concern for all jurisdictions considering a truth process. The argument that truths are coming out regardless is certainly relevant to this discussion. Similarly, there is a wealth of psychological and psychiatric literature that focuses on the long-term consequences of violence associated with civil or political conflict. Of course, the subjective experience of victims or survivors is not universal, and some may well cope better than others. Nonetheless, as Hamber, Nageng, and O'Malley have summed up (2000: 19) "[F]rom a psychological (psychoanalytic) perspective, sleeping dogs do not lie and past traumas do not simply pass or disappear with the passage of time." Truth recovery does not provide a miracle cure for those traumatised by violence, but it

---

[225] "A Truth Commission is one proposal by which some people think that 'closure' can be brought on what has happened. In somewhere as small as Northern Ireland this proposal is unlikely to be successful and while the State would have to be fully accountable and would be required to co-operate fully and to disclose all information fully to such a Commission, the terrorist groups would have full control over their level, or lack, of participation. We feel that a Truth Commission would not only be unworkable in Northern Ireland but would serve only to hold those who served in the Crown Forces to account for their actions while terrorists can hide behind the cloak of anonymity" (Democratic Unionist Party 2003: 9).
[226] "Even had we a Truth Commission here, I believe that once again the British government would evade the truth. We would never get past the private or the sergeant, the colonel or the general to establish the fact of state terrorism, sanctioned from the top. The hearings would be dragged out for years upon years. Documents will have been shredded or gone missing, witnesses have died off, memories 'faded'. We should be wary of clamouring for a Truth Commission" D. Morrison "Buried Secrets and Buried Truths", *Andersonstown News*, 19 January 2004.

can at least provide a basis for more long-term personal and societal healing (Hamber 1995, 1998, 2003a; Lykes, Terre Blanche & Hamber 2003).[227] Indeed, it could be argued that a decision not at least to attempt truth recovery would represent a moral and political failure to provide the platform for healing which some victims undoubtedly require.

The view that the piecemeal approach to truth might represent a bespoke alternative to the more traditional transitional processes such as a truth commission emerged largely in a context where the chances of such a broader process appeared highly unlikely. As Bell (2003) acknowledges in perhaps the best-known article written in this genre, the absence of such an official process for establishing a broader social truth represents an ongoing obstacle to more far-reaching institutional transformation. Therefore, it might be better to view the range of truth-recovery initiatives to date as different critical junctures, or what Bell refers to as "stages" of an evolving process, wherein a society is gradually becoming better ready for such a far-reaching initiative. As to the argument from primarily loyalist and unionist sources that "enough is enough" of these inquiries and other discrete incident-focused initiatives, this would appear to be an equally persuasive argument for a more far-reaching and generalist truth-recovery process which would deal with issues arising from all parts of the community rather than attempt to "put a lid on" the emergence of more uncomfortable truths.

With regard to the question of whether the war is "over", this remains fundamentally a question of political judgement. Clearly, the announcement by the IRA that its armed struggle was over and subsequent further acts of decommissioning have considerably changed the political landscape. The considerable scaling-down of security force commitments and installations, the testimony of the Independent International Commission on Decommissioning, the independent witnesses and the reports of the Independent Monitoring Commission in January and then September 2006, have all further contributed to a widespread sense that a watershed has been reached in the transition. Of course, while internal discussions as to their future direction appear to be ongoing within both major paramilitary organisations, loyalist paramilitaries have not as yet made any similar statement to the IRA's or begun a process of widespread weapons decommissioning. Sporadic acts of violence continue to be carried out by dissident republicans, and large numbers of security force and intelligence resources remain committed to the jurisdiction. That said, the context of 2006 is still sufficiently different from that of 2003/4 (and a world away from 1994), at least to warrant a re-examination of the assertion of those who contended then that "war" was still not over.[228]

The specific points emanating from loyalism, in particular with regard to the reasons for its opposition to truth recovery, warrant closer examination, not least because of the importance that the contribution of loyalist paramilitaries and former paramilitaries might make to any truth-recovery process. To recap, these arguments are essentially that: a new generation of young loyalist militants might be inspired to re-engage in violence by "digging up the past"; republicans through their political skills and organisation would be able to turn any further truth recovery to their political advantage; and such a process would play into the hands of those who seek to criminalise loyalism further, in particular those loyalists describe as "middle unionism".

It is important to acknowledge that a detailed examination of the actions of loyalists (as well as republicans and security forces) is, indeed, likely to expose what Cohen (2001) has referred to as "ugly truths". Indeed, that is the whole point. As has been highlighted in the former Yugoslavia in particular, one of the contexts in which violence occurs is where there is a combination of the mystique associated with past acts of heroism emanating from one's community and an associated denial or partial reading or understanding of one's own past (Ignatieff 1998). The reason that some former loyalist combatants have been amongst the most persuasive advocates for a peaceful future is precisely their keen awareness of the ugliness of past violence, including acts of violence in which some of them were intimately involved. For a generation of young loyalists who have little personal memory of the brutality of the conflict in and about Northern Ireland, it is, therefore, arguable that exposure to a process that leads to a "warts and all" account of the past is precisely what is required to undermine the potential for a return to conflict.

---

[227] "There is no magic solution to the problem of dealing with the impact of extensive violence. Truth Commissions, criminal trials, or even extensive counselling and support, will not miraculously deal with the legacies of violence in a society. Healing is inevitably a lengthy and culturally bound process. There is often no clear starting point and there will be few markers along the way - indeed, it is rare for the psychological impact of the past ever to be completely dealt with. This does not, of course, mean that programmes in pursuit of healing are a waste of time - quite the contrary. Assistance with healing can be invaluable for individuals and their communities. But the inherent limitations of attempts to deal with the legacies of extreme violence and the long-term nature of any such project must be accepted." (Hamber 2003a: 77).

[228] For example, in 1993 (the year before the IRA and loyalist cease-fires) 84 deaths were attributed by the police to the security situation in Northern Ireland. In both 2004 and 2005, there were 5 deaths similarly attributed. http://www.psni.police.uk/deaths_cy-57.doc

The view that republicans would be able to turn a truth-recovery process entirely to their own political advantage also requires closer scrutiny. Certainly, the exposure of issues such as collusion between the security forces and loyalist paramilitarism or the involvement of the security forces in extra-judicial killings would fit within a republican analysis of the conflict. However, such activities, which were undoubtedly denied with vehemence throughout the conflict in and about Northern Ireland and in the immediate wake of the ceasefires, are now more or less taken for granted. Sir John Stevens and Justice Peter Cory have already found that there was evidence of collusion in the Finucane case and, indeed, Cory also found such evidence in the Nelson, Hamill, and Wright cases. The attempt by the British government to include members of the security forces in the abandoned "On The Runs" Legislation was an effective admission of the involvement of some such individuals in the most serious of illegal activities. Recent revelations of the extent of British intelligence and police Special Branch infiltration into the ranks of the IRA have raised the possibility of state collusion in republican violence. In addition, if one considers the actions more broadly of republicans themselves, the *Lost Lives* account of deaths in the conflict suggests that republican paramilitaries were responsible for 2,139 deaths between 1969 and 1999. The Provisional IRA alone was responsible for 1,771 deaths, 636 of whom were civilians (McKittrick et al. 1999: 1484). Indeed, some of the most notorious actions which resulted in the largest number of civilian deaths in Northern Ireland and elsewhere were carried out by republicans. Even if one accepts the loyalist view of republicans' supposed organisational and political skills, it stretches credibility to suggest that they will be able to manage a detailed analysis of such "ugly truths" to their own exclusive political advantage.

Finally, from a loyalist perspective there is the argument concerning the criminalisation of loyalist violence, in particular from "middle unionism", and the view that further truth recovery might contribute to such a process. However, an alternative perspective might be to suggest that one of the functions of a truth-recovery process such as a truth commission is normally to examine not just the acts of violence, but the causes and context of such actions. One of the long-standing frustrations expressed by former loyalist paramilitaries and their political spokespersons is precisely the denial by "middle unionism" of their contribution in creating a political context where loyalist paramilitaries resorted to violence. In effect, their argument is that a "middle unionist" analysis of loyalist violence is often deliberately removed from the context in which it occurred. A key feature of any truth process would undoubtedly be to place the context and causes of loyalist violence front and centre. Thus, far from contributing to the further criminalisation of past loyalist violence, a truth-recovery process could contribute to a better understanding of the political context in which such violence occurred, as well as exploring the contribution of those elements of "middle unionism". For the first time in the history of Northern Ireland, such an exploration would be occurring in a context where the laws of libel did not apply.

The last argument to consider from those who would support the "drawing a line under the past" option is based upon the premise that no genuine truth recovery will occur with regard to the conflict. At first glance, such a perspective is understandable. Loyalists have, to date, generally set their face against such a process. Republicans have only comparatively recently appeared more publicly receptive to the issue. While the Chief Constable has declared himself in favour of a truth process (Orde 2005) and the British Prime Minister has at least hinted at a similar mindset, it should not be assumed that such a perspective is shared universally by the military, all of the branches of the intelligence services, or even other elements of the criminal justice system. Indeed, it is possible that various institutions such as the judiciary, Public Prosecution Service, government departments, the media, educational establishments, and other bodies which might well be asked to account for their actions during the conflict in any far reaching truth-recovery initiative, have given little substantive thought to their possible contribution to such a process.

Of course, there is slight circularity to the argument that no-one will speak the truth in a process of truth recovery. Certainly, it is harder to make the case that substantial truth recovery will happen in the absence of an organised process.

In addition, one of the key lessons of the Northern Ireland peace process has been the regularity by which the initially unimaginable has become quite common-place as political circumstances have evolved. The achievement of the first ceasefires, the political negotiations and conclusion of the Agreement, the early release of paramilitary prisoners, the Patten reforms of policing, the establishment (albeit sporadic) of a devolved administration which included unionists and republicans and included the latter taking seats at Stormont, the apparent completion of IRA decommissioning, and the formal announcement of the end of armed struggle – these and other milestones in the process would have been predicted by few but the most optimistic commentators right up until they were realised. Taking this longer view would suggest that, with the appropriate political will, truth recovery, too, is achievable. True, it would be an immensely complex and socially painful process, but so too have many of the previous achievements which have defined the peace process.

Option Two - Internal Organisational Investigations

Introduction

This model would draw upon the experience of a number of the paramilitary organisations and elements of the security forces in conducting their own internal investigations or audits into historical events. Thus, by way of illustration, this option might be regarded as building upon previous initiatives such as the IRA's internal investigation into the fate of those killed and disappeared by its members in the 1970s, or the PSNI's internal investigation into the convictions of Robert Hindes and Hugh Hanna for the killing of Peter Johnston in 1973 by loyalist paramilitaries.[229] This option would entail the voluntary involvement of different paramilitary organisations and different elements of the security and intelligence services establishing such a mechanism and responding to victim requests for information concerning particular events. This option does not necessarily require the establishment of an over-arching truth-recovery process with associated legal powers and administrative infrastructure. However, in order to maximise quality control with regard to the information being provided, as well as provide some form of structure to manage the liaison between victims and organisations that have been involved in violence, it might require some form of central co-ordinating and liaising entity. This option is perhaps best thought of as a model wherein these organisations take primary responsibility for attempting to provide victims with the truth about what happened to their loved ones.

Rationale

The principal rationale for this style of truth recovery is that both the non-state and state organisations which have been directly involved in violent actions are arguably more likely to cooperate with a truth-recovery process over which they have some degree of ownership. Without such co-operation, it is likely that in many cases complete truth will be difficult to ascertain. Such organisations would arguably receive considerable political plaudits for genuine efforts to provide victims the maximum available truth with regard to incidents in which they were injured or their loved ones were killed. Although this option would obviously work best if it involved simultaneous cooperation from all relevant organisations, the fact that such cooperation would be voluntary would provide the possibility of staged involvement with one or more organisations "jumping first". The possibility of staged involvement in the process of truth recovery would, in turn, provide a context of moral and political pressure for non-cooperating organisations (and ultimate censure in any final report for organisations who retained such a stance throughout the process), as well as remove any apparent de facto veto on progress from such organisations.

Process

This option would entail the acquisition of necessary resources and the establishment of a central body that would have responsibility for liaising with the different paramilitary organisations and relevant elements of the security and intelligence services. Given the experiences of the commissions established by the ANC to examine abuses committed by their members (see Chapter Two), it would appear sensible that this central co-ordinating body should be international and independent to maximise the trust and confidence both of the various organisations involved and the general public and victims who would be coming to it in search of truth.

In consultation with all interested parties including the two governments, that body would draw up and seek consensus on the terms of reference for governing the conduct of the internal inquiries to be carried out by the different organisations. Obvious issues to be considered would include the range of issues discussed in Chapter One, including the naming of names, the extent to which any hearings would be public, the publication and legal consequences of any report, and the mechanisms in place to try to maximise quality control with regard to information coming back from the different organisations. Without wishing to prejudge such discussions, given the heavy reliance of this option upon the good will of the organisations most directly involved in the conflict, it would seem highly likely that they would seek to achieve maximum anonymity for their members past and present. Such an emphasis would suggest that names would not be named, that much of the process would be conducted in private and that there would be no possibility of prosecution emanating from any evidence which was received.

This option could operate as follows: (a) the process would be preceded by a public campaign to encourage those victims seeking truth to come forward to the central co-ordinating body; (b) the victims would then "tell

---

229 The two men were 15 and 17 years old when they were convicted on the basis of admissions made during interrogation. Following correspondence from Mr Hanna's father expressing his belief that his son was innocent of the murder, the RUC carried out a reinvestigation of the original investigation under the direction of Assistant Chief Constable Sam Kincaid. Mr Kincaid became convinced of their innocence and expressed his concerns to the Criminal Cases Review. The Criminal Cases Review referred the case back to the Northern Ireland Court of Appeal who found that the convictions were indeed unsafe. In reaching that conclusion the Court made particular reference to the internal police investigation as having been highly persuasive in directing them to that conclusion (*The Queen v Robert James Hindes and Hugh Richard Hanna*, LJ Campbell, 2005 NICA 36).

their story" to the co-ordinating body; (c) the latter would in turn liaise with the relevant organisation involved in the incident; (d) the relevant organisation would conduct an investigation designed to uncover the maximum truth possible and report back to the central co-ordinating body (the practical element of this work being conducted by members or former members of the different organisations in whom other members would place their trust and confidence); (e) verifying the version of events received back as much as possible, this body would then report back to the relevant victims; and (f) this body would finally produce a report on the findings unearthed.

The actual conduct of the investigations could take a number of overlapping forms. The investigations could be conducted in a truth commission format, wherein the particular security force/intelligence organisation or paramilitary group would investigate the actions through a combination of testimony from combatants, witnesses, documentation or (if the process had been so designed) victims. Alternatively, the investigation could take a mock tribunal format, wherein an external liaison person from the central organisation would oversee the investigation and, in effect, preside over a case in which facts and competing interpretations of events are presented.

Having outlined a possible model as to how this option might be put into practice, the Sub Group then examined the relative strengths/opportunities and obstacles/weaknesses presented by such an option.

Option 2: Internal Organisational Investigations

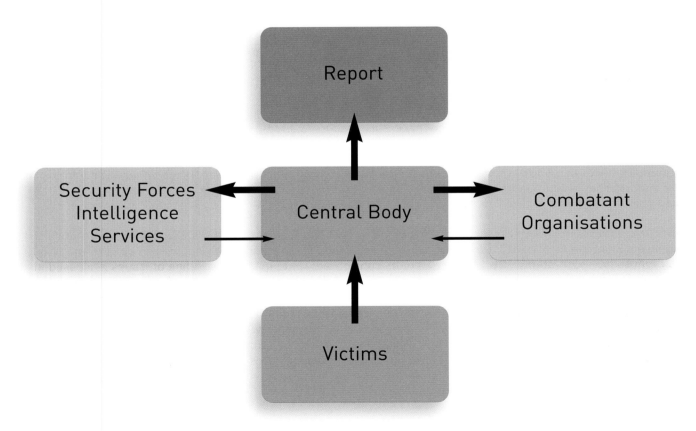

Strengths and opportunities

Ex-combatants and post-conflict healing and reconciliation
This option would facilitate those organisations (as well as individual members or former members) that had been involved in violence to contribute further to the process of post-conflict healing and reconciliation. To date in the transition, former paramilitary activists and, some former members of security forces have engaged in a wide range of largely unpublicised work aimed at both healing and reconciliation. This work includes involvement in initiatives such as the Glencree Ex-Combatants programme, encounters between former republicans and British Army veterans, interface mediation efforts involving former combatants, and the involvement of former republican and loyalist ex-prisoners, together with members of the security forces and victims of violence in the work of Healing Through Remembering. Given the significant degree of ownership amongst former combatants envisaged by this option, this option would enable such individuals to build upon that work in a structired and managed fashion. Ex-combatants would be the most likely individuals to garner the required information from the different organisations. This option would permit them the opportunity to give practical expression to their ongoing commitment to the goals of healing and reconciliation.

Victims and post-conflict healing
As was discussed above, there is no magical relationship between truth recovery and healing or closure for the victims of political violence. Nonetheless, to the extent that this option might provide the opportunity to access truth concerning past events which might otherwise not be fully uncovered, it could make a contribution to that process. It would certainly be feasible to build into the process sufficient support structures to assist with the psychological and emotional stresses involved for victims who chose to come forward to the central co-ordinating institution. However, as is discussed below, this model would arguably fail to deliver on a number of important victim indices.

Obstacles and weaknesses
The obstacles and weaknesses discussed may be grouped under the following headings.

Trust and public confidence
Obviously, the higher degree of ownership and involvement of the different paramilitary organisations and relevant elements of the security forces in unearthing their own "ugly truths" could have an inverse effect on levels of public confidence in the process. Obvious questions would be raised about the willingness of organisations which had been involved in extreme acts of violence to expose their members and the organisation to further social or political opprobrium. Even if an independent intermediary structure were used which would also be tasked with checking the validity of data, the willingness of victims to come forward and expose themselves to possible further hurt might well be affected by the extent to which the organisations involved would have input into the truths exposed. The fact that much of the work of such a process would also most likely be conducted in private might further undermine its general credibility.

Why would the relevant organisations participate?
An obvious question with regard to this option is the incentive for participation by organisations which had been involved in acts of violence. There is considerable cynicism in some quarters as to the possibilities of cooperation by such organisations in any truth-recovery processes. What sets this option apart from some of those discussed below is that it does not contain any obvious "carrot" for former combatants, such as a formal amnesty process. This option is largely premised on the possibility of at least some protagonist organisations becoming involved in truth recovery in order to assist practically with individual and societal healing and as a symbolic gesture that the conflict is indeed finished. While, if some organisations did become involved in such a process and others refused, the latter would be subject to whatever social or political censure that might ensue, the members of such recalcitrant organisations would not be in a materially different position from those individuals who had cooperated fully.

The capacity of organisations to deliver truth
Even if one sets aside concerns regarding the commitment of the different organisations concerned to engage in genuine truth recovery, there are clearly different levels of capacity between the different groups. State organisations which have been involved in conflict, such as the police, military, and intelligence agencies, may have kept detailed records - although the reliability of such records at key "intense" periods of the conflict may also be questionable. They do, however, have considerable investigative and auditing experience within their own ranks, and certainly would have the technical skills and capacity to deliver considerable amounts of detailed information on deaths and injuries at the hands of the state. Paramilitary organisations, on the other hand, may have considerable technical difficulties in carrying out such work. Clearly, some of the larger and better-organised groupings have a greater general capacity than others. Given the nature of their activities during the conflict, there will have been a general cultural aversion to keeping detailed written records across

all of the illegal organisations. Much of the truth recovery work in this sector would by definition rely on the memories of people involved. Apart from the general vagaries of human memory, in some instances stretching back over thirty five years, many key players may well have died of natural causes or been killed, or have long since left the relevant organisation and, even, the jurisdiction. The chaotic reality of different periods of the conflict may well have seen internecine feuds, changes in leadership, and a genuine diminution in the required level of local knowledge which would be required to unearth the necessary level of detail. Even in a context where there was a genuine effort being made by the relevant organisation to provide the necessary information, these capacity issues might well lead to the hopes of victims being raised, only to be cruelly dashed again when the process failed to deliver.

The lack of institutional and political accountability
A further weakness of such a proposed option discussed by the Sub Group was a concern that the particular focus in this option on the centrality of those who had been actually involved in acts of violence might encourage a concurrent lack of attention on the role of institutions or indeed political leaders in contributing to the conflict. Thus, for example, the institutions discussed above or indeed what loyalists refer to as "middle unionists" might be largely exempt from analysis if this option were adopted. Of course, much would depend on the remit of the central co-ordinating institution. Given that much of their practical work would involve liaising with ex-combatants and victims concerning particular incidents, it would hardly be surprising if any resultant report of the process had a similarly narrow gaze.

Victims' needs beyond truth recovery
While there is considerable attention paid to the difficult process of liaising between victims, a central body, and ex-combatants to uncover truth (and, as noted above, that process could include emotional and psychological support for victims), such a focus does not really engage with the much broader range of victims' needs. Some victims may well have needs which include a sense that "justice is being done", and such a need may be an integral part of their healing process. As outlined in Chapter One, there is now a quite well-developed set of international standards that focus on such needs, including the right to reparations which include restitution, compensation, rehabilitation, and satisfaction and guarantees of non-repetition. As currently envisaged, this model would probably fall short of those guarantees on reparations.

Personnel
This process would probably require a range of international members to sit as members of the central co-ordinating institution, an appropriate staff who were deemed acceptable to both ex-combatants and victims to conduct the liaison work, former members of the combatant organisations to conduct the internal investigations, and sufficient support staff to ensure that the emotional and psychological needs of victims were met before, during and after the process.

Resources
Although this process would require resources to support the establishment of the central structure, as well as staff who could liaise with both ex-combatant organisations and support of victims, the cost would be considerably less than that of some of the larger or more legalistic options discussed below.

Timeframe
One to two years.

Outcomes
Possible outcomes to this option might include feedback to individual victims or their families, a report of investigation findings, including mention of who cooperated and who did not, and some form of organisational acknowledgement of responsibility for individual past acts.

Option Three – Community-Based "Bottom-Up" Truth Recovery

Introduction

This option would seek to build on previous experiences of community-based truth recovery and replicate similar "bottom-up" initiatives in other communities affected by the conflict in and about Northern Ireland.[230] It would also overlap to some extent with ongoing storytelling initiatives, although it would seek to do more investigative and verification work. Local communities themselves would be involved in devising the parameters and process of truth recovery. This option would view truth recovery as a vehicle through which to achieve community development as well as localised healing and reconciliation. The option would require the establishment of an oversight body to arrange staffing, organise training, manage documentation and so forth. However, it is envisaged that, as much as possible, the actual process of collecting testimony from victims, witnesses, and combatants would be conducted by individuals from the local communities affected. These individual testimonies would also be supplemented by collecting additional information from documentary sources (e.g. newspaper reports, coroners' reports, the work of local historians), all of which would be included in a series of final reports from the different communities affected. These reports would then be fed back to the overall co-ordinating body, who could in turn produce a report which drew together the various localised findings and thematised them as much as possible. This option would facilitate moving forward on truth recovery even in a context wherein the state had decided not to establish a more traditional "top-down" initiative. Although, as is discussed below, this option might work better in conjunction with such an initiative, it would remove any apparent veto over progress on truth recovery by the state or other political elites.

Rationale

The rationale for this style of truth recovery would be to maximise individual and collective ownership and empowerment at grassroots level concerning the process of truth recovery in communities most directly affected by political violence. As discussed in Chapter One, such an option may operate as either a stand-alone model or as a mechanism to supplement a more traditional "top-down" official process. The involvement of local people in the process of documenting local truth would be designed to serve as both a community development vehicle as well as a mechanism for communal healing and reconciliation. The option could be designed in such a way that it took account of the impact of structural and systemic aspects of the conflict and in turn feed into a broader process of truth recovery. It would resonate strongly with some of the storytelling work previously documented by HTR (Kelly 2005).[231] It would also provide the opportunity to give voices to victims and marginalised communities, record previously untold stories, underline the validity of different experiences between and within communities, and provide an alternative to dominant macro narratives which de-emphasise the importance of individual and grassroots experiences.

Process

This option would require the acquisition of sufficient resources and most probably a central resource which local interested community groups, NGOs or other elements of civil society could approach for support and assistance in how to establish and conduct a local "bottom-up" truth-recovery programme. That resource would draw upon the methodological and technical experience of other projects which have already conducted such programmes in order to assist with devising a bespoke programme tailored to meet the needs and capacities of the local projects.

In order to maximise the participation of victims, ex-combatants, and other significant actors, this option would require the drafting of protocols with regard to the development of trust, confidentiality, anonymity (where necessary), consent, and other matters related to the management of the data generated. Ideally, such protocols should also be accompanied by a guarantee from the Public Prosecution Service and the Police Service of Northern Ireland (PSNI) that such localised truth-recovery efforts will not be jeopardised by, for example, police raids designed to garner information to prosecute individuals.

Local staff and volunteers would be appointed from within the relevant communities who would be tasked with establishing and managing the local community truth-recovery initiative. Such programmes would draw upon the considerable skills base in community development and community work generally that exist in many

---

[230] While the notion of "community" envisaged with regard to this model is primarily geographical, it could also potentially include "communities of interest" wherein groups of victims or other affected individuals could band together to organise a collective "bottom-up" approach to truth recovery.

[231] The original Healing Through Remembering Report recommended "A storytelling process known as 'Testimony'. Stories and narratives will be collected from all who wish to tell of their experiences of the conflict in and about Northern Ireland. These stories - collected by those already undertaking this type of work and by community groups through a flexible but standard method - would form part of an archive housing the stories of the past and serving as a vehicle to learn lessons for the future." (Healing Through Remembering 2002: v).

areas affected by the conflict in and about Northern Ireland, and apply those to the process of truth recovery. The staff and volunteers would engage in a process of consultation with the local affected community as to the likely parameters and working methods of the programme.

Once the local consultation process was completed and the working methods agreed, the local staff and volunteers would begin the process of taking testimony, liaising with the relevant ex-combatant and victim organisations, and framing the events within the broader context of the local history of the affected community. This latter part of the process could take a number of forms, including use of storytelling or oral history techniques, sampling as diverse a range of individuals as possible to capture the breadth of local views on conflict-related events, returning transcripts to local interviewees for checking and verifying as much as possible these personal remembrances with other available documentary and human sources. Those interviewed would include victims, witnesses, and where possible and relevant, former combatants and members of the security forces. The process of interviewing such individuals who had been engaged in acts of violence within that community would most likely include a guarantee not to name names as a condition for assistance with the project.

Following the collation of all of the testimony and documentary sources, the local community projects would undertake the task of writing an account of what had occurred within their community. Again, where necessary, such projects should be able to draw on technical support and assistance from a central resource. Depending upon the views of the different participating communities, the central resource could also undertake a process of writing up a more general account of the experience of "bottom-up" truth recovery by those affected by the conflict in and about Northern Ireland.

Option 3: Community-Based "Bottom-Up" Truth Recovery

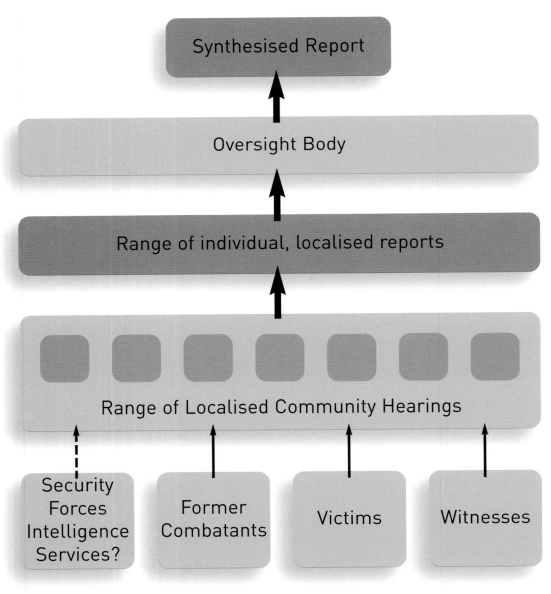

Strengths and opportunities

The strengths and opportunities discussed with regard to this option were grouped under the following headings.

A broad notion of community

One of the perennial concerns in doing any form of grassroots justice or reconciliation work is the question as to how to define the concept of community (see Crawford 1997; Roche 2002). As was noted above, while communities as envisaged in this options are most likely to be geographical, the option would also be sufficiently flexible for groups to coalesce as "communities of interest" and to establish a truth-recovery process focused on their particular concern. Thus, for example, it might be possible to envisage such processes established to seek truth concerning the families of those killed or injured as informers by loyalist or republican paramilitaries or, alternatively, families of security forces' casualties coming together to work on truth recovery where it appears that loved ones were killed in order to protect intelligence or Special Branch agents. In this vein, the notion of community is neither narrow nor static, but rather a fairly broad one which could encompass a range of "bottom-up" activities.

The importance of ownership and legitimacy

One of the key strengths of this approach to truth recovery would be the indigenous legitimacy potentially garnered by having the process so firmly rooted in local communities. A common criticism of more traditional approaches to truth recovery is that often victims and local communities feel that they lose ownership over their own stories as the official process takes them and then translates them into a usable discourse of national reconciliation (e.g. Wilson 2001; Gibson 2004a, 2004b). The organic legitimacy of the process would be increased by the fact that much of the face-to-face work done under this option, as well as the actual transcribing, checking, and writing (where possible), would be completed by local friends and neighbours.

The importance of local networks and relationships for the quality of data

Another obvious strength of a localised approach to truth recovery is that those involved will already have an established network of relationships, which should assist with the process and quality of the information garnered. Engendering trust is crucial to any process of truth recovery. Providing that the process of consultation concerning the parameters and working practices of the option is properly handled, local key actors will already be aware of the process and its intentions. In particular, the involvement of local people in conducting and managing the process should enhance the credibility of the project for local victims and witnesses. In addition, if a programme is seen to have widespread legitimacy in a local community, this may in turn lead to a more calibrated and effective organic pressure upon ex-combatant organisations or local individual combatants or former combatants to assist the community in its search for truth.[232]

Truth recovery as community development and healing

As noted above, this option would seek to take advantage of the skills and experience base in many local communities affected by violence and apply them to the process of truth recovery. Based upon experiences internationally (e.g. Lykes et al. 2003) and in Northern Ireland (Ardoyne Commemoration Project 2002), there is considerable evidence that actual involvement in such a process can contribute towards the healing and empowerment of those involved. In some instances, this may be quite literally a process of "mastering the past", wherein, for example, the victims of violence could develop sufficient confidence to speak out about their experiences of loss and to gain a sense that their story has value and worth.[233] Such a process could be of value to all victims. It may be particularly important, however, where deaths or injuries as a result of the conflict in and about Northern Ireland do not fit with the more familiar templates of who was responsible. Thus, for example, the families of individuals living in a republican or loyalist community who have been killed by paramilitaries "from their own side" for allegedly being informers, or the victims of an internecine feud, or punished for alleged anti-social behaviour – all of these victims may take considerable comfort that their stories can at last be told, particularly to other members of their local community. "Bottom-up" truth recovery may open up space for reflection and healing on internal communal divisions in local communities where, from the outside at least, such communities are often assumed to be homogenous. Such deliberations could also in turn feed into broader societal processes of truth recovery.

---

[232] For a discussion of the complexities of the relationship between paramilitary organisations and responses to communal pressures see e.g. Sluka 1989; McAuley 1996; and McEvoy & Mika 2002.

[233] For example, the Ardoyne Commemoration Project (2002) notes that a surprising number of those victims interviewed had never spoken of the deaths of their loved ones to friends, neighbours or indeed witnesses who had been present at the event.

Obstacles and weaknesses
The obstacles and weaknesses identified were outlined as follows.

"Bottom-Up" truth recovery may facilitate institutional and security force denial
One obvious criticism of any community-based truth-recovery initiative is that it is likely to focus on those actors from whom its members may feel that some information is likely to be forthcoming. In the context of working class republican and loyalist communities, the combatant actors addressed are likely to be those organisations with a presence in the communities affected. A by-product of this "inward-looking" dynamic is that it is unlikely to apply any real pressure to either the state security forces or indeed other institutions that arguably have a case to answer in the broader process of social truth recovery. While, of course, it would be possible in the writing of any report emanating from a community-based truth-recovery process to reflect on the actions or policies of state institutions, without direct access to information from the latter, such a report would arguably have less impact. Community-based truth-recovery initiatives are unlikely to have any particular powers of discovery or compelling witnesses. In addition, whatever "organic" power they may have to be directed towards encouraging cooperation from indigenous combatant actors who live and work in their own community,[234] such power would arguably be considerably blunted against individuals who are from outside those affected communities and who work for agencies which may be engaged in institutional denial of their culpability regarding particular past actions during the conflict. Of course, individual security force members or former members would be free to engage in such a process regardless of the organisational positions adopted by the British Army, PSNI, or relevant veterans organisations. The resultant effect of such community initiatives, at least if they were acting in isolation from any broader official truth-recovery process, might arguably be a diminution of pressure upon such agencies to provide the necessary information.

"Bottom-Up" truth recovery may be too "single identity" focused
A related by-product of the inward-looking nature of any "bottom-up" truth-recovery process would be a likely "single identity" focus of the model. Of course, there is a lively debate within community development and community relations work more generally about the respective merits of cross-community versus single-identity work (e.g. Church, Visser & Johnson 2004; Hamber et al. 2005). Indeed, as some commentators on single-identity work have argued, finding and acknowledging the diversity within groupings may well be a necessary first step towards creating a greater receptiveness towards difference in other groups or traditions (Leichty & Clegg 2000: 216). That said, there are obvious dangers in single-identity-focused truth recovery. For example, if a project was not properly managed to reflect the diversity of views within a given community, there are dangers that particularly powerful narratives could dominate the option. Similarly, if left unchallenged, socially and personally damaging narratives of victimhood or perceptions of "otherness" with regard to other communities could both overly influence the process within a given community and also (as a worst case scenario) lessen rather than improve the possibility of acknowledgement of the suffering of other "outside" communities.

Capacity differences between different communities
A third and related difficulty of this option is that its commendable reliance on local ownership and participation is also a weakness, in that it would be dependent upon the variations in capacity between different affected communities. Variations in capacity between different communities could lead to an uneven quality of data, project management, and final report and follow-up services to those affected. In communities which wished to establish such a programme, but where indigenous capacity was lacking, there would obviously be a need for greater support and technical assistance from any central resource. Such a central resource could include international and local expertise in the same way that many of the previous community-led inquiries have drawn upon such experience. However, increased involvement of "outsider" expertise would require careful balancing in terms of maintaining the trust of local victims, witnesses, and combatants or ex-combatants.

Victims' needs beyond truth recovery.
As with the internal investigations option, this option for truth recovery might struggle to meet the needs of victims beyond telling and recording their story and having it published. As noted above, it would not provide institutional recognition, acknowledgement or accountability. In particular, if this option were instituted in lieu of an official truth-recovery process and its presumed attention to such needs, it too would be failing such victims.

---

[234] Similar to the Internal Investigation option above, obviously whatever power this initiative would have is also curtailed by its inability to offer substantial incentive for cooperation, such as an amnesty.

Personnel

This process would require trained researchers and interviewers to serve as a central resource to assist with the development and training of the local community-based programmes. In addition, local staff and volunteers from the communities who undertook "bottom-up" truth recovery would have to be employed and managed during the process of data collation, verification, and report-writing.

Resources

Given that the process would not require legal investigation, representation or even necessarily large-scale public hearings,[235] the costs would not be prohibitive. Certainly, the British or Irish governments could fund such processes without significant dents in relevant national budgets. In any case if either government did not provide ring-fenced funding for such initiatives, it might be possible to secure funding from other sources.

Timeframe

One to three years.

Outcomes

Possible outcomes to this option might include feedback to individual victims or their families, a report of local community truth-recovery findings, and, if local communities deemed it appropriate, a larger report which would collate and thematise the findings from across the community-based initiatives and include recommendations to the two governments as to how this process might be built upon.

---

[235] Such hearings might be organised on a much smaller scale in local communities if deemed appropriate by the local communities themselves.

Option Four - A Truth-Recovery Commission

Introduction
This option would draw explicitly on the breadth of international experience concerning the establishment and running of truth commissions. Specifically, a commission would be established and tasked with examining the conflict in and about Northern Ireland. The Commission would focus on events of the past over a particular period of time. The parameters of the timeframe would be a matter for public debate, but, for example, the Commission might decide to choose two definitive dates (e.g. 1969 to 1998) and allow sufficient flexibility in exploring the context of violence to incorporate discussions on events which happened before or after those dates. The Commission would investigate patterns of abuse over the period in question. It would explore the causes, context, and consequences of violence as well as examine specific events and patterns. After consultation, the Commission would be established by new legislation put forward by the two governments, but as an independent institution free from interference by either the British or Irish government. In the UK context, it should explicitly not be established within the framework of the Inquiries Act.

The Commission would sit in Northern Ireland, but make arrangements to take evidence from a range of affected communities. Its remit would be sufficiently broad to examine events which occurred in relation to the conflict in and about Northern Ireland anywhere on these islands, or indeed overseas. It could be given extensive investigative powers. It could have the same power to compel witnesses to attend as the High Court. It could have the power to grant amnesties to those who came forward and made full disclosure with regard to past events, as well as the power to recommend prosecutions against those who did not but who were found to have a case to answer. The Commission would sit for a finite period. It would hear evidence from victims, witnesses, former combatants, members of the security forces, intelligence agencies, institutional spokespeople from the different institutions it considered relevant to take evidence from, and a number of other civic and political actors. It would have the power to hear testimony both in public and private, although the assumption would be that hearings would be held in public unless there were compelling reasons for a private hearing. The Commission would also have the power to order appropriate reparations to the victims of the conflict. The Commission would produce a final report outlining key findings with recommendations to address past wrongs and prevent recurrence. The two governments would then be tasked with establishing an oversight mechanism (similar to that which occurred in wake of the Patten Report) for a period of time (e.g. five years) which would produce annual reports on the extent to which the Commission's recommendations had been implemented.

Rationale
The rationale for the establishment of a truth-recovery commission is that it is intended as a practical and symbolic expression of a willingness of a society to deal with its violent past as part of the transition to becoming a more healthy society. As British Prime Minister Tony Blair has suggested, there is a need in the Northern Ireland transition for a mechanism to prevent the past from continuing to dominate the present and the future. The rationale for having one body with a cross-jurisdictional remit to examine events that occurred in Northern Ireland, Great Britain, and the Irish Republic (although it could conceivably look at relevant events that happened elsewhere) would be (a) in recognition of the number of individuals and communities affected by the conflict in these different sites; (b) as a way of moving beyond the piecemeal approach to truth that has been the dominant approach to date; and (c) learning from the experience of previous initiatives which have been hampered by cross-border jurisdiction issues (e.g. the Barron Inquiries into the Dublin/Monaghan bombings and the Seamus Ludlow murder). The Commission would be designed as an institution to give a voice to both victims and those who had been involved in violence. However, its remit to explore the causes, nature, context, and consequences of political violence would be sufficiently broad to also provide an opportunity for a range of institutions (e.g. government departments beyond the security forces, churches, political leaders, judiciary) to explore the actions or inactions of their institutions during the conflict in and about Northern Ireland.

Process
As the Commission would require legislation in both jurisdictions, its establishment should be preceded by a time-limited but intense period of consultation on its role, terms of reference, and powers. In order to give the consultation focus, the governments should outline their views as to how the Commission should function. Such a consultation should not take longer than three months. The consultation should be informed by previous work completed in the field. Whilst it would be open to the public at large to contribute to the public consultation, particular efforts should be made to solicit the views of the victims of political violence.

Following the consultation period, both governments should pass the required enacting legislation. In the British context, this should be done explicitly outside the terms of the current Inquiries Act.

The Commissioners appointed should include either an entirely international membership, or a mixture of respected local and international figures, but with a chairperson and deputy chairperson of impeccable international reputation.

The Commission must be given sufficient staff and resources to complete its remit. These would most likely include lawyers, researchers, investigators, psychologists, social workers, psychiatrists, an information and public relations office, and related administrative and technical support. With regard to lawyers in particular, the Commission would, from the outset, establish rules and regulations designed as much as possible to prevent the proceedings from becoming overly adversarial. For example, the rules should permit individuals who are interviewed or give evidence to the Commission to be represented by skilled workers (e.g. from the NGO sector) who are not necessarily lawyers. It is also suggested that a financial cap should be placed on the funds available to lawyers and other professionals working for the Commission, and that all such professionals would undertake to carry out work relevant to the Commission until that work was completed and within the agreed limitations on the funds available.

The research and investigative branches of the Commission would undertake an extensive programme of statement taking and research concerning past acts of violence. This would be done by face-to-face interviews with victims, witnesses, former combatants, security force and intelligence services, and anyone else who could shed light on such events. Localised meetings and hearings would be held in affected communities throughout Northern Ireland, the Republic, and Great Britain. Thematic hearings focusing on the role of different institutional actors (e.g. the media, the churches, the judiciary, the health service) in the conflict, as well as the impact of the conflict on different sectors (e.g. women, children) could also be part of this process. Primary data on past events would then be verified and corroborated as much as possible against other sources of information, including police or court files, coroners' reports, contemporaneous media accounts, and any other relevant secondary sources. As the process of collating information gathered momentum, preliminary findings would be entered in order to inform the themes explored at a later stage by the Commissioners themselves.[236]

Depending on the volume of information gathered through this route and the wishes of the individual victims, a system could be devised to have "representative" victims give evidence in person to the Commission proper. However, any victim who wished to give public testimony should be permitted to do so. As noted above, the Commission would operate under a presumption of holding hearings in public, although it would have the power to hold hearings in private where warranted for compelling reasons. Whilst the Commission would be located in Northern Ireland, Commissioners would undertake a process of public consultation and hearings in local communities throughout these islands. All of those individuals contributing to the work of the Commission (but victims in particular) would receive the necessary psychological support before, during and after their involvement in either the original interviews, process of information recording or subsequent appearance before the Commission itself.

In tandem with the process of information-gathering and documentation, the Commission would oversee a separate process with the power to grant amnesty to former combatants who made full disclosures of past actions. Such an amnesty would entail the legal expunging of the relevant criminal record for those who fully satisfy the requirements of the Commission and a guarantee of non-prosecution for acts fully admitted to the satisfaction of the Commission. This process would be open to all members and former members of paramilitary organisations (including those currently "on the run," who would be free to return to give evidence without fear of arrest), state security and intelligence agencies, and other individuals liable for prosecution for past actions. Following the completion of the deliberations of the amnesty element of the Commission, the Commission would also have the power to recommend prosecution to the Public Prosecution Service of any actors who had not benefited from such an amnesty and against whom there was a case to answer.[237]

Following the process of research, investigation, validation, and hearings and amnesty deliberations, the Commissioners would produce a report on their deliberations detailing events, causes, nature, context, and consequences of the conflict in and about Northern Ireland, as well as make findings with regard to the culpability for human rights violations. The enabling legislation would include a commitment to publish that report within a reasonable time from the completion of the work of the Commission. That report would also

---

236 In the South African and other examples this stage of the process was followed by either rejection of the data because it was outside the terms of reference of the Commission or deemed untrue or accepted on the basis of the evidence and the balance of probability (Wilson 2001: 40).

237 In cases where the Commission had heard evidence from a former combatant but not been satisfied that a full disclosure had been made and therefore refused to grant an amnesty, none of the admissions made could be used to prosecute such an individual.

include a series of recommendations as to how Northern Ireland and other affected jurisdictions should deal with the past and prevent human rights violations from happening again. Recommendations for reparations to victims should also be made.

Following the release of the Commission's report, both governments would establish an independent overview mechanism which would report to the Dáil and British Parliament on an annual basis for a defined period as to progress on implementation of the report recommendations.

Option 4: Truth-Recovery Commission

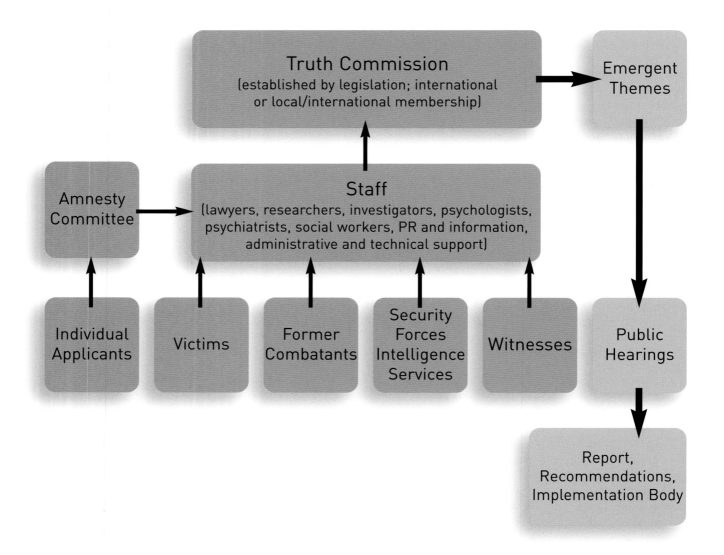

Strengths and opportunities
The strengths and opportunities discussed with regard to the establishment of a truth-recovery commission may be grouped under the following headings.

A powerful institutional tool of truth recovery
A properly funded independent truth-recovery commission with a sufficiently broad remit, adequate resources, legal powers, and staffed by appropriately skilled commissioners and staff is a powerful institutional tool for truth recovery. As is discussed at length above, truth commissions cannot miraculously undo all of the hurt and pain caused by conflict. Indeed, it is now generally accepted that the early days of the South African Truth and Reconciliation Commission (SATRC) saw its reconciliatory potential somewhat

oversold by some commissioners and an over-enthusiastic public relations agency (Boraine 2000; Wilson 2001). That said, a truth-recovery commission with appropriate legal powers would gain access to official documentation and institutions that a less formal, non-governmental process could not. Such a process could contribute more significantly to some form of limited accountability at least. In addition, if it were also equipped with legal incentives to encourage full disclosure from former combatants from state and non-state organisations (e.g. an amnesty process), a truth-recovery commission would also arguably be the institution most likely to garner the maximum information possible from such actors. As in the South African context, this would not necessarily mean that such individuals must apologise, show remorse or request forgiveness (although the procedures should be sufficiently flexible to permit the recording of any of these actions) in order to qualify for amnesty. Rather, it could be stipulated that, if the acts in question were scheduled under the Emergency Legislation and the individual was adjudged to have made a full disclosure of all relevant facts or information, he or she should be granted an amnesty.[238]

A statement of intent to deal with the past
At a more symbolic level, a fully independent truth-recovery commission would signify a serious societal intent to begin the painful process of dealing with the past in a holistic and meaningful fashion. Such a Commission could build on the truth-recovery work that has already taken place but do so in a much more inclusive fashion, which would not only cover a much broader range of incidents, but also locate all such events investigated and documented in a broader framework of the causes, nature, context, and consequences of violence. Such a process should, in particular, focus on the needs of victims to know the truth concerning the events of the past. In order to deal effectively with the past, it should be framed as an inquisitorial process which would seek to avoid (as much as possible) becoming enmeshed in the legalistic adversarialism which has characterised some of the other inquiries regarding the conflict in and about Northern Ireland.

A chance to "set the record straight"
A truth-recovery commission would also afford the opportunity to "set the record straight" as definitely as possible about past events that remain contentious. Whilst not all truths about every event may necessarily be unearthed, the Commission should at least, as Michael Ignatieff has suggested, "narrow the range of permissible lies". Certainly, the focus of any such Commission on the context of the conflict in and about Northern Ireland or the role of institutions during it would make less feasible the "uninvolved" or "neutral" stance adopted by some political actors who have steadfastly maintained that only "the men of violence" should be held responsible for their actions. At the very least, it would be a definitive and authoritative source of historical record which will make the denial of "ugly truths" by any of the relevant political, military or paramilitary actors less intellectually or morally tenable.

A vehicle for reconciliation?
One of the most oft-stated rationales for a truth commission is that it could serve as an important vehicle for reconciliation in Northern Ireland. In the South African context, some of the most prominent supporters of the SATRC have argued strongly that it made a major contribution to the process of national reconciliation (Boraine 2000; Tutu 1999; Villa-Vicencio & Verwoerd 2000; Villa-Vicencio 2003). Given the importance of the assumed relationship between truth and reconciliation more generally in transitional societies (e.g. Hayner 2001; Kriesberg 2004) it is worth exploring its intricacies in some detail.

The complexities of the meaning of reconciliation are borne out by the failure of a number of truth commissions properly to define its meaning. For example, as Richard Wilson (2001) points out, and as was noted in Chapter Two, the concept of reconciliation was included in the nomenclature of the SATRC but the Commission never defined what was meant by the term. Similarly, as noted above, the East Timorese Commission on Reception, Truth and Reconciliation also does not contain a definition of the term, although a criterion is laid down as to how individuals may qualify for community-based reconciliation as opposed to prosecution. This lack of definitional clarity has led to predictable difficulties for the work of both bodies.

The contested meaning of the term "reconciliation" with regard to Northern Ireland is an excellent case in point. For some community relations practitioners, faith-based activists, academics and others, it is a common-sense term which speaks to the need in a divided society for individuals and communities to reconcile a tragic history and alternative political aspirations in a small geographical space (e.g. Love 1995; Faith & Politics Group 2002).

---

[238] For example, Section 20(1) of the South African Promotion of National Unity and Reconciliation Act 1995 established the Amnesty Committee. That section states that, "If the Committee, after considering an application for amnesty, is satisfied that (a) the application complies with the requirements of this Act; (b) the act, omission or offence to which the application relates is an act associated with a political objective committed in the course of the conflicts of the past in accordance with the provisions of subsections (2) and (3); and (c) the applicant has made a full disclosure of all relevant facts, it shall grant amnesty in respect of that act, omission or offence".

For others, however, particularly elements of both republicanism and loyalism, the connection of the term "reconciliation" with the community relations paradigm is viewed with suspicion as either assimilationist or integrationist. For some such actors, community relations is a framework which negates causes of the conflict beyond the "two tribes" analogy, seeks to delegitimise expressions of culture or history which do not fit neatly within an illusory "middle ground" view of the jurisdiction, and overstates the potential of the contact hypothesis between Catholics and Protestants, despite dubious returns on its dominance of funding strategies over a twenty-year period (e.g. Shirlow et al. 2005; Hamber & Kelly 2005). For still others, notably those who approach transition from a human rights or humanitarian law perspective, the fusion of reconciliation with community relations is a process which may obscure the need for accountability of those guilty of gross human rights violations (Mageean & McEvoy 2000).

As Hamber and Kelly (2005: 13) point out, the concept of reconciliation has been subject to a number of quite distinct interpretations internationally, including as a "soft" concept or euphemism for political compromise, a profound process involving forgiveness and repentance (which often carries theological overtones), or as a practical programme of work designed to re-establish workable relationships in deeply divided societies. After a substantial review of the literature, Hamber and Kelly (2005) concluded that reconciliation should be best viewed as a voluntary process which involves addressing conflictual and fractured relations through a number of practical interwoven strands. These include developing a shared vision of an interdependent and fair society; acknowledging and dealing with the past; building positive relationships; ensuring cultural and attitudinal change; and making substantial social, economic and political change (Hamber & Kelly 2005: 7). Their definition has subsequently been adopted by the European Union Peace and Reconciliation funding initiatives.

In the context of the truth-recovery debate regarding the conflict in and about Northern Ireland, the notion of reconciliation as synonymous with the SATRC in the eyes of many further complicates the picture. For some, reconciliation in the South African context became a byword for a process that was too "perpetrator-friendly", wherein those guilty of gross violations were granted amnesty in return for comparatively little, despite the huge pain that amnesty inflicted upon victims (Hamber et al. 2000; Wilson 2001). Alternatively, reconciliation was viewed by others as a fuzzy and imprecise term which perpetuated a simplistic perpetrator/victim divide and left those reluctant to offer apology or seek forgiveness for acts of armed struggle (which they regarded as justified) as political scapegoats for the SATRC's inability to hold institutions properly accountable for the sins of the past. In addition, the SATRC has also been criticised for exaggerating its potential to contribute to "healing" and "closure" (Hamber & Wilson 2002), and related reconciliation-related terms without providing an objective set of empirical indicators by which such impact might be assessed or evaluated (Gibson 2004a, 2004b).

To summarise, in assessing the potential impact of a truth-recovery commission on the broader process of reconciliation, there are a number of elements to the process which must be given careful consideration.
An early step in the process of establishing a Commission would be to define what was meant by reconciliation. That process should be informed by the considerable international literature on the complexity of the term in Northern Ireland. It should also be cognisant of the particular meaning and history of the term in Northern Ireland, both positive and negative. Obvious questions would include whether, for example, it means reconciliation at an individual level (e.g. between victims and those who killed or injured them or their loved ones), at a community level (between particular communities e.g. Shankill/Falls or between Catholics and Protestants) or at an even more abstract national level (e.g. between the peoples of Ireland and Great Britain). As well as developing the meaning of the term, any truth-recovery commission would arguably have to develop benchmarks by which its reconciliatory impact might be assessed at the individual, communal or national level. Once these substantive preliminary issues were addressed, the Commission should also be careful not to overstate the ambition or potential of reconciliation in its organisational culture and working practices.

In particular, victims cannot and should not feel pressurised by the process to forgive those who have harmed them or their families.[239] Similarly, with regard to people who have been previously involved in acts of violence, as suggested above, if there is any suggestion of a requirement for penitence or contrition as a pre-condition towards achieving reconciliation, then this is likely to impede severely the work of the Commission. Reconciliation cannot be forced upon the protagonists to any conflict; rather it must grow organically from

---

[239] As one member of the Human Rights Violations Committee of the SATRC recounted to Richard Wilson: "By being politically independent, by listening to all sides of the conflict, we can deal with our past and move away from bitterness. We must reconcile with our past as opposed to promoting reconciliation between individuals. It is too much to ask victims to forgive. They may get some satisfaction from knowing the truth of what happened and who ordered what. But it's their right to hate the perpetrators" (cited in Wilson 200: 107).

whatever process is established.[240] Thus, for example, it is highly unlikely that the proceedings of the truth-recovery commission would include many formal victim/offender reconciliation encounters in the full glare of publicity. While such one-to-one sessions might grow organically once the process is established, and indeed be facilitated by organisations with established skills or experience in such interactions, such as restorative justice or mediation practitioners, it is more likely that such work would be done away from the spotlight of the Commission's formal hearings.

Informed by such a cold-eyed and pragmatic approach to those difficulties and limitations, a truth-recovery commission could nonetheless arguably play a useful function in this area. While the HTR Sub Group chose not to include the word in the title of this proposed option for the reasons outlined above, it is to be hoped that such a Commission would act as a catalyst designed to promote reconciliation for individuals, communities and the societies affected by the conflict rather than as the vehicle which would ultimately achieve such a goal.

A basis for a new political accommodation?
Finally, and more optimistically, the actual practice of truth recovery on this scale, the production of an authoritative report, and the establishment of a rigorous oversight mechanism to ensure implementation of the Commission's recommendations – could, cumulatively, serve as a key foundation block for the development of a new polity in Northern Ireland. A formal and organised recognition of the suffering of the "other" is a fundamental element of a new political accommodation in this jurisdiction. This does not mean that reconciliation will have been achieved on an individual, communal or societal level once the work of truth recovery and implementation is completed. It does mean, however, that the Commission would be accepted as a milestone along the journey from a violent political conflict towards peaceful co-existence during which a deeper form of reconciliation may occur.

Weaknesses and obstacles
The weaknesses and obstacles identified with this option were as follows.

Difficulty in garnering public support and confidence
There are serious misgivings in some quarters in Northern Ireland about the value of a truth-recovery commission. One of the key tasks of the two governments in the consultation process leading to establishment of the Commission would be to persuade those who are cynical of its value and of the respective commitment of the two governments to genuine "warts and all" truth recovery. Clearly, the introduction of the Inquiries Act to deal with the Finucane case and any subsequent public inquiries is viewed by many in the nationalist community in Northern Ireland as indicative of a desire amongst elements of the British political and security establishment to obfuscate rather than illuminate uncomfortable truths concerning the conflict in and about Northern Ireland. The transfer of national security responsibility from the PSNI to MI5 as the potential for devolved justice functions has inched forward has been viewed by some as evidence of a desire of parts of the intelligence services, at least, to ensure that local politicians do not gain access to the truth of what has occurred in the past. With regard to elements of the unionist and loyalist community, as was discussed at length above, they have serious misgivings about such a process being open to manipulation by republicans for their own political objectives. Whilst either set of objections is not necessarily insurmountable, they do represent formidable political obstacles for both governments. Guaranteeing the independence of the Commission from government or any of the major political actors, ensuring that the remit, powers and resources of the Commission were such that genuine and holistic rather than partial truth recovery was achievable – these and other features would certainly go some way to countering such objections.

Resourcing and the dangers of legalism
Undoubtedly, a truth-recovery commission would be the most expensive of the options yet explored. It should be possible to keep expenditure well below that which has been spent on the Bloody Sunday Inquiry through careful planning, capping of the funds available for lawyers and other professionals, and concerted efforts to avoid the pitfalls inherent in a process which becomes too adversarial or legalistic. Such a drive would require clear terms of reference, which would need to include provision for the representation of victims, witnesses or alleged perpetrators of violent acts by non-lawyers, and firm stewardship of the proceedings by the Commissioners. Even with such provisions in place, the process would inevitably involve lawyers and legal argumentation. In addition, the research, investigation, victim support, information and other technical support would require adequate resourcing to ensure that the task was properly conducted. With sensible

---

[240] For example, Huyse (2003) argues that there are three stages to reconciliation: replacing fear by non-violent coexistence, building confidence and trust, and moving towards empathy. The final stage, according to Huyse, needs to be accompanied by building democracy and a new socio-economic order. For him, empathy also does not imply forgiveness or absolute harmony, and does not exclude feelings of anger (cited in Hamber & Kelly 2005: 21).

planning and financial systems in place, and a strong steer in the enabling legislation and guidelines for the conduct of the Commission to avoid the pitfalls of legalism as much as possible, the two governments would (in undertaking this initiative) be making a concurrent undertaking not to attempt to do truth recovery "on the cheap".

Ensuring the participation of victims, ex-combatants and relevant institutions
Another key challenge for any Commission will be the participation of victims, those who have been involved in acts of violence, and relevant institutions.

Whilst many individual victims and victims' organisations have actively campaigned for a truth commission, others have been opposed for a variety of reasons. Once established, it would be important to secure the participation of as broad a cross section as possible, including those who had opposed the establishment of the institution in the first place. A key feature in the process of maximising victim participation will be the investment of time and resources in working with and providing psychological and legal support to victims before, during and after the truth-recovery commission process.

Considerable efforts will also have to be made to seek to maximise the participation of former combatants. If the Commission has the legal power to compel attendance and testimony, this offers a solid foundation to attempt truth recovery. In addition, the "carrot" of a formal amnesty process in return for full disclosure may also encourage some actors to come forward. As noted above, the guarantees of non-prosecution from information which was given in the Bloody Sunday Inquiry and the Commission to uncover the remains of the disappeared were seen as vital elements of the broader truth-recovery process. Of much more importance potentially would be the efforts at discussion and persuasion between former combatants, their organisations and individuals or groups in whom they have confidence and trust. In this vein, the Commission could draw to some extent on the Internal Investigations option to explore creative ways in which relationships might be developed in order to maximise the potential for truth recovery from those constituencies.

Finally, the Commission could be faced with the challenge of maximising participation by institutions that, although not necessarily directly involved in committing acts of violence, may nonetheless have useful insights into the Commission's broader work on the causes, nature, context, and consequences of violence. Some such institutions may be reluctant to participate. For example, in South Africa there was a lively and heated debate as to whether the judiciary should come before the SATRC (Dyzenhaus 1998). With such institutions, and with others such as non-security-focused government departments, the churches, business, educational establishments and authorities, the media, and other major social institutions, ensuring their participation (without resort to subpoena where possible) will require nuanced and delicate discussions about the role and function of a truth-recovery commission and the importance of their contribution to the work of that commission and to the future of the jurisdiction.

Personnel
As mentioned above, the Commissioners appointed should include either an entirely international membership, or a mixture of respected local and international figures, but with a chairperson and deputy chairperson of impeccable international reputation. To build confidence, the Commissioners should be appointed through a transparent and public nomination process. The Commission would also have to be assisted by sufficient numbers of suitably qualified staff including lawyers, researchers, investigators, psychologists and psychiatrists, an information and public relations office, and related administrative and technical support.

Resources
A truth-recovery commission would be expensive. However, as suggested above, with appropriate planning and stewardship, it should be possible to have a truth-recovery commission which covers the entire spectrum of the conflict cost less than the Bloody Sunday Tribunal, which was focused on one event.

Timeframe
Three to four years.

Outcomes
The expected outcomes include an official in-depth truth-recovery process, a report with conclusions of its investigation and a series of recommendations (including recommendations concerning reparations for victims), and an oversight mechanism to ensure implementation of those recommendations. Other associated outcomes might include the other elements of HTR's work, such as a museum or other memorials, educational and storytelling programmes, art and drama exhibitions, a Day of Reflection and so forth.

Option Five - A Commission of Historical Clarification

Introduction
The fifth option discussed by the HTR Truth Recovery and Acknowledgement Sub Group was a Commission of Historical Clarification. A Commission of Historical Clarification would differ from a truth commission in a number of ways. It would have a different mandate and approach. The focus would be predominantly a historical one on the causes of conflict in and about Northern Ireland. While the Commission of Historical Clarification could take individual submissions, it would not necessarily report on all of them. If the Commission did decide to report on individual cases, its task would not be to assign legal or indeed individual culpability. To that end, such a commission would have much less emphasis on either victims or those who had been involved in acts of past violence. Rather, the focus would be on devising an independent, authoritative, historical narrative about what occurred during the conflict in and about Northern Ireland and why, in order to encourage a broader sense of collective (rather than individual) responsibility for what occurred.

Rationale
The primary rationale for this style of truth recovery would be that, for whatever combination of social, political or ideological reasons, the post-conflict transition concerning the conflict in and about Northern Ireland could not sustain a full-blown truth commission. In the absence of reverting to the "do nothing further" option with regard to some form of official body undertaking a truth-recovery process, a Commission of Historical Clarification might prove a more acceptable vehicle. The Commission would be tasked with adding clarity to analysis and investigation of recent events through exploration of historical roots of conflict. It would be premised on the fact that, without addressing history (and conflicted interpretations of that history), the individuals, communities, and societies affected by the conflict in and about Northern Ireland cannot fully understand more recent events or indeed move beyond those events. While the Commission may seek to clarify unaddressed incidents/cases, this would be in the context of placing them within a historical narrative rather than shaping them through legal initiatives such as an amnesty for those who committed such acts, or indeed recommendations for prosecutions or reparations for individual victims. The Commission and its staff would comprise primarily researchers and historians rather than lawyers or professionals skilled in supporting victims.

Process
A Commission would be established independent from the two governments, but with their financial backing. The Commissioners could be either international or local or a combination of the two and specialists in Irish/British history and politics. They would, however, be individuals whose collective reputations for objectivity and scholarly rigour would command widespread support for the Commission's final report as an authoritative account of the conflict and its causes. As the Commission would have no legal powers, it would not require new legislation to set it up. The Commission would be supported by a relatively small staff of research and administrative/technical support.

The Commission would invite written and oral submissions from any individuals, groups, communities or institutions involved in the conflict in and about Northern Ireland. Where necessary, they and their staff would engage in a process of community outreach in order to hear at first hand the experiences of local people affected by the conflict in and about Northern Ireland. The Commission could also invite oral public submissions to its plenary sessions. All of the evidence coming forward to the Commission would be done on a completely voluntary basis, as the Commission would not have the power to subpoena witness or access official documentation.

Following the collection of information from these primary sources, these accounts would be verified against all available secondary sources (court and coroners' records, media accounts, academic, and policy publications). Once this information had been properly collated and verified as much as possible, the writing of the Commission report would begin.

The Commission report would most likely be written in at least two volumes. One of these volumes would focus on the broader narrative of the conflict in and about Northern Ireland and its causes, the other might detail the individual cases submitted to or discussed by the Commission. The Commission report could also contain recommendations to the two governments as to how those killed or injured in the conflict in and about Northern Ireland should be best remembered.

Option 5: Commission of Historical Clarification

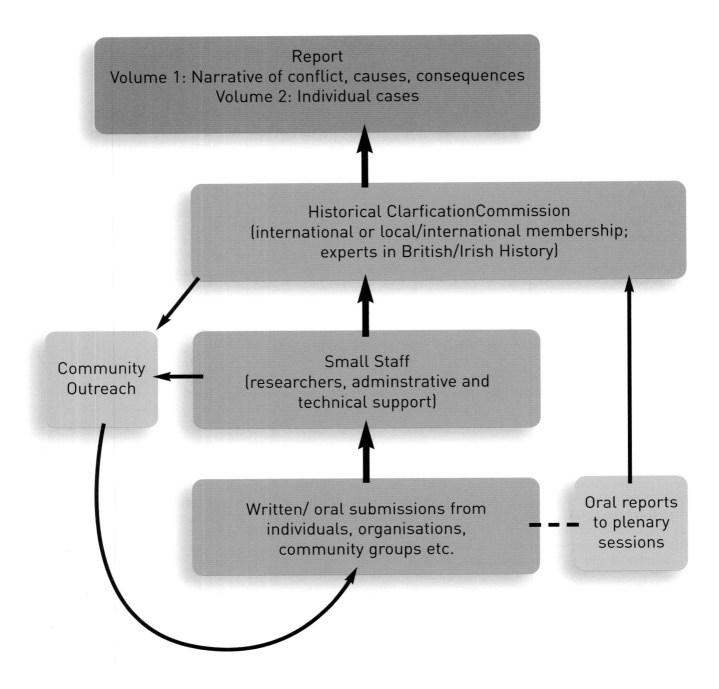

Strengths and opportunities
The strengths and opportunities of a Commission of Historical Clarification as a vehicle of truth recovery were thematised under the following headings.

The need for a definitive official historical account of the conflict
As was discussed above, competing claims concerning the history of any period of communal violence may serve as an impediment to political and social progress even long after a conflict has finished. Long-held grudges, some of them of dubious historical accuracy, have often been deployed as the justification of renewed conflict in troubled jurisdictions (e.g. Majstorovic 1997). An objective, official account of the historical causes of the conflict as well as a detailed narrative clof events would make the denial of responsibility for the conflict from any of the relevant individual or institutional players much more difficult to sustain.

Less likely to generate intense political opposition
Given the reduced legal powers of a Commission of Historical Clarification, it would arguably generate less intense political opposition than a fully fledged truth commission. Although there are undoubtedly individuals and organisations that would bridle at the suggestion that the origins of the conflict in and about Northern Ireland were not monocausal (i.e. the cause which best fits their own political analysis), such opposition would possibly be somewhat muted by the historical and scholarly rather than legal approach of such a Commission.

Capacity to generate a public debate concerning the past
Despite its limitations, a Commission of Historical Clarification would still arguably be able to generate a considerable level of social and political debate concerning the past in Northern Ireland. Other, not-dissimilar initiatives such as the Opsahl Commission[241] or the hearings associated with the Patten Commission on policing, or the Opsahl Commission have arguably played an important role in generating a public debate about the past and the mistakes and abuses which have occurred. Certainly, the heated debates heard by the Patten Commissioners concerning the history of the RUC in both nationalist and unionist communities highlighted two completely distinct historical narratives, both of which were arguably true (Mulcahy 2005). Even the process of hearing and recording such competing narratives is sometimes a valuable process in itself in challenging all sides to consider that others may have had a totally different experience. For many people who attended those hearings, they represented their first opportunity to tell their stories with regard to policing, and the power and conviction of feeling certainly impressed itself upon the Patten Commissioners listening (Shearing 2001). In a similar vein, a Commission of Historical Clarification would generate a lively public debate and, if properly managed, allow a diverse range of individuals, groups, and communities to make their contribution to that debate.

Weaknesses and obstacles
The weakness and obstacles identified were as follows.

Danger of an arid scholarly process
If the danger of a truth commission is that it may become too legalistic in tone and in the way it conducts is business, the parallel danger of a Commission of Historical Clarification is that it could appear too scholarly and removed from the realities of either the conflict in and about Northern Ireland or the transition. Thus, for example, historians, economists, or political scientists could spend considerable energies arguing about the "real" levels of discrimination against Catholics in the old Stormont era, or the "true" intentions of the Dublin government towards the North in the early 1970s, or the myriad of other academic preoccupations with regard to the conflict in and about Northern Ireland. While such questions are, of course, important and of interest, it would not be difficult to envisage the process becoming an increasingly arid series of technical debates which might only sustain the interest of the political elites.

Insufficient focus on the needs of victims from a "top-down" process
A related difficulty with a Commission of Historical Commission as envisaged is that it is a process that pays insufficient attention to the specific needs of victims. While the process would include the opportunity for individual written and perhaps oral submissions, and these might appear in a separate volume of the ensuing report, the focus of the Commission would be on the broader themes and collective causes of conflict rather than on providing definitive "truths" concerning individual cases in order to assist individual healing or closure. Even if the community outreach hearings were handled imaginatively, it would be hard to shake off the impression that this was other than an elites-driven and elites-focused process. It would be difficult to engender a sense of genuine ownership amongst victims in any such process.

Lack of legal powers would hamper truth recovery
A further potential difficulty with this option would be its lack of legal powers of investigation, subpoena or amnesty. Whilst there might conceivably be a degree of moral pressure applied to those who had been involved in acts of violence to hand over documents or come forward (if, for example, other rival individuals or organisations did likewise), the lack of either a "carrot" in the shape of an amnesty or a "stick" in the shape of legal powers of compulsion would be a serious impediment to the process.

---

[241] The Opsahl Commission was established as a "Citizens Inquiry" in 1992 into the ways forward for Northern Ireland. The independent, international commission was chaired by the widely respected Norwegian human-rights lawyer Prof Torkel Opsahl. The Commission sought and indeed achieved a large number of submissions concerning different aspects of politics in the jurisdiction and also held a series of high profile public hearings. Although opinions vary as to the impact of the report, the process of the hearings and the weight and range of the submissions were certainly evidence that the Commission had sparked serious debate not just amongst Northern Ireland's politicians but throughout civil society.

Research fatigue
A final impediment to such a process would again relate to the scholarly approach of such a Commission. Relative to its size, Northern Ireland is the most academically researched region in the world (O'Leary & McGarry 1995). There are literally hundreds of books and thousands of academic articles written on every aspect of the conflict in and about Northern Ireland. Given the questionable capacity of such a Commission to unearth "new" facts through first-hand testimony or previously suppressed documentation being made available, the Commission would inevitably be shaping its views from existing secondary sources. While there is a case for the production of a definitive and objective historical account of the conflict which is widely accessible, this was arguably achieved by those who wrote the history curricula for Northern Ireland school children at least a decade ago. The Commission might arguably, therefore, raise public expectations unreasonably that it was going to produce a "new" definitive truth document which many school children might well regard as "old hat" once they read and digest it.

Personnel
The Commission would include a range of historical and/or political experts and scholars and a small staff of researchers and related support.

Resources
A Commission of Historical Clarification would be a relatively cheap option, given the lack of legal involvement. Although it would ideally be funded by government (or the two governments), it could probably also access funds from elsewhere.

Timeframe
One to two years.

Outcomes
A final report which would seek to offer (as definitively as possible) an account of the causes of the conflict with the possibility of another volume detailing individual cases.

CHAPTER FIVE

Truth Recovery, Trust and Political Generosity

It has not been the intent of Healing Through Remembering (HTR) to offer a definitive view as to how or whether Northern Ireland should have some form of a truth-recovery process. Indeed, as is detailed in Chapter Four, the option of "drawing a line under the past" and thereby taking a conscious decision not to undertake any new process of truth recovery was viewed as sufficiently important to warrant a full analysis alongside other options for truth recovery. Rather, the purpose of this document is to provide as much relevant detail and context as possible in order to inform the broader debate concerning truth recovery regarding the conflict in and about Northern Ireland. In particular, HTR has sought to avoid the discussion on truth recovery becoming narrowed to the question of whether or not a South African-style truth and reconciliation commission is a "good idea". The intention has been to deepen and broaden discussions on the topic.

In discussing the various options for truth recovery in Chapter Four, we have sought to outline a range of practical issues which would inevitably arise as a result of any such process. Thus, matters such as the makeup and remit of each truth-recovery option; how each would impact upon victims, former combatants, security forces or other institutions or organisations; whether hearings would be held in public and private and so forth, are explored in each option. Much of the detail in operationalising each of these options would quite properly generate considerable debate. Throughout the document, we have also sought to explore some of the broader values or issues of principle around which any truth-recovery process must be framed. Thus, it would also be an early task in setting up any of the truth-recovery options to outline the principles and values which would inform their work.[242] Some would presumably cause little controversy. Thus, principles such as the primacy of international law, the prioritising of the needs of victims, the independence of any truth-recovery mechanism from the state, ex-combatant groups, political parties or civil society would conceivably meet with little opposition. Others however, such as the difficult relationship between accountability and incentivising those with information to come forward (including the question of amnesties and prosecutions), or the extent to which any truth-recovery process would contribute to individual or societal reconciliation - these could conceivably be more difficult principles around which to reach consensus. It is our hope that the various pros and cons of the arguments as to how these and other thorny issues might be resolved can be informed by the contents of this report. In this last section we would like to make a few final points which may be of relevance concerning the creation of a space for this debate, the assumed "ugliness" of truth, the role of trust, and the creation of political generosity.

For many years preceding the ceasefires in Northern Ireland, it became something of a truism that the conflict in and about Northern Ireland was so multifaceted as to be practically insoluble. At times, some of us who have lived and worked in the jurisdiction appeared to take a silent pleasure in the complexity of our situation and to acquiesce in the intractability of our conflict. As has been argued elsewhere, the prolonged nature of the conflict in and about Northern Ireland, and its deep historical, political, cultural, and social origins, arguably became reified in some quarters into a tired resignation that little could be done to achieve change (McEvoy & Ellison 2003). Thankfully, such pessimism was not shared by all, many of whom took considerable risks over the past fifteen years in seeking to achieve and sustain the peace process.

At times, one detects a similar pessimism with regard to the question of truth recovery regarding the conflict in and about Northern Ireland. Such a view suggests that truth recovery is just too difficult, politically impractical, and emotionally challenging even to discuss properly. As was noted previously, concerns that the timing was not right for such a widespread debate appear to have played a major part in the British government's decision to suspend their efforts at exploring the issue in 2005. It could be contended, however, that the process which led to the production of this report is a practical counterweight to such a sense of pessimism. The HTR Truth Recovery and Acknowledgement Sub Group includes members who are strong supporters of different styles of truth recovery. It also includes members who are opposed to the establishment of any new truth-recovery initiatives at all, and still others who might be best described as agnostic. Despite those different positions, and their very diverse backgrounds, the group members listed at the beginning of the report have collectively engaged in the lively and spirited process of debate and discussion that resulted in this document. If individuals from such different constituencies can engage in such a process, then surely this suggests that individuals and communities affected by the conflict in and about Northern Ireland are well capable of a similarly reasoned debate.

---

[242] For a useful outworking of similar values and principles see e.g. EHSSB Trauma Advisory Panel (2006).

Much of the discussion which went into the production of this report has been informed by an awareness that the debate on truth recovery cannot be divorced from politics more generally and from the ongoing attempts to re-establish and sustain a local power-sharing Executive and Assembly in particular. The specific arguments for and against truth recovery in the context of attempting to get Sinn Féin, the DUP, and the other major parties to share power are explored in some detail in Chapter Four. More generally, however, truth recovery has direct consequences for the body politic of any society which undertakes such a process. Indeed, apart from the desire for individual healing and reconciliation amongst individuals directly affected by violence, the most oft-stated rationale for engagement in truth recovery is to assist with the societal and political process of healing and reconciliation for jurisdictions emerging from conflict (Biggar 2001; Hamber 2002; Hayner 2001; Ignatieff 1998; Wilson 2001).

With regard to the conflict in and about Northern Ireland, any process of truth recovery would inevitably become a site wherein competing versions of history would be strongly advocated by the various protagonists. The term "whataboutery",[243] apparently originally coined by former Catholic Archbishop Cathal Cardinal Daly, well captures the longstanding tradition concerning Northern Ireland of using past sins visited by either community (or indeed the British or Irish state) upon each other in order to avoid uncomfortable questions about one's own past role or indeed contemporary responsibilities for making peace. For some of those who are doubtful as to the merit of truth recovery, this is precisely their concern. They fear that any such mechanism would provide a platform for further propagation of such discussion – in effect, a process for the institutionalisation of "whataboutery".

The counter argument to such concerns is that it is precisely through the institutionalisation of truth recovery that societies may provide a regulated space wherein such competing versions of histories may be asserted and, more importantly, tested. Forging shared narratives of the past is a key element to making political agreements possible (Forsberg 2001; Hunt 2004). One of the elements that characterise political cultures which promote variations of "whataboutery" is the lack of an objective and authoritative source of truth.[244] In truth recovery, the contest concerning the events of the past is not a political "free-for-all". Instead, formalised truth recovery usually entails a systematic attempt to uncover, research, record, and validate as much as possible what actually happened. An objective and respected source of truth narrows the capacity of politicians, ex-combatants, victims or other actors to simply assert partial or untrue versions of history. Indeed, the very process of constructing such an authoritative source of truth, albeit one which would undoubtedly be fiercely contested in the making, could make a significant contribution to the broader maturation of the political culture of the jurisdiction. Part of the value of truth recovery is precisely that whatever mechanism is chosen becomes a key site of struggle and contest, albeit a regulated one.[245]

A further, related theme which has received considerable emphasis throughout this document has been the fact that "ugly truths" would be likely to emerge or be confirmed in any process of truth recovery. Quite apart from the potential of political destabilisation, in a conflict which has seen 3,700 deaths and the popular held view that there were 40,000 injuries, further detailed examination of the shattered lives behind these statistics would inevitably be a deeply painful and traumatic process for many thousands of families involved. As has been detailed in this report and persistently argued by influential actors such as the Police Service of Northern Ireland (PSNI) Chief Constable Sir Hugh Orde, for example, in explaining the rationale for the establishment

---

243 Fealty (2005) has described the term "whataboutery" thus: "Some define it as the often multiple blaming and finger pointing that goes on between communities in conflict. Political differences are marked by powerful emotional (often tribal) reactions as opposed to creative conflict over policy and issues...both communities use the terrible burden of past events to lay obstacles in the way of peace. Evasion may not be the intention but it is the obvious effect. It occurs when individuals are confronted with a difficult or uncomfortable question. The respondent retrenches his/her position and rejigs the question, being careful to pick open a sore point on the part of questioner's 'tribe'. He/she then fires the original query back at the inquirer. Historical subjects can be the worst. Rational perspective disappears and opponents are forced to assume moral responsibility for their community's past sins. The substance of the issue is foregone for an emotional power play that comprises the solipsistic concerns of the participants, with little regard for fact or quality of argument"
(Available at http://www.sluggerotoole.com/archives/2005/02/glossary_what_i.php).
244 See generally Osiel (2000) and Cohen (2001).
245 Justice Albie Sachs, former South African Constitutional Court Judge and anti-apartheid activist, has well captured this with regard to the work of the South African Truth and Reconciliation Commission in his own country. "I think the TRC Report is a brilliant document. I loved it because it was so uneven, it was rough, it had its seams, you could see the stitching, and it was authentic, it was real. It was not one of these boring, homogenised commissioned reports that are read only by a few experts. It contained the passion, the variety, and even the contradictions of the process itself. There are a number of findings that I did not feel all that comfortable with, but that was not important. The important thing was that in the process, the TRC put its findings down on the table, and was itself a protagonist, it was not simply recording history. It was a very active participant in the process. The TRC was a site of struggle, an ideological, conceptual, political, emotional, personal struggle" Memorandum submitted by Justice Albie Sachs, Appendix 4, Evidence to the Northern Ireland Affairs Select Committee (NIAC 2005: Ev 262).

of the Historical Enquiries Team (Orde 2005), many families simply want to know the truth about what happened to their loved ones and why. That said, no one involved with the HTR Initiative underestimates the real anguish that some of the broader truth recovery options outlined earlier may entail.

However, as has been demonstrated in other processes of truth recovery, such harrowing accounts are likely to be accompanied by other compelling tales of bravery, self-sacrifice, generosity, forgiveness, and so forth. Even in the most horrific of circumstances, such as the aftermath of genocide in Rwanda, wherein the capacity of human beings for almost unimaginable brutality might appear psychologically overwhelming for a nation trying to reconstruct itself, other more redemptive tales of individual heroic actions and great personal bravery have emerged as Rwandans have struggled to come to terms with the past (Gourevitch 1999; Hatzfeld 2005). Of course, such "up-lifting" narratives cannot and should not be viewed as offsetting the horror that has gone before. Arguably, however, they do underline that in exploring even the darkest events in human history, therein will lie at least some seeds of hope for the future.

For those who advocate for truth recovery regarding the conflict in and about Northern Ireland, an additional objective of stimulating debate on the topic is to broaden ownership of and responsibility for the process of conflict transformation. In stark terms, they would argue that the necessity for political arrangements which accommodate competing political and national traditions cannot be understood unless a serious debate takes place on how the failures of the past contributed directly to a thirty-year conflict. Beyond the obvious armed actors and the organisations in Northern Ireland discussed in this report who may have a case to answer for their role in the conflict in and about Northern Ireland (e.g. politicians, judiciary, Public Prosecution Service, government departments, the media, educational establishments, churches), other significant organisations and individuals in Britain, the Republic or elsewhere remain largely inured to their previous history or potential role in such a process. As Hamber (1999) has argued previously, some may have covertly supported state or paramilitary violence merely by their silence or disrespect for the dead of the other community. For those who advocate it, truth recovery is also designed to responsibilise those from outside the jurisdiction who played a part in the conflict in and about Northern Ireland. For example, for those who were involved directly in armed actions, this may mean telling what they know about events in which they were involved. More generally, however, there is arguably a broader process required in, for example, both the Republic of Ireland and Britain to consider the impact that the conflict in and about Northern Ireland had on the political, social, economic, and indeed cultural life of both states.[246]

Two final issues which are of relevance in the consideration of truth recovery regarding the conflict in and about Northern Ireland are the interrelated themes of trust and political generosity.

As in many other examples of conflict transformation, the absence of trust has been widely viewed as core to the stop-start nature of the peace process in the jurisdiction (Peatling 2004). In broad terms, most of the political parties at different times have expressed their distrust of the British government. Unionists fear the meddlesome intent of the Irish government. Unionists have also had longstanding concerns as to republicans' commitment to permanently ending violence (Farrington 2006). Many republicans and nationalists, on the other hand, contend that this latter concern (which focused for so long upon the decommissioning of paramilitary weapons) masked a fundamental unwillingness to share power with Catholics (Rafter 2006). When one adds to this the manifest concerns between the different major political parties within their own political communities and constituencies (e.g. between the Ulster Unionists and the DUP, Sinn Féin and the SDLP or Sinn Féin and the Coalition partners in the Republic) the absence of trust can appear somewhat daunting.

Despite these longstanding tensions, those tasked with directing the interminable negotiations (together with the political protagonists themselves) have deployed an impressive array of strategies to circumnavigate the lack of trust and sustain the process thus far. These have included the deployment of independent and/or international involvement in the most sensitive of areas, complex sequencing procedures concerning key proposals, the production (and re-drafting) of a host of legislative initiatives as evidence of intent on the part of the governments, as well as the darker arts of political manoeuvring.

As discussed previously, most of the various protagonists have also developed skills in their capacity to "stretch" their different political constituencies. Dixon (2002, 2004) has detailed the deployment of a number of political techniques (by both governments and other actors) in the process which have included what he

---

[246] For useful illustrations of this kind of work in the British context, see for example the work of the Warrington Project in developing curriculum and other materials so that British school children might better understand the causes and context of the conflict in and about Northern Ireland http://www.childrenforpeace.org/index.asp. For a discussion on the Republic of Ireland see Cleary (2002).

refers to as "choreography and play-acting", "smoke screens", "kite-flying", "constructive ambiguity", "necessary fictions", and "political theatre". He concludes that while there are obviously real constraints which restrict the ability of politicians to be truthful, "[t]he point also occurs at which manipulation becomes counterproductive to the peace process because the public is no longer able to make the distinction between truth and lies" (Dixon 2002: 740). For advocates of truth recovery, it is precisely the capacity to distinguish between the truth and the lies of the past that is required to build the basis for a stable political future.

The constituency which has apparently lost most confidence in the political process is unionism (Aughey 2002; Farrington 2006).[247] In tandem with this apparent political disillusionment, the different variants of unionism and loyalism have also expressed serious misgivings about the role of truth recovery (EPIC 2004; Lundy & McGovern 2005a, 2006; Unionist Group 2006). As was detailed in Chapter Four, such concerns have included the notion of truth as a "Republican Trojan Horse", contributing to "nationalist revisionism", playing into nationalist cultures of victimhood – all of which are manifestations to a greater or lesser extent of a lack of trust in the "other".

However, one might also argue that this sense of ambivalence regarding truth recovery is more complex and suggests a lack of confidence or trust in "self" and an apparent fear that loyalists or unionists may lose more as a result of any truth-recovery process. For example, the EPIC document on loyalist attitudes to truth recovery speaks explicitly of their concern that such a process might contribute to what they regard as ongoing attempts to stigmatise and criminalise loyalism, most of which they regard as historically emanating from "middle unionism" (EPIC 2004).

As noted previously, the argument advanced by the DUP against a truth commission in particular is that it would "serve to hold accountable only those who served in the Crown Forces while terrorists could hide behind the cloak of anonymity" (Democratic Unionist Party 2003: 9).

With regard to the Ulster Unionist Party, while they remain at the time of writing engaged in a process of internal discussion on the issue of truth recovery, individual members of that party have also indicated a lack of confidence as a key impediment to truth recovery.[248] Each of these sources suggests that the lack of trust with regard to truth in the unionist community is more complex than simply being directed against nationalists or republicans.

As was discussed in Chapter One, both of the main nationalist parties have declared themselves more or less in favour of some form of organised truth-recovery process. That said, a lack of trust on the nationalist side is no less palpable. The relevant Sinn Féin discussion document calls for a debate on the timing and purpose of truth-recovery processes. However, it also talks of "genuine doubts and fears concerning the issue of truth" and notes that "the expectations of truth commissions are almost always greater than what they can eventually achieve" and stipulates that "there should be no hierarchy of victims" and also that "humility and generosity should inform the parties seeking to reach agreement on this issue. It should not be about getting one over on one's opponents" (Sinn Féin 2003: 3-6). Similarly, the suggestion by the SDLP that a victims' forum should be the body tasked with designing any truth-recovery process is underpinned by a number of principles including again that there should be no hierarchy of victims and that "any truth-finding process must be completely independent of all parties to the conflict, including the state" (SDLP 2005: 2-3). Beyond the two main parties, other important voices within nationalism and republicanism have expressed deep cynicism about any such initiative. For example, the critical comments discussed earlier from both Brian Feeney and Danny Morrison regarding truth recovery are illustrative of a broader lack of trust both of the motives of those who had proposed the establishment of a truth commission, and of the willingness of the main players within unionism or the state to participate with good faith.[249] Nationalists and republicans, too, appear concerned that victims from their community might not be treated fairly by any such process.

[247] For example, there is now much research that suggests that despite the lack of empirical evidence that Catholics have materially benefited disproportionately from the peace process and Protestants have suffered proportionately, such a belief is widely held in sections of the Protestant community. See Cairns, Van Til & Williamson (2003), Leonard (2004), Deloitte (2004), Healy (2005), and CAJ (2006 in press) for an overview of this debate.

[248] "Many people who lost close relatives and friends wish to talk about their experiences. They want to be frank, open and confident with people around them but this is only possible when the setting and context are carefully and sensitively established. Truth is subjective we all know, and there is a serious risk that inquiries seeking forensic or objective truth would prove partial, inconclusive and unlikely to seriously address the hurts in society" (Unionist Group 2006: 1).

[249] "...there's not a pup's chance of a truth and reconciliation commission working here...What would happen if people had amnesty granted and then came in to testify chapter and verse on currently elected Sinn Féin politicians? Or DUP politicians? How many years would it continue as layer after layer was peeled away? Do you think current PSNI and former RUC personnel would allow MI5, MI6 and FRU personnel to get off scot free? Do you think the British government would contemplate for an instant exposing MI5, MI6 or FRU to public scrutiny? Could there ever be any approach to truth about what went on here without such exposure? Of course not." From B. Feeney, "An NI Truth Inquiry Would Never Work", *Irish News*, 26 February 2004. See also D. Morison "A Truth that Tells a Lie", *Andersonstown News*, 24 February 2004.

To varying degrees, therefore, difficulties remain concerning a lack of trust with regard to the issue of truth recovery in both of the principal communities in Northern Ireland. Both communities manifest distrust as to the willingness or capacity of the "other" (and in the case of republicans and nationalists at least, the British state is considered an "other" as well) to engage in any such process with bona fides. Both also demonstrate fears that their victims or their community might be treated unfairly or might lose more. Whilst such concerns may be more pronounced in the unionist community in tandem with other indicators of more general political disenchantment, one should not underestimate the political obstacles presented by the lack of trust amongst nationalists or republicans, too.

In other contexts, the bonds developed between former enemies during the process of tortuous negotiations have been viewed as crucial in the development of political trust (e.g. Spitz & Chaskalson 1999; Lieberfeld 1999). In the Northern Ireland context, the development of such relationships of trust has been hampered by a number of factors, including the cumbersome ways in which some of the negotiations have been conducted (Dixon 2006). However, while trust between the main political actors may be some way off, it is possible to explore conditions which might contribute to a culture of greater political generosity amongst the different protagonists.

A theme which runs through some of the discussions on the work of the South African Truth and Reconciliation Commission (SATRC) is the notion that individual and national engagement in such a process contributed to a greater spirit of political generosity amongst some political protagonists (Boraine 2000; Hamber 2003b). One of the by-products of the engagement was to inculcate a measure of humility amongst the political elites, a diminution in absolute moral certainties concerning the past actions of "their side" and a concurrent greater willingness to see beyond the victimhood of one's own community to countenance the suffering of the "other" (Boraine 2000; Govier & Verwoerd 2002; South African Truth and Reconciliation Commission 1998). Political generosity does not diminish the cut and thrust of normal adversarial politics. It does, however, speak to the capacity to accept the common humanity of one's political adversaries and to treat them individually and politically with the civility and respect which that humanity demands, regardless of their past deeds (Leach & Sabatier 2005).

Despite appearances to the contrary, all of the main political actors in Northern Ireland have shown themselves capable of generosity to political opponents, both within and without their own communities. Often such actions have been taken despite criticism from within their own political bloc in particular.[250]

For example, the origin of the peace process has been widely attributed to the determination of John Hume to pursue the Hume/Adams dialogue with Sinn Féin, despite the potential political cost to his party and the opprobrium that was heaped upon him from many quarters during the most difficult days of those negotiations (Murray 1998). Republicans would point to a number of concrete and symbolic compromises, including taking their seats in the "partitionist assembly" at Stormont, or former Sinn Féin Lord Mayor Alex Maskey laying a wreath at the Cenotaph in 2002 as acts of political generosity (Adams 2004).[251] Similarly, with regard to the Ulster Unionist Party, the various efforts at power-sharing with Sinn Féin prior to complete IRA decommissioning, and in the face of considerable internal and external opposition, are widely regarded as politically generous acts (McDonald 2001; Dixon 2006). As for the Democratic Unionist Party, which on the face of it has defined its political identity by its intransigence and unwillingness to compromise: in fact it, too, would frame its proximity to a political deal with Sinn Féin in 2004/2005 as politically generous.[252] Smaller parties, such as the Progressive Unionist Party or the Alliance Party, would also point to acts such as their respective support for funding towards the Belfast St Patrick's Day Parade or support of a Sinn Féin candidate for mayor as acts of a similar nature.[253]

---

[250] From amongst the armed actors too, each of their significant moves in the peace process have been in the face of some opposition from their own constituencies. Thus, for example, the decisions relating to the calling of the original IRA and loyalist ceasefires, the IRA decommissioning of its weaponry or the reduction in security measures or security force numbers, as well as of course the changes to policing wrought under the Patten Commission in light of the changed context; all of these moves have met with institutional or organisational resistance from within (see generally, English 2004; Wood 2006; Mulcahy 2005). While some might balk at the description of these moves as politically generous, they did entail some considerable efforts at managing the discontent within their own ranks and they were designed at least in part to contribute to the broader social good.

[251] Maskey's initiative in particular was widely credited as a significant act of political generosity. It was described by the strident anti-republican critic Kevin Myers as "generous and courageous" (An Irishman's Diary, *Irish Times*, 16 July 2002). The *Irish News* (3 June 2003) referred to it as "one of the most significant gestures of reconciliation witnessed in Northern Ireland in recent years" and the *Belfast Telegraph* described it as a "historic" gesture which gave "hope for the future" ("Maskey Lays Somme Wreath", *Belfast Telegraph*, 1 July 2002 and "Giving Hope to the Future", *Belfast Telegraph* 6 July 2002,).

[252] "Dr Paisley said that if the IRA gave up its weapons and abandoned its criminal activity he would have to 'swallow hard' to do business with republicans. 'Once they quit their terrorist path, I will have to do a good deal of swallowing' he said 'I'll have to do a good deal of biting my lip in future days'" (*BBC News*, 3 December 2005, http://news.bbc.co.uk/1/hi/northern_ireland/4067175.stm).

[253] See "The Changing Face of Politics", *Irish News*, 16 January 2006

Of course, more cynical commentators would immediately point to other selfish or strategic motivations which may have influenced some or all of these actions. This may well be true. Indeed, it is arguably an intrinsic element of the process of politics to frame political movement or shifts in positions which appear to favour one's opponents as being in the strategic interest of one's own constituency, or as resonating with one's existing political ideology.[254] That said, each of these moves by the various actors required facing opposition within their own constituencies. They also required an acknowledgement, sometimes unstated, that movement on the part of the actors themselves was required in order to accommodate their political opponents for the broader good of society. While they may not always have been framed in terms of political generosity, they do at least speak to the potential that such generosity is at least possible.

As was noted above, a key concern from a political management perspective with regard to truth recovery regarding the conflict in and about Northern Ireland is that the re-examination of the violence of the past would hamper the capacity of the political parties to re-establish and sustain a power-sharing executive. In effect, it would narrow the potential for political generosity. Certainly, quite a number of the individuals and political parties in the Executive and Assembly would be likely to experience a degree of political embarrassment concerning their past acts if a rigorous truth-recovery mechanism were to be established. For example, the armed actions of loyalists, republicans, and the security forces; histories of discrimination and exclusion; historical relationships between constitutional political parties and paramilitarism; an exploration of the consequences of political and religious rhetoric – these and many other themes likely to feature in truth recovery would suggest that such discomfort would be shared amongst many of the political parties.

For those who advocate truth recovery, this is exactly the point. Truth recovery exposes the myth of blamelessness (Ignatieff 1998). This is its contribution to the body politic. It is in significant part through engagement in a process in which no-one will emerge untarnished that the possibility for increased political generosity is established. Greater political generosity may, in time, lead to the workable levels of trust which are in turn required to maintain the political process. In the long run, the sustainability of a political process which is free from political violence will be the best benchmark to judge whether or not we have succeeded in making peace with the past.

The need to engage with that past is not just a question of politics; it is a question of morality. While there are inevitable differences about whether a truth-recovery process is feasible or not, or whether one mechanism might be more effective than another, the reality is that all sections of the community contain victims who have been deeply affected by the conflict in and about Northern Ireland. Indeed, many of the leading political actors in Northern Ireland share the experience of having been victimised, or have been involved in or witnessed traumatic events or lost friends or family as a direct result of the conflict in and about Northern Ireland. Many victims from all sides have indicated that they wish to know more about what happened to them or their loved ones and why. In both governments and across all of the main political parties, church organisations, civil society, and elsewhere, there is a widespread consensus on the desirability of processes and structures which prioritise the needs of victims. If we accept that there is a relationship between those needs and truth, then there is a moral imperative for all of us affected by the conflict to engage seriously in a debate on truth recovery. This report from HTR is designed to contribute to that debate.

---

254 Thus for example, the developments in Sinn Féin's position on truth recovery has been framed explicitly in the party's language of transforming the conflict (Sinn Féin 2003). If the DUP were to shift with regard to their position on truth recovery, one might expect some of that discussion to be framed within evangelical Christian notions of truth, forgiveness, and repentance. For a useful discussion of the influence on the latter in the institutional thinking of the DUP see Southern (2005).

Reference List

Adams, G. (2004). *Hope and History: Making Peace in Ireland.* Cork: Brandon Press.

Afzali, A., & Colleton, L. (2003). Constructing Coexistence: A survey of Coexistence Projects in Areas of Ethnic Conflict. In A. Chayes & M. L. Minow, *Imagine Coexistence: Restoring Humanity After Violent Ethnic Conflict.* San Francisco: PON Books/Jossey-Bass, 1-19.

Aguilar, P. (2001). Justice, Politics and Memory in the Spanish Transition. In B. de Brito, G. Enríquez & P. Aguilar (eds), *The Politics of Memory.* Oxford: Oxford University Press.

Amnesty International (1994). *Political Killings in Northern Ireland.* London: Amnesty International.

Anderson, K. (2004). Humanitarian Inviolability in Crisis: The Meaning of Impartiality and Neutrality for U.N. and NGO Agencies Following the 2003-2004 Afghanistan and Iraq Conflicts. *Harvard Human Rights Journal,* 17, 41-74.

Anthony, G., & Mageean, P. (2006). Habits Of Law And Truth Telling In Post-Conflict Northern Ireland: The Story Of Article 2 ECHR. In J. Morison, K. McEvoy & G. Anthony (eds), *Judges, Human Rights and Transition: Essays in Honour of Stephen Livingstone.* Oxford: Oxford University Press.

Ardoyne Commemoration Project (2002). *Ardoyne: The Untold Truth.* Belfast: Beyond the Pale.

Article 19 (2000). Who Wants To Forget? Truth and Access to Information about past Human Rights Violations. http://www.article19.org/pdfs/publications/freedom-of-information-truth-commissions.pdf

Asmal, K. (2000). Truth, Reconciliation and Justice: The South African Experience in Perspective. *Modern Law Review,* 63, 1, 1-24.

Asson, D. (2003). *Never Again: Struggling for Humanness in Postconflict Rwanda And Guatemala.* Unpublished M.A. dissertation. http://www.ptsview.com/thesis/final.pdf

Aughey, A. (2002). The Art and Effect of Political Lying in Northern Ireland. *Irish Political Studies,* 17, 2, 1-16.

Ballengee, M. (1999). The Critical Role of Non-Governmental Organizations in Transitional Justice: A Case Study of Guatemala. *UCLA Journal of International Law and Foreign Affairs,* 4, 2, 477-510.

Barkan, E. (2000). *The Guilt of Nations: Restitution and Negotiating Historical Injustices.* New York: WW Norton.

Barria, L., & Roper, S. (2005). How Effective are International Criminal Tribunals? An Analysis of the ICTY and the ICTR. *The International Journal of Human Rights,* 9, 3, 349-368.

Barron, H. (2003). *Interim Report of the Report of the Independent Commission of Inquiry into the Dublin and Monaghan Bombings.* http://cain.ulst.ac.uk/events/dublin/barron03.pdf

Bass, G. (2000). *Stay the Hand of Vengeance: The Politics of War Crimes Tribunals.* Princeton: Princeton University Press.

Bassiouni, M. (1996). Searching for Peace and Achieving Justice: The Need for Accountability. *Law & Contemporary Problems,* 59, 9-28.

Beevor, A. (2001). *The Spanish Civil War.* New York: Random House.

Bell, C., & Keenan, J. (2004). Human Rights Nongovernmental Organizations and the Problems of Transition. *Human Rights Quarterly,* 26, 2, 330-374.

Bell, C., & Keenan, J. (2005). Lost on the Way Home: The Right to Life in Northern Ireland. *Journal of Law and Society,* 32, 1, 68-89.

Bell, C. (2003). Dealing with the Past in Northern Ireland. *Fordham International Law Journal*, 26, 4, 1095-1147.

Biggar, N. (ed.) (2003). *Burying the Past: Making Peace and Doing Justice after Civil Conflict.* Washington, DC: Georgetown University Press.

Blakeley, G. (2005). Digging Up Spain's Past: Consequences of Truth and Reconciliation. *Democratization*, 12, 1, 44-59.

Bloomfield, K. (1998). *"We Will Remember Them": Report of the Northern Ireland Victims Commissioner.* Belfast: HMSO. The Stationary Office Northern Ireland.

Boed, R. (1999). An Evaluation of The Legality and Efficacy of Lustration as a Tool Of Transitional Justice. *Columbia Journal of Transnational Law*, 37, 357-402.

Boraine, A. (2000). *A Country Unmasked: Inside South Africa's Truth and Reconciliation Commission.* Oxford: Oxford University Press.

Borneman, J. (1997). *Settling Accounts: Violence, Justice, and Accountability in Postsocialist Europe.* Princeton: Princeton University Press.

Borneman, J. (2005). Public Apologies as Performative Redress. *SAIS Review of International Affairs*, 25, 2, 53-66.

Brooks, R. (1999). The Age of Apology. In R. Brooks (ed.) *When Sorry Isn't Enough.* New York: New York University Press.

British Irish Rights Watch (1999). *Deadly Intelligence.* London: British Irish Rights Watch.

British Irish Rights Watch (2003). *British Irish Rights Watch Response to Stevens 3.* http://www.birw.org/BIRW%20response%20to%20Stevens%203.html

Cabrera, R. (1998). Should We Remember? Recovering Historical Memory in Guatemala. In B. Hamber (ed.), *Past Imperfect: Dealing with the Past in Northern Ireland and Societies in Transition.* Derry: INCORE.

Cairns, E., Mallet, J., Lewis, C. A., & Wilson, R. (2003). *Who are the victims? Self-assessed victimhood and the Northern Ireland conflict* (NIO Research and Statistical Series No. 7). Belfast: NIO.

Cairns, E., Van Til, J., & Williamson, A. (2003). *Social Capital, Collectivism-Individualism and Community Background in Northern Ireland: A Report to OFMDFM and Head of the Voluntary & Community Unit of the Department for Social Development.* Coleraine: University of Ulster.

CAJ (1999). *Additional Submission to the Criminal Justice Review (in relation to the Patrick Finucane case), October 1999.* Belfast: Committee on the Administration of Justice. http://www.caj.org.uk/keydocuments.html

CAJ (2006). *Equality in Northern Ireland.* Belfast: Committee on the Administration of Justice.

Campbell, C. (2005). Wars on Terror and Vicarious Hegemons: The UK, International Law, and the Northern Ireland Conflict. *International and Comparative Legal Quarterly*, 54, 2, 321-356.

Campbell, C., Ní Aoláin, F., & Harvey, C. (2003). The Frontiers of Legal Analysis: Reframing the Transition in Northern Ireland. *Modern Law Review*, 66, 3, 317-345.

Cassese, A. (2003). *International Criminal Law.* Oxford: Oxford University Press.

CEH (1999). *Memory of Silence: Report of the Guatemalan Commission of Historical Clarification.* http://shr.aaas.org/guatemala/ceh/report/english/toc.html

Chigara, B. (2002). *Amnesty in International Law.* London: Longman.

Church, C., Visser, A., & Johnson, L. (2004). A Path to Peace or Persistence? The "Single Identity" Approach to Conflict Resolution in Northern Ireland. *Conflict Resolution Quarterly*, 21, 3, 273-294.

Cleary, J. (2002). *Literature, Partition and the Nation-State: Culture and Conflict in Ireland, Israel and Palestine*. Cambridge: Cambridge University Press.

Clio Evaluation Consortium (2002). *Evaluation Of The Core Funding Programme For Victims' / Survivors' Groups*.
http://www.brandonhamber.com/projects_clio.htm

Cohen, S. (2001). *States of Denial*. Cambridge: Polity Press.

Collier, P., Elliott, L., Hegre, H., Hoeffler, A., Reynol-Querol, M & Sambanis, N. (2003). *Breaking the Conflict Trap: Civil War and Development Policy*. Washington DC: World Bank & Oxford University Press.

Corey, A., & Joireman, S. (2004). Retributive Justice: The Gacaca Courts in Rwanda. *African Affairs*, 103, 73-89.

Cory, P. (2004). Cory Collusion Reports into Rosemary Nelson, Pat Finucane, Robert Hamill, Billy Wright, Chief Superintendent Breen and Superintendent Buchanan and Lord Justice and Lady Gibson.
http://cain.ulst.ac.uk/issues/collusion/cory

Crandall, J. (2004). Truth Commissions In Guatemala and Peru: Perpetual Impunity and Transitional Justice Compared. *Peace, Conflict and Development*, 4 April.
http://www.peacestudiesjournal.org.uk/docs/perpetualimpunity.PDF

Crawford, A. (1997). *The Local Governance of Crime: Appeals to Community and Partnerships*. Oxford: Oxford University Press.

Crocker, D. (2000). Truth Commissions, Transitional Justice and Civil Society. In R. Rotberg & D. Thomas (eds), *Truth vs Justice: The Moral Efficacy of Truth Commissions, South Africa and Beyond*. Princeton: Princeton University Press.

Cueva, E. (2004). The Contribution of the Peruvian Truth and Reconciliation Commission to Prosecutions. *Criminal Law Forum*, 15, 1-2, 55-66.

Cunningham, M. (1999). Saying Sorry: The Politics of Apology. *Political Quarterly*, 70, 3, 285-293.

CWRIC (1997) *Recommendations, Personal Justice Denied: Report of the Commission on Wartime Relocation and Internment of Civilians*. Washington DC: University of Washington Press.

Daly, E. (2000). *Mister, Are You a Priest?* Dublin: Four Courts Press.

Daly, E. (2002). Between Punitive and Reconstructive Justice: The Gacaca Courts in Rwanda. *York University Journal of International Law and Politics*, 34, 355-396.

Daly, E. (2003). Reparations In South Africa: A Cautionary Tale. *University of Memphis Law Review*, 33, 367-407.

David, R. (2003). Lustration Laws in Action: The Motives and Evaluation of Lustration Policy in the Czech Republic and Poland (1989–2001). *Law and Social Inquiry*, 28, 2, 387-440.

David, R., & Choi, S. (2005). Victims on Transitional Justice: Lessons from the Reparation of Human Rights Abuses in the Czech Republic. *Human Rights Quarterly*, 27, 2, 392-435.

Davis, M. (2005). Is Spain Recovering its Memory? Breaking the Pacto del Olvido. *Human Rights Quarterly*, 27, 3, 858-880.

De Greiff, P. (ed.) (2006). *The Handbook on Reparations*. Oxford: Oxford University Press.

Deloitte MCS Ltd (2004). *Research to Develop A Methodology for Identifying Areas of Weak Community Infrastructure*. Belfast: Consultation Paper for Department of Social Development.

Democratic Unionist Party (2003). *A Voice for Victims: The Democratic Unionist Party's policy on Innocent victims of terrorism*. Belfast: Democratic Unionist Party.
http://cain.ulst.ac.uk/issues/politics/docs/dup/dup03victims.pdf

Dickinson, L. (2003). The Promise of Hybrid Courts. *American Journal of International Law*, 97, 295-310.

Dixon, P. (2002). Political Skills or Lying and Manipulation? The Choreography of the Peace Process. *Political Studies*, 50, 4, 725-41.

Dixon, P. (2004). 'Peace within the Realms Of The Possible'? David Trimble, Unionist Ideology and Theatrical Politics. *Terrorism and Political Violence*, 16, 3, 462-482.

Dixon, P. (2006). Performing the Northern Ireland Peace Process on the World Stage. *Political Science Quarterly*, 121, 1, 61-92.

Dobell, L. (1997). Silence in Context: Truth and/or Reconciliation in Namibia. *Journal of Southern African Studies*, 23, 2, 371-382.

Drumbl, M. (2000). Sclerosis: Retributive Justice and the Rwandan Genocide. *Punishment & Society*, 2, 3, 287-308.

Drumbl, M. (2001). Punishment, Postgenocide: From Guilt To Shame to Civis in Rwanda. *New York University Law Review*, 75, 5, 1221-1326.

Duggen, A. (2002). The Politics of Apology between Japan and Korea. In M. Bradley & P. Petro (eds), *Truth Claims: Representation and Human Rights*, Rutgers NJ: Rutgers University Press.

Dyzenhaus, D. (1998). *Judging the Judges: Judging Ourselves*. Oxford: Hart.

EHSSB Trauma Advisory Panel (2006). *Dealing with the Past, Looking to the Future: Values, Principles and Recommendations for the Care and Support of Participants in any Potential 'Dealing with the Past' Process*. Belfast: Eastern Health and Social Services Board.

Ellis, M. (1996). Purging the Past: The Current State of Lustration Laws in the Former Communist Bloc. *Law and Contemporary Problems*, 59, 4, 181-196.

Ellison, G., & Smyth, J. (2000). *The Crowned Harp: Policing Northern Ireland*. London: Pluto.

English, R. (2004). *Armed Struggle: The History of the IRA*. New York: Oxford University Press.

Ensalaco, M. (1994). Truth Commissions for Chile and El Salvador: A Report and Assessment. *Human Rights Quarterly*, 16, 4, 656-675.

Ensalaco, M. (1999). *Chile Under Pinochet: Recovering the Truth*. Penn: University of Pennsylvania Press.

Eolas (2003). *Consultation Paper on Truth and Justice: A Discussion Document*. Belfast: Eolas.

EPIC (2004). *Truth Recovery: A Contribution from Within Loyalism*. Belfast: EPIC.

Evenson, E. (2004). Truth and Justice in Sierra Leone, Co-ordination between Court and Commission. *Columbia Law Review*, 104, 730-767.

Faith and Politics Group (2002). *A Time to Heal: Perspectives on Reconciliation*. Belfast: Faith and Politics Group.

Farhang, M. (2004). The Coalition Provisional Authority Took Giant Steps to Guarantee Iraq a Functioning Criminal Justice System. *Los Angeles Lawyer*, 27, 45.

Farrington, C. (2006). *Ulster Unionism and the Peace Process in Northern Ireland*. London: Palgrave.

Fay, M., Morrissey M., & Smyth, M. (1999). *Northern Ireland's Troubles: The Human Costs*. London: Pluto.

Fealty, M. (2005). What is Whataboutery?
http://www.sluggerotoole.com/archives/2005/02/glossary_what_i.php

Findlay, M., & Henham, R. (2005). *Transforming International Criminal Justice: Retributive and Restorative Justice in the Trial Process*. Cullompten: Willan.

Forsberg, T. (2001). The Philosophy and Practice of Dealing with the Past: Some Conceptual and Normative Issues. In N. Biggar (ed), *Burying the Past: Making Peace and Doing Justice After Civil Conflict*. Washington, DC: Georgetown University Press.

Forsberg, T., & Teivainen, T. (2004). *Past Injustice in World Politics: Prospects of Truth Commission Like Global Institutions*. http://www.cmi.fi/files/Truth_Commission.pdf

Freeman, M., & Hayner, P. (2003). Truth-Telling: The Truth Commissions of South Africa and Guatemala. In D. Bloomfield, T. Barnes & L. Huyse (eds), *Reconciliation After Violent Conflict: A Handbook*. Stockholm: International Institute for Democracy and Electoral Assistance.

Gauck, J. (1994). Dealing with a Stasi Past. *Daedelus*, Winter, 1-27.

Geula, M. (2000). South Africa's Truth And Reconciliation Commission As An Alternate Means Of Addressing Transitional Government Conflicts In A Divided Society. *Boston University International Law Journal*, 18, 57-84.

Gibney, M., & Roxstrom, E. (2001). The Status of State Apologies. *Human Rights Quarterly*, 23, 4, 911-939.

Gibson, J. (2004a). Overcoming Apartheid: Can Truth Reconcile a Divided Nation? *Politikon*, 31, 2, 129–155.

Gibson, J. (2004b). Does Truth Lead to Reconciliation? Testing the Causal Assumption of the South Africa Truth and Reconciliation Commission. *American Journal of Political Science*, 48, 2, 201-217.

Gifford, Lord (1971). *Inquiry into the Circumstances Surrounding the Deaths of Seamus Cussack And George Desmond Beattie*. Belfast: Northern Ireland Socialist Research Centre.

Gilligan, C. (2006). Traumatised by Peace? A Critique of Five Assumptions in the Theory and Practice of Conflict-related Trauma Policy in Northern Ireland. *Policy and Politics*, 34, 2, 325-44.

Godoy, A. (2002). Lynchings and the Democratization of Terror in Postwar Guatemala: Implications for Human Rights. *Human Rights Quarterly*, 24, 3, 640-661.

Goldstein, R. (2004). Morocco's New Truth Commission: Turning the Page on Human Rights Abuses? Carnegie Endowment for International Peace. *Arab Reform Bulletin*.
http://www.carnegieendowment.org/publications/index.cfm?fa=view&id=16504

Goldstone, R. (2000). *For Humanity: Reflections of a War Crimes Investigator*. New Haven: Yale University Press.

Golob, S. (2002). Forced to be Free: Globalized Justice, Pacted Democracy, and the Pinochet Case. *Democratization*, 9, 25–9.

Gourevitch, P. (1999). *We Wish To Inform You That Tomorrow We Will Be Killed With Our Families: Stories From Rwanda*. New York: Picador.

Govier, T., & Verwoerd, W. (2002). Trust and the Problem of National Reconciliation. *Philosophy of the Social Sciences*, 32, 178-205.

Graybill, L. (2004). Pardon, Punishment, and Amnesia: Three African post-conflict methods. *Third World Quarterly*, 25, 6, 1117–1130.

Green, E. C., & Honwana, A. (1999). Indigenous Healing of War-affected Children in Africa. *World Bank, IK Notes*, No. 10. July. New York: World Bank.

Guelke, A. (2005). The Lure of the Miracle: The South African Connection and the Northern Ireland Peace Process. Paper Presented as part of the ESRC New Security Challenges Series. http://www.qub.ac.uk/csec/Guelke%20paper.pdf

Hamber, B. (1995). *Do Sleeping Dogs Lie? The Psychological Implications of the Truth and Reconciliation Commission in South Africa*. Johannesburg, South Africa: The Centre for the Study of Violence & Reconciliation.

Hamber, B. (1998). The Burdens of Truth: An evaluation of the psychological support services and initiatives undertaken by the South African Truth and Reconciliation Commission. *American Imago*, 55, 1, 9-28.

Hamber, B. (ed.) (1999). *Past Imperfect: Dealing with the Past in Northern Ireland and Countries in Transition*. Derry: INCORE.

Hamber, B. (2002). 'Ere Their Story Die': Truth, Justice and Reconciliation in South Africa. *Race and Class*, 44, 1, 61-79.

Hamber, B. (2003a). Healing. In D. Bloomfield, T. Barnes & L. Huyse (eds), *Reconciliation after Violent Conflict: A Handbook*. Stockholm, Sweden: International Institute for Democracy and Electoral Assistance.

Hamber, B. (2003b). Rights and Reasons: Challenges for Truth Recovery in South Africa and Northern Ireland. *Fordham International Law Journal*, 26, 4, 1074-1094.

Hamber, B. (2004). Submission to the Northern Ireland Affairs Committee: Reconciliation, Ways of Dealing with Northern Ireland's Past. Oral submission given on Wednesday 2 March 2005, Ev206. http://www.publications.parliament.uk/pa/cm200405/cmselect/cmniaf/303/303i.pdf

Hamber, B. (2006). The dilemmas of reparations: In search of a process-driven approach. In K. De Feyter, S. Parmnetier, M. Bossuyt & P. Lemmens (eds), *Out of the Ashes: Reparation for Victims of Gross and Systematic Human Rights Violations*. Antwerpen, Oxford: Intersentia.

Hamber, B., & Kelly, G. (2005). *A Place for Reconciliation? Conflict and Locality in Northern Ireland* (Report 18). Belfast: Democratic Dialogue.

Hamber, B., Nageng, D., & O'Malley, G. (2000). Telling It Like It Is...: Understanding The Truth And Reconciliation Commission From The Perspective Of Survivors. *Psychology in Society* (PINS), 26, 18-42.

Hamber, B., & Wilson, R. (2002). Symbolic Closure through Memory, Reparation and Revenge in Post-Conflict Societies. *Journal of Human Rights*, 1, 1, 35-53.

Hamber, B., & Wilson, R. (eds) (2003). *Recognition and Reckoning: The Way Ahead on Victims Issues*. Belfast: Democratic Dialogue.

Harrell, P. (2003). *Rwanda's Gamble: Gacaca and a New Model of Transitional Justice*. Lincoln NE: Writers Club Press.

Hatzfeld, J. (2005). *Into the Quick of Life: The Rwandan Genocide - The Survivors Speak*. London: Serpents Tale.

Hayashi, B. (2004). *Democratizing the Enemy: The Japanese American Internment*. Princeton: Princeton University Press.

Hayes, P., & Campbell, J. (2003). *Bloody Sunday: Trauma, Pain and Politics*. London: Pluto.

Hayner, P. (1997). International Guidelines For The Creation And Operation Of Truth Commissions: A Preliminary Proposal. *Law and Contemporary Problems*, 59, 4, 173-180.

Hayner, P. (2001). *Unspeakable Truths: Facing the Challenge of Truth Commissions*. London: Routledge.

Healing Through Remembering (2002). *Report of the Healing Through Remembering Project*. Belfast: Healing Through Remembering.

Healing Through Remembering (2006a). Healing Through Remembering Website. http://www.healingthroughremembering.org

Healing Through Remembering (2006b). *Acknowledgement and Its Role In Preventing Future Violence: Discussion Paper and Proposal.* Belfast: Healing Through Remembering.

Healy, K. (2005). *Future Support of Areas of Weak Community Infrastructure.* Belfast: CFNI.

Hegarty, A. (2003). Dealing With The Past: The Government Of Memory: Public Inquiries And The Limits Of Justice In Northern Ireland. *Fordham International Law Journal,* 26, 4, 1148-1192.

Hegarty, A. (2004). Truth, Law and Official Denial: The Case of Bloody Sunday. *Criminal Law Forum,* 15, 1-2, 199-246.

Hermon, J. (1997). *Holding the Line: An Autobiography.* Dublin: Gill & Macmillan.

HET (2006). *Policing the Past: Introduction to the Work of the Historical Enquiries Team.* Belfast: PSNI.

Hirsh, D. (2003). *Law against Genocide: Cosmopolitan Trials.* London: Glass House Press, Cavendish Publishing.

Human Rights Watch (1999). *The Sierra Leone Amnesty in International Law,* 3 August 1999. http://www.hrw.org/campaigns/sierra/int-law2.htm

Humphrey, M. (2003). From Victim to Victimhood: Truth Commissions and Trials as Rituals of Political Transition and Individual Healing. *The Australian Journal of Anthropology,* 14, 2, 171-187.

Hunt, T. (2004). Whose Truth? Objective Truth and a Challenge for History. *Criminal Law Forum,* 15, 1-2, 193-198.

Huyse, L. (2003). The process of reconciliation. In D. Bloomfield, T. Barnes & L. Huyse (eds), *Reconciliation after Violent Conflict: A Handbook,* Stockholm: International Institute for Democracy and Electoral Assistance.

ICTJ (2004). *Legal Analysis Prepared for the International Centre for Transitional Justice on the Applicability of the United Nations Convention on the Prevention and Punishment of the Crime of Genocide to Events which Occurred During the Early Twentieth Century (February 2003).* New York: International Centre for Transitional Justice. http://www.ictj.org

ICTR (2005). 10th Annual Report of the International Criminal Tribunal for Rwanda. http://69.94.11.53/ENGLISH/annualreports/a60/534e.pdf

Ignatieff, M. (1996). Articles of Faith. *Index on Censorship,* 25, 5, 110-122.

Ignatieff, M. (1998). *The Warrior's Honor: Ethnic War and the Modern Conscience.* New York: Henry Holt & Co.

Ignatieff, M. (2000). *Newshour* with Jim Lehr 31 May 2000.

Joinet, L. (1996). *Question of Impunity for Perpetrators of Violations of Human Rights (Civil and Political): Final Report Prepared by Mr. Louis Joinet Pursuant to Subcommission Resolution 1995/35 - Annex II: Set of Principles for the Protection and Promotion of Human Rights through Action to Combat Impunity,* E/CN.4/Sub.2/1996/18, Commission on Human Rights, Geneva (29 June 1996). http://www.derechos.org/nizkor/impu/joinet2.html

Joint Committee (2005). *Final Report on the Report of the Independent Commission of Inquiry into the Dublin Bombings of 1972 and 1973.* Dublin: Joint Committee on Justice, Equality, Defence and Women's Rights, Office of the Houses of the Oireachtas.

Kerr, R. (2004). *The International Criminal Tribunal for the Former Yugoslavia: An Exercise in Law, Politics and Diplomacy.* Oxford: Oxford University Press.

Kelly, G. (2005). *Storytelling Audit. An Audit of Personal Story, Narrative and Testimony Initiatives Related to the Conflict in and about Northern Ireland.* Belfast: Healing Through Remembering.

Kittichaisaree, K. (2001). *International Criminal Law*. Oxford: Oxford University Press.

Kriesberg, L. (2004). Comparing Reconciliation Actions within and between Countries. In Y. Bar-Siman-Tov, *Conflict Resolution to Reconciliation*. New York: Oxford University Press, 81-110.

Kritz, N. (1995). *Transitional Justice: How Emerging Democracies Reckon with Former Regimes*. Washington DC: USIP.

Krog, A. (1998). *Country of My Skull*. New York: Random House.

Landsman, S. (1996). Alternative Responses to Serious Human Rights Abuses: Of Prosecution and Truth Commissions. *Law and Contemporary Problems*, 59, 4, 81-92.

Lashmar, P. (2003). The Stalker Affair. Violations of Rights in Britain Series 3 No.27. London: Charter 88. http://www.charter88.org.uk/publications/violations/lashmar2.html

Lawyers Committee for Human Rights (2003). *Beyond Collusion: The UK Security Forces and the Murder of Patrick Finucane*. New York: Lawyers Committee for Human Rights. http://www.humanrightsfirst.org/pubs/descriptions/beyond_collusion.pdf

Leach, W. & Sabatier, P. (2005). To Trust an Adversary: Integrating Rational and Psychological Models in Collaborative Policymaking. *American Political Science Review*, 99, 4, 491-504.

Leichty, J., & Clegg, C. (2000). *Moving Beyond Sectarianism: Religion, Conflict and Reconciliation in Northern Ireland*. Dublin: Columba Press.

Leman-Langlois, S. (2002). Constructing a Common Language: The Myth of Nuremberg in the Problematization of Post-Apartheid Justice. *Law and Social Inquiry*, 27, 1, 79-100.

Leonard, M. (2004). Bonding and Bridging Social Capital: Reflections from Belfast. *Sociology*, 38, 5, 927-943.

Letki, N. (2002). Lustration and Democratisation in East-Central Europe. *Europe Asia Studies*, 54, 4 529-552.

Lieberfeld, D. (1999). *Talking with the Enemy: Negotiation and Threat Perception in South Africa and Israel/Palestine*. Westport CT: Praeger.

Livingstone, S., McEvoy, K., Rebouche, R. & Mageean, P. (2006). *Judges, Lawyers and Transition in Northern Ireland*. Belfast: Queens University Belfast Human Rights Centre.

Los, M. (1995). Lustration and Truth Claims: Unfinished Revolutions in Central Europe. *Law And Social Inquiry*, 20, 117-161.

Love, M. T. (1995). *Peace Building Through Reconciliation in Northern Ireland*. Aldershot: Avebury Press.

Lundy, P., & McGovern, M. (2005a). *Northern Ireland Life and Times Survey Political Attitudes: Truth Commissions*, Brief Overview. 1 July 2005. Copy on file with the author.

Lundy, P., & McGovern, M. (2005b). *Community, "Truth-telling" and Conflict Resolution: A Critical Evaluation of the Role of Community-based "Truth-telling" Processes for Post-Conflict Transition. A Case Study of the Ardoyne Commemoration Project*. http://cain.ulst.ac.uk/issues/victims/ardoyne/lundymcgovern05.pdf

Lundy, P., & McGovern, M. (2006). Trust, Testimony and Post-Conflict Transition: Unionist Attitudes to Truth Recovery Processes in Northern Ireland. Article under review, copy on file with the author.

Lykes, B., Terre Blanche, M., & Hamber, B. (2003). Narrating Survival and Change in Guatemala and South Africa: The Politics of Representation and a Liberatory Community Psychology. *American Journal Of Community Psychology*, 31, 1-2, 79-90.

Maga, T. (2001). *Judgment at Tokyo: The Japanese War Crimes Trials*. Kentucky: University of Kentucky Press.

Mageean, P., & McEvoy, K. (2000). Human Rights, Reconciliation and Justice: The Work of Human Rights NGOs in Conflict Transformation. Paper presented at the *Robben Island Symposium on the Voluntary Sector and Conflict Resolution*. Copy on file with the author.

Majstorovic, S. (1997). Ancient Hatreds or Elite Manipulation? Memory and Politics in the Former Yugoslavia. *World Affairs*, 159, 4, 170-182.

Mallender, L. (2005). Can Amnesty Laws and International Justice be Reconciled? At the *6th Annual Conference of the Association of Human Rights Institutes (AHRI)*, National University of Ireland, Galway (1 October 2005). Copy on file with the author.

Mansfield, M. (1992). *Report of the Public Inquiry into the Killing of Fergal Caraher and the wounding of Miceal Caraher 30th December 1990*. Cullyhanna: Cullyhanna Justice Group.

Manuel, A., & Schabus, N. (2005). Indigenous Peoples at the Margin of the Global Economy: A Violation of International Human Rights and International Trade Law. *Chapman Law Review*, 8, 229-267.

Martin, S. (2004). Taking Another Brick from the Wall: Conditions for an Effective Truth Process in Northern Ireland. Unpublished Diploma Dissertation, University of Cambridge. Diploma/Master of Studies (M.St.) Degree in Applied Criminology and Police Management. Copy on file with the author.

McAdams, A. J. (ed.) (1986). *Transitional Justice and the Rules of Law in New Democracies*. Notre Dame IN: University of Notre Dame Press.

McAuley, J. (1994). *The Politics of Identity: A Loyalist Community in Belfast*. Aldershot: Avebury.

McCann, E. (1992). Bloody Sunday in Derry: What Really Happened. Dingle: Brandon.

McCann, E. (2005). *The Bloody Sunday Inquiry: The Families Speak Out*. London: Pluto.

McClean, R. (1997). *Road to Bloody Sunday*. Swords: Ward River Press.

McDonald, H. (2001). *Trimble*. London: Bloomsbury.

MacEntee, P. (2006). *Commission of Investigation into the Dublin Monaghan Bombings in 1974: Second Interim Report*. Dublin: Office of the Taoiseach.

McEvoy, K. (2001). *Paramilitary Imprisonment in Northern Ireland*. Oxford: Oxford University Press.

McEvoy, K. (2003). Beyond the Metaphor: Political Violence, Human Rights and 'New' Peacemaking Criminology. *Theoretical Criminology*, 7, 3, 319-346.

McEvoy, K., & Conway, H. (2004). The Dead, the Law and the Politics of the Past. *Journal of Law and Society*, 31, 4, 539-562.

McEvoy, K. & Ellison, G. (2003). Criminological Discourses in N. Ireland: Conflict and Conflict Resolution. In K. McEvoy & T. Newburn (eds), *Criminology, Conflict Resolution and Restorative Justice*. London: Palgrave.

McEvoy, K. & Ericcson, A. (2006). Restorative Justice in Transition: Ownership, Leadership and "Bottom Up" Human Rights. In D. Sullivan & L. Tift (eds), *Handbook of Restorative Justice*. London: Routledge.

McEvoy, K. & McGregor, L. (eds) (2007 in press). Transitional Justice From Below. In edited special issue of *Journal of International Criminal Justice*.

McEvoy, K., & Mika, H. (2002). Restorative Justice and the Critique of Informalism in Northern Ireland. *British Journal of Criminology*, 43, 3, 534-563.

McEvoy, K., & Morison, J. (2003). Beyond the Constitutional Moment: Law, Transition and Peacemaking in Northern Ireland. *Fordham International Law Journal*, 26, 3, 961-1014.

McEvoy, K. & White, C. (1998). Security Vetting in Northern Ireland: Loyalty, Redress and Citizenship. *Modern Law Review*, 61, 3, 341-361.

McGoldrich, D., Rowe, P., & Donnelly, E. (eds) (2004). *The Permanent International Criminal Court: Legal and Policy Issues*. Oxford: Hart Publishing.

McGregor, L. (2001). Individual Accountability in South Africa: Cultural Optimum or Political Façade? *American Journal of International Law*, 95, 1, 32-45.

McGregor, L. (2003). Challenging the Orthodox Approach to Establishing Central Institutions in Transitional Justice. Northern Ireland: An Opportunity for Innovation? Unpublished LLM Dissertation, School of Law, Harvard University. Copy on file with the author.

McKittrick, D., Kelters, S., Feeney, B., Thornton, C., & McVea, S. (1999). *Lost Lives: The Stories of the Men, Women and Children Who Died Through the Northern Ireland Troubles*. London: Mainstream Publishing.

McKittrick, D., & McVea, D. (2000). *Making Sense of the Troubles*. Belfast: Blackstaff Press.

McLaughlin, C. (2002). Reparations in South Africa - a visit to Khulumani. *Race & Class*, 44, 1, 81-86.

Merry, S., & Milner, N. (1993). Introduction. In S. Merry & N. Milner (eds), *The Possibility of Popular Justice*. Ann Arbor: The University of Michigan Press.

Miller, J. (1988). Settling Accounts with a Secret Police: The German Law on the Stasi Records. *Europe Asia Studies*, 50, 2, 305-330.

Miller, S. (2003). Spain Begins To Confront Its Past: A Campaign To Dig Up The Mass Graves Of Thousands Murdered During The Civil War Has Begun. *Christian Science Monitor*, 6 February.

Morgan, A. (2002). The Northern Ireland (Location of Victims' Remains) Act 1999: Amnesty, Immunity or What? *Irish Jurist*, 37, 306-322.

Morrissey, M., & Smyth, M. (2002). *Northern Ireland after the Good Friday Agreement: Victims, Grievance and Blame*. London: Pluto.

Mowbray, A. (2004). *The Development of Positive Obligations under the European Convention on Human Rights by the European Court of Human Rights*. Oxford: Hart.

Mulcahy, A. (2005). *Policing Northern Ireland: Legitimacy, Reform and Social Conflict*. Cullompten: Willan.

Mullan, D. (1997). *The "Bloody Sunday" Massacre in Northern Ireland: The Eyewitness Accounts*. Boulder Co: Roberts Reinhart Publishing.

Mullan, D. (2001). *The Dublin Monaghan Bombings*. Dublin: Merlin Publishing.

Mullan, D. (2003). (Chairperson) *New Lodge Six Report of the Community Inquiry into The Killings Of Jim McCann, Jim Sloan, Tony Campbell, Brendan Maguire, John Loughran, Ambrose Hardy.* http://www.thebarrack.com

Murray, G. (1998). *John Hume and the SDLP: Impact and Survival in Northern Ireland*. Dublin: Irish Academic Press.

Murray, R., & Livingstone, S. (2004). The Effectiveness of National Human Rights Institutions. In S. Halliday & P. Schmidt (eds), *Human Rights Brought Home: Socio-Legal Perspectives on Human Rights in the National Context*. Oxford: Hart.

Nagata, D. (1993). *Legacy of Injustice: Exploring the Cross-generational Impact of the Japanese-American Internment*. The Hague: Kluwer.

NIAC (2005). *The Functions of the Office of the Police Ombudsman for Northern Ireland* (HC 344) Evidence to the Northern Ireland Affairs Committee. London: Stationary Office.

NIACRO & Victim Support (2000). *All Truth is Bitter: A Report of the Visit to Northern Ireland of Dr Alex Boraine*. Belfast: NIACRO/Victim Support.

Ní Aoláin, F. (2002). Truth Telling, Accountability and the Right to Life in Northern Ireland. *European Human Rights Law Review*, 5, 572-590.

Nino, C. (1991). The Duty to Punish Past Abuses of Human Rights Put into Context: The Case of Argentina. *Yale Law Journal*, 100, 8, 2619-2640.

NIO (2003). *Proposals in Relation to On the Runs.* Belfast: Northern Ireland Office.
http://www.nio.gov.uk/proposals_in_relation_to_on_the_runs_(otrs)_-_april_2003.pdf

Nobles, M. (2003). Assessing the Effects of International Human Rights on the Emergence of Domestic Official Apologies. Paper prepared for the American Political Science Meeting, Philadelphia, PA 28-31 August 2003.
http://web.mit.edu/polisci/research/mnobles/HR_and_official_apologies.pdf

Nordstrom, C. (1997). *A Different Kind of War Story.* Pennsylvania: University of Pennsylvania Press.

Northern Ireland Human Rights Commission (2003). *Human Rights and Victims of Violence.* Belfast: Northern Ireland Human Rights Commission.

O'Brien, M. (1996). Northern Ireland at the United Nations, 1960-1996. Unpublished LLM Thesis, School of Law, Queen's University Belfast.

O'Brien, J. (2002). *A Matter Of Minutes: The Eduring Legacy of Bloody Sunday.* Cork: Merlin Press.

O'Brien, J. (2005). *Killing Finucane: The Inside Story of Britain's Intelligence War.* Dublin: Gill & MacMillan.

OFMDFM (2004). *Reshape, Rebuild, Recover: Delivering Practical Help and Services to the Victims of the Northern Ireland Conflict.* Belfast: Office of the First Minister Deputy First Minister.
http://www.victimsni.gov.uk/pdf/victimsbrochure.pdf

O'Leary, B., & McGarry, J. (1995). *Broken Images: Explaining Northern Ireland.* Oxford: Blackwell Press.

OPONI (2001a). Police Ombudsman Releases Findings on Devenny Investigation. Press Release, 4 October 2001. Belfast: Office of the Police Ombudsman for Northern Ireland.
http://www.policeombudsman.org//Publicationsuploads/devenny.pdf

OPONI (2001b). Statement by The Police Ombudsman For Northern Ireland On Her Investigation Of Matters Relating To The Omagh Bombing On August 15th 1998. 12 December 2001. Belfast: Office of the Police Ombudsman for Northern Ireland.
http://www.policeombudsman.org//Publicationsuploads/omaghreport.pdf

OPONI (2004). The Investigation by Police of the Murder of Mr Sean Brown on 12 May 1997. Belfast: Office of the Police Ombudsman for Northern Ireland.
http://www.policeombudsman.org//Publicationsuploads/SeanBrownreport.pdf

OPONI (2005a). *Annual Report of the Police Ombudsman for Northern Ireland.* Belfast: Office of the Police Ombudsman for Northern Ireland.

OPONI (2005b). Statement under Section 62 of the Police (NI) Act 1998 on the Investigation by Police of the Murder of Eoin David Morley on 15 April 1990. Belfast: Office of the Police Ombudsman for Northern Ireland.
http://www.policeombudsman.org/publicationsuploads/FEB%2017%20-%20MORLEY%20REPORT.pdf

Opsahl, T. (1993). *A Citizens' Inquiry: The Opsahl Report on Northern Ireland.* Dublin: Lilliput Press.

Orde, H. (2005). War is easy to declare, peace is an elusive prize. Paper presented at the *Telling the Truth in Northern Ireland* Conference. Dublin: Trinity College, 10 June 2005.

Orentlicher, D. (1991a). Settling Accounts: The Duty to Prosecute Human Rights Violations of a Prior Regime. *Yale Law Journal*, 100, 8, 2537-2615.

Orentlicher, D. (1991b). A Reply to Professor Nino. *Yale Law Journal*, 100, 8, 2641-2643.

Orentlicher, D. (2004). *Independent Study On Best Practices, Including Recommendations, To Assist States In Strengthening Their Domestic Capacity To Combat All Aspects Of Impunity*. E/CN.4/2004/88. New York: UN Economics and Social Council.

Orentlicher, D. (2005). *Report of Diane Orentlicher, independent expert to update the set of principles to combat impunity / updated set of principles for the protection and promotion of human rights through action to combat impunity*. E/CN.4/2005/102. Geneva: Office of the United Nations High Commissioner for Human Rights.

Orr, W. (2000). *From Biko to Basson: Wendy Orr's Search for the Soul of South Africa as a Commissioner of the TRC*. Johannesburg: Contra Press.

Osiel, M. (1997). *Mass Atrocity, Collective Memory and the Law*. New Brunswick: Transaction Publishers.

Osiel, M. (2000). Why Prosecute? Critics of Punishment for Mass Atrocity. *Human Rights Quarterly*, 22, 1, 118 -147.

Patten, C. (1999). *A New Beginning: Policing in Northern Ireland. The Report of the Independent Commission on Policing in Northern Ireland*. Belfast: HMSO.

Peatling, G. (2004). *Failure of the Northern Ireland Peace Process*. Dublin: Irish Academic Press.

Porter, N. (2003). *The Elusive Quest: Reconciliation in Northern Ireland*. Belfast: The Blackstaff Press.

Portillo, M. (2005). Article by Michael Portillo about Bosnia for *The Sunday Times*, 30 October 2005.

Posel, D. (1999). *The TRC Report: What Kind of History? What Kind of Truth?* Johannesburg: University of Witwatersrand.

Posel, D. (2002). The TRC Report: What Kind of History? In D. Posel & G. Simpson (eds), *Commissioning the Past: Understanding South Africa's Truth and Reconciliation Commission*. Johannesburg: Witwatersrand University Press.

PRI (2004). Research Report on the Gacaca Report VI: From camp to hill, the reintegration of released prisoners. http://www.penalreform.org/download/Gacaca/Rapport%20VI_AG.pdf

Pringle, P. & Jacobson, P. (2000). *Those Are Real Bullets, Aren't They? Bloody Sunday Derry 1972*. London: Fourth Estate.

Pritchard, R. (1996). The gift of clemency following British war crimes trials in the Far East, 1946–1948. *Criminal Law Forum*, 7, 1, 15 -50.

Quinn, J. (2003). Lessons Learned: Practical Lessons Gleaned from Inside the Truth Commissions of Guatemala and South Africa. *Human Rights Quarterly*, 25, 4, 1117-1149.

Rafter, K. (2006). *Sinn Fein 1905-2005: In the Shadow of Gunmen*. Dublin: Gill and Macmillan.

Ratner, S., & Abrams, J. (1997). *Accountability for Human Rights Atrocities in International Law*. Oxford: Oxford University Press.

Reynolds, L. (2003). Handling the Truth. In B. Mitchell (ed), *Truth Recovery After Conflict: Conflict Transformation Papers* (Vol. 3). Belfast: LINC Resource Centre.

Roberts, A., & Guelff, R. (2000). *Documents of the Laws of War, Third Edition*. Oxford: Oxford University Press.

Roche, D. (2002). Restorative Justice and the Regulatory State in South African Townships. *British Journal Of Criminology*, 42, 3, 514-533.

Roht-Arriaza, N. (1996). Combating Impunity: Some Thoughts On The Way Forward. *Law and Contemporary Problems*, 59, 4, 93-102.

Rolston, B. (1996). *Turning the Page without Closing the Book: the Right to Truth in the Irish Context.* Dublin: Irish Reporter Publications.

Rolston, B. (2000). *Unfinished Business: State Killings and the Quest for Truth.* Belfast: Beyond the Pale.

Rolston, B. (2002). Assembling The Jigsaw: Truth, Justice And Transition In The North Of Ireland. *Race and Class,* 44, 1, 87-106.

Rolston, B., & Scraton, P. (2005). In Full Glare of English Politics: Ireland, Inquiries and the British State. *British Journal of Criminology,* 45, 4, 547-564.

Rombouts, H. (2002). *The Legal Profession and the TRC: A Study of a Tense Relationship.* Johannesburg: CSVR.

Roper, S., & Barria, L. (2005). Assessing the Record of Justice: A Comparison of Mixed International Tribunals versus Domestic Mechanisms for Human Rights Enforcement. *Journal of Human Rights,* 4, 4, 521 – 536.

Rosenberg, T. (1999). What Did You Do in the War, Mama? *New York Times Magazine,* 7 February.

Rowe, P. (2004). War Crimes. In D. McGoldrich, P. Rowe & E. Donnelly (eds), *The Permanent International Criminal Court: Legal and Policy Issues.* Oxford: Hart.

RUC (1990). *Chief Constable's Annual Report.* Belfast: HMSO.

Ryder, C. (2000). *The RUC 1922-2000: A Force under Fire* (4th ed). London: Arrow.

Sarat, A. (1999). Rhetoric and Remembrance: Trials, Transcriptions and the Politics of Critical Reading. *Legal Studies Forum,* 23, 4, 355-378.

Sarkin, J. (1999). The Necessity and Challenges of Establishing a Truth and Reconciliation Commission in Rwanda. *Human Rights Quarterly,* 21, 3, 767-823.

Sarkin, J., & Daly, E. (2004). Too Many Questions, Too Few Answers: Reconciliation in Transitional Societies. *Columbia Human Rights Law Review,* 66, 661-728.

Schabas, W. (2003). The Relationship Between Truth Commissions and International Courts: The Case of Sierra Leone. *Human Rights Quarterly,* 25, 4, 1035-1066.

Schabas, W. (2004). *An Introduction to the International Criminal Court* (2nd Edition). Cambridge: Cambridge University Press.

Schabas, W. (2005). Genocide Trials and Gacaca Courts. *Journal of International Criminal Justice,* 3, 4, 879-895.

Scott, J. (2001). *Seeing Like a State.* New Haven: Yale University Press.

SDLP (2005). *Vindicating the Rights of Victims and Survivors: Proposals for Truth, Recognition and Remembrance.*
http://www.sdlp.ie/policy/documents/policydocs.shtm#OFMDFM

Shea, D. (2000). *The South African Truth and Reconciliation Commission.* Washington: USIP.

Shearing, C. (2000). A New Beginning for Policing. *Journal of Law and Society,* 27, 3, 386-393.

Shearing, C. (2001). A Nodal Conception of Governance: Thoughts on a Policing Commission. *Policing and Society,* 11, 3-4, 259-72.

Shirlow, P., Graham, B., McEvoy, K., Purvis, D., & Ó hAdhmaill, F. (2005). *Politically Motivated Former Prisoner Groups: Community Activism and Conflict Transformation.* Belfast: Community Relations Council.

Šimonović, I. (2004). Dealing with the Legacy of Past War Crimes and Human Rights Abuses: Experiences and Trends. *Journal of International Criminal Justice*, 2, 3, 701-710.

Sinn Féin (2003). *Truth: A Sinn Féin Discussion Document.* http://cain.ulst.ac.uk/issues/politics/docs/sf/sf03truth.pdf

Skweyiya (1992). Report of the Commission Of Enquiry Into Complaints By Former African National Congress Prisoners And Detainees. http://www.anc.org.za/ancdocs/misc/skweyiya.html

Sluka, J. (1989). *Hearts and Minds, Water and Fish: Support for the IRA and INLA in a Northern Ireland Ghetto.* London: JAI Press.

Smith, P. (2001). Memory without History: Who Owns Guatemala's Past? *The Washington Quarterly*, 24, 2, 59-72.

Southern, N. (2005). Ian Paisley and Evangelical Democratic Unionists: An Analysis of the Role of Evangelical Protestantism within the Democratic Unionist Party. *Irish Political Studies*, 20, 2, 127-145.

South African Truth and Reconciliation Commission (1998). *Truth and Reconciliation Commission of South Africa Report* (Vol. 1-6). Cape Town: Juta.

Spitz, R., & Chaskalson, M. (1999). *The Politics of Transition: A Hidden History of South Africa's Negotiated Settlement.* Johannesburg: Wits University Press.

Stalker, J. (1988). *The Stalker Affair.* London: Penguin.

Stanley, E. (2005). Truth Commissions and the Recognition of State Crime. *British Journal of Criminology*, 45, 4, 582-597.

Steinert, H. (1997). Fin De Siècle Criminology. *Theoretical Criminology*, 1, 1, 111-129.

Stevens, D. (2004). *The Land of Unlikeness: Explorations into Reconciliation.* Dublin: Columba Press.

Stevens, J. (2003). *Stevens Three: Overview and Recommendations.* http://cain.ulst.ac.uk/issues/collusion/stevens3/stevens3summary.htm

Taylor, P. (1987). *Stalker.* London: Faber.

Teitel, R. (2000). *Transitional Justice.* New York: Oxford University Press.

Tim Parry and Johnathan Ball Trust (2003). *The Legacy: A Study of the Needs of GB Victims and Survivors of the Northern Ireland 'Troubles'.* Warrington: Tim Parry and Johnathan Ball Trust.

Tomlinson, M., & Hillyard, P. (2000). Patterns of Policing and Policing Patten. *Journal of Law and Society*, 27, 3, 394-415.

Tully, L. D. (2003). Human Rights Compliance and the Gacaca Jurisdictions in Rwanda. *Boston College International and Comparative Law Review*, 26, 385-441.

Tutu, D. (1999). *No Future without Forgiveness.* New York: Double Day.

UN (2005). *Tenth Annual Report of the International Criminal Tribunal for the Prosecution of Persons Responsible for Genocide and Other Serious Violations of International Humanitarian Law Committed in the Territory of Rwanda and Rwandan Citizens Responsible for Genocide and Other Such Violations Committed in the Territory of Neighbouring States between 1 January and 31 December 1994.* http://69.94.11.53/ENGLISH/annualreports/a60/534e.pdf.

UN Security Council (2004). *The Rule of Law and Transitional Justice in Conflict And Post-Conflict Societies: Report of the Secretary-General.* S/2004/616. New York: United Nations.

Unionist Group (2006). *Drawing a Line under the Past.* 16 March 2006. Copy on file with the author.

van der Merwe, H. (2000). *Evaluation of the Health Sector Hearing.* Johannesburg: CSVR.

Victims Unit (2002). *Reshape, Rebuild, Achieve: Delivering Practical Help and Services to the Victims of the Conflict in Northern Ireland.* Belfast: Office of First Minister Deputy First Minister, Victims Unit (VU).

Villa-Vicencio, C. (2003). Restorative Justice in South Africa. In N. Biggar (ed), *Burying the Past: Making Peace and Doing Justice After Civil Conflict.* Washington, DC: Georgetown University Press.

Villa-Vicencio, C., & Verwoerd, W. (2000). *Looking Back, Reaching Forward: Reflections on the Truth and Reconciliation Commission of South Africa.* Cape Town: University of Cape Town Press.

Walsh, D. (2000). *Bloody Sunday and the Rule of Law in Northern Ireland.* Basingstoke: Macmillan.

Watters, D. (2003). Is there need for a Truth and Reconciliation Commission within the Peace Process in Northern Ireland? In B. Mitchell (ed), *Truth Recovery after Conflict: Conflict Transformation Papers* (Vol. 3). Belfast: Linc Resource Centre.

Widgery, J. (1972). *Report of the Tribunal Appointed to inquire into the Events on Sunday, 30th January 1972, which Led to Loss of Life in Connection with the Procession in Londonderry on that Day* (1971/72 H.C. 220).

Williams, K. (2003). Lustration as the Securitization of Democracy in Czechoslovakia and the Czech Republic. *Journal of Communist Studies and Transition Politics*, 19, 4, 1-24.

Williamson, A., Scott, D., & Halfpenny, P. (2000). Rebuilding civil society in Northern Ireland: the community and voluntary sector's contribution to the European Union's Peace and Reconciliation District Partnership Programme. *Policy & Politics*, 28, 1, 49-66.

Wilson, J. (1999). *A Place and a Name: Report of the Victims Commission of the Republic of Ireland.* Dublin: Stationary Office.

Wilson, R. (2001). *The Politics of Truth and Reconciliation in South Africa: Legitimizing the Post-Apartheid State.* Cambridge: Cambridge University Press.

Wood, I. (2006). *Crimes of Loyalty: A History of the UDA.* Edinburgh: Edinburgh University Press.

Zalaquett, J. (1993). *Report of the Chilean National Commission on Truth and Reconciliation: Volume 1 & 2.* Notre Dame IN: University of Notre Dame Press.

Appendix One

Truth Recovery and Acknowledgement Sub Group Members

Sarah Alldred works for the Tim Parry Johnathan Ball Trust on the Legacy Project. The project offers GB victims/survivors and veterans of the Northern Ireland "Troubles" voices and tools for recovery by providing a peer support service, a user-led website, story sharing residentials and an advocacy service. Prior to this Sarah studied for a Masters in Peace Studies at the University of Bradford, and a PhD at the Centre for the Study of Forgiveness and Reconciliation in Coventry, England.

Marie Breen Smyth is Reader in International Politics at the University of Wales, Aberystwyth, and previously founded and directed the Institute for Conflict Research in Belfast. She was a Senior Fellow in the United States Institute of Peace, Washington DC, and taught at University of Ulster. She initiated The Cost of the Troubles Study, and has published extensively on various aspects of the Northern Ireland conflict.

Emily Brough manages the Student Diversity Programme of NUS-USI. She became concerned about issues of truth and justice in relation to the past through her involvement with a research project on the impact of the conflict on young people, work with community relations and human rights organisations, and friendships with people from different walks of life affected by conflict-related violence. Originally from Scotland, Belfast has been her home for the past ten years.

Pat Conway is currently Director of Services with the Northern Ireland Association for the Care and Resettlement of Offenders (NIACRO). He is primarily responsible for adult services for ex-offenders, prisoners and ex-prisoners as well as policy development and communications. Pat has worked in London and Belfast as a Social Worker and has been involved in the Healing Through Remembering Project for the past six years.

Séamas Heaney is Project Director with the Old Library Trust Healthy Living Centre, Derry. Provision of a Community Healing Programme is one of the core elements of the project, focusing on individual and community trauma. The project has recently carried out research into the impact of the "Troubles" on community life.

Gareth Higgins has worked as an academic and activist, and is a writer, broadcaster, and research consultant. He is a founding member of the zero28 project, a faith-based peace and justice community. He has written widely on the conflict in and about Northern Ireland, as well as on culture and society generally, and art and spirituality.

Avila Kilmurray has been Director of the Community Foundation for Northern Ireland (previously the Northern Ireland Voluntary Trust) since 1994. Born in Dublin, Avila holds a B.A. (Hons.) degree from University College Dublin and a M.A. in International Relations from the Australian National University. Avila has been involved in a range of community and anti-poverty initiatives. In 1990, Avila was appointed the first Women's Officer for the Transport & General Workers' Union (T.G.W.U.) (Ireland) and has served on the Executive Council of the Irish Congress of Trade Unions. She has written extensively on community development, women's issues and civil society.

Patricia Lundy is a Lecturer in Sociology at the University of Ulster, Jordanstown. Together with colleagues she has been involved in a number of community-based truth-recovery projects including the Ardoyne Commemoration Project. Patricia holds a Ph.D. from Queen's University Belfast (1993).

Stephen Martin is a Superintendent in the Police Service of Northern Ireland. He has been a police officer for 20 years, serving in a range of operational and headquarters support roles throughout Northern Ireland. He is currently Head of Operational Development Programmes at the Police College, Garnerville.

Roy McClelland is Professor Emeritus of Mental Health in the School of Medicine and Dentistry at Queen's University Belfast, and a Consultant Psychiatrist at Belfast City Hospital Trust. He is Chairman of the Review of Mental Health and Learning Disability (NI), and Chairman of the Privacy Advisory Committee (NI). Roy is also the Chair of Healing Through Remembering.

Kieran McEvoy is Professor of Law and Transitional Justice and Director of the Institute of Criminology and Criminal Justice, School of Law, Queen's University Belfast.

Jackie McMullan is a former republican prisoner. He has been involved in HTR since 2001 and is Chairperson of the Truth and Acknowledgement Sub Group. He and his partner Laoise have a son. He is currently working in a voluntary capacity with a number of community projects.

Raymond Murray is parish priest in Cookstown parish. He was prison chaplain in Armagh's women's prison from 1968. Monsignor Murray was a founding member of the Association of Legal Justice in 1970, and Relatives for Justice in 1991, and has documented and published extensively on human rights abuses during the conflict in the North of Ireland. He provided pastoral care to many families bereaved by all actors during the conflict. An Irish historian and archivist, he is a founder member of the Ó Fiaich Library, established in memory of the late Cardinal Tomás Ó Fiaich.

Paul O'Connor is the Project Co-ordinator at the Pat Finucane Centre. He did his degree in Peace and Conflict studies at the University of Ulster. He has two children and lives in Derry City.

David W. Porter is Director of the Centre for Contemporary Christianity in Ireland. He was appointed to the Northern Ireland Civic Forum as a community relations nominee.

Dawn Purvis lives in South Belfast. She is currently Chairperson of the Progressive Unionist Party and an Independent Member of the Northern Ireland Policing Board.

Andrew Rawding is a former British Army officer who served in Northern Ireland from 1991-94. He currently works for St Ethelburga's Centre for Reconciliation and Peace in the City of London.

Joe Rice has been a practising solicitor in Northern Ireland since 1980 and is the Senior Partner at John J. Rice & Company, Solicitors. He holds Masters Degrees in Human Rights, Emergency Law and Discrimination Law from Queen's University. He is the present Secretary of the Belfast Solicitors' Association and his main legal work concerns criminal law and human rights law cases.

Mike Ritchie has been Director of Coiste na nIarchimí, the national network of Irish republican ex-prisoners, since 1998. He previously worked as Information and Research Manager for the NI Association for the Care and Resettlement of Offenders and as Research Officer for the Committee on the Administration of Justice. He has an MA (Hons) in History from Edinburgh University (1977) and a Post Graduate Certificate in Education from Queen's University, Belfast (1981). Mike has lived in Belfast since 1980 and has three daughters.

Tom Roberts is a former UVF prisoner. He is currently Director of ex-prisoner support group EPIC.

Mark Thompson is currently the Director of Relatives for Justice, a human rights NGO working with and on behalf of people affected by the conflict. Mark has long advocated for an inclusive truth-recovery process as part of the transition and has played a key role in the debate within the nationalist and republican community. Mark contributed to the Eolas Consultation Document around truth recovery published in 2003.

Irwin Turbitt retired as an Assistant Chief Constable from the PSNI this year having served almost 30 years in the RUC and the PSNI. He has been involved in voluntary peace-building work for a number of years, and plans now to be more so along with academic and consulting work in the areas of leadership, innovation and governance at Warwick Business School.

Alan Wardle is Project Development Manager for Shankill Stress and Trauma Group in Belfast. He has participated in international training delivery programmes, in both Kosovo and Croatia, delivering conflict management theories as well as mediation models.

Healing Through Remembering Board Members

Marie Breen Smyth is Reader in International Politics at the University of Wales, Aberystwyth, and previously founded and directed the Institute for Conflict Research in Belfast. She was a Senior Fellow in the United States Institute of Peace, Washington DC, and taught at University of Ulster. She initiated The Cost of the Troubles Study, and has published extensively on various aspects of the Northern Ireland conflict.

Sean Coll is Community Victim Support Officer with the Sperrin Lakeland Health and Social Care Trust. He is Chair of the Healing Through Remembering Day of Reflection Sub Group. Living in County Cavan, he has worked in Fermanagh and Tyrone for over 15 years.

Claire Hackett is the Co-ordinator of the Falls Community Council's oral history archive which records the experience of the conflict in West Belfast. She has been an activist in the women's movement for over 20 years. Claire is the Chair of the Healing Through Remembering Sub Group on Storytelling.

Maureen Hetherington is the Co-ordinator of the Junction, a community relations resource and peace building centre in Derry/Londonderry. Maureen has an M.A. in Humanities and has been working in the field of community relations in a full-time capacity for twelve years. She was a founder member and former chair of An Crann/The Tree, an organisation set up to help people tell and hear the stories of the "Troubles". She then set up (in collaboration with Holywell Trust) Towards Understanding and Healing, an organisation that facilitates "positive encounter dialogue groups" between all those involved in and affected by the conflict. [HTR Board member 2001 – 2006].

Alan McBride is Youth Worker at the WAVE Trauma Centre and columnist with Sunday Life. Alan has been involved in reconciliation work for the last 20 years.

Roy McClelland is Professor Emeritus of Mental Health in the School of Medicine and Dentistry at Queen's University Belfast and a Consultant Psychiatrist at Belfast City Hospital Trust. He is Chairman of the Review of Mental Health and Learning Disability (NI). Roy is also Chairman of the Privacy Advisory Committee (NI). He is also the Chair of Healing Through Remembering.

Jackie McMullan is a former republican prisoner. He has been involved in HTR since 2001 and is Chairperson of the Truth Recovery and Acknowledgment Sub Group. He and his partner Laoise have a son. He is currently working voluntarily with a number of community projects.

Dawn Purvis lives in South Belfast. She is currently Chairperson of the Progressive Unionist Party and an Independent Member of the Northern Ireland Policing Board. [HTR Board member 2006 – present].

Geraldine Smyth is a Dominican theologian from Belfast, working in both Dublin and Belfast as Senior Lecturer at the Irish School of Ecumenics, Trinity College Dublin. She holds a Ph.D. in theology from Trinity College Dublin (1993) and an honorary doctorate from Queen's University Belfast (2003) for service to reconciliation and public life. She is also a registered psychotherapist. [HTR Board member 2006 – present].

Oliver Wilkinson is the Chief Executive Officer of the Share Centre in Lisnaskea, Co. Fermanagh. He was previously CEO of Victim Support Northern Ireland and has also worked within the criminal justice system with people affected by ordinary criminal activity and also with people affected by the conflict in and about Northern Ireland.

Healing Through Remembering Staff

Elaine Armstrong has been the Administrative Assistant with Healing Through Remembering since August 2004.

Lainey Dunne has been the Communications Officer with Healing Through Remembering since August 2005. She has been working in the field of communications and public relations for the last five years.

Kate Turner has been the Project Co-ordinator with Healing Through Remembering since December 2000. She has twenty years experience in the voluntary sector.

Healing Through Remembering Core Consultant

Brandon Hamber was born in South Africa and currently lives in Belfast, where he works as an independent conflict transformation consultant. He trained as a clinical psychologist in South Africa and holds a Ph.D. He is an Honorary Fellow of INCORE at the University of Ulster. He is also co-founder of the Office of Psychosocial Issues, Berlin. He is a board member of Khulumani Victim Support Group in South Africa. He has worked extensively in South Africa and Northern Ireland but has also consulted in Liberia, Sierre Leone, Brazil, Moçambique, Malawi and the Basque Country. He is the core consultant to Healing Through Remembering.

NOTES

NOTES

NOTES

NOTES

NOTES